CONFLICTING WORLDS
New Dimensions of the American Civil War

T. Michael Parrish

RAILROADS IN THE CIVIL WAR

The Impact of Management on Victory and Defeat

JOHN E. CLARK JR.

Louisiana State University Press · *Baton Rouge*

Manufactured in the United States of America
First printing
10   09   08   07   06   05   04   03   02   01
5   4   3   2   1

Designer: Melanie O'Quinn Samaha
Typeface: Galliard
Typesetter: Coghill Composition Co. Inc.
Printer and binder: Thomson Shore, Inc.

Library of Congress Cataloging-in-Publication Data:

Clark, John Elwood, 1940–
    Railroads in the Civil War : the impact of management on
victory and defeat / John E. Clark, Jr.
        p.   cm. — (Conflicting worlds)
Includes bibliographical references and index.
    ISBN 0-8071-2726-4 (alk. paper)
    1. United States—History—Civil War,
1861–1865—Transportation.   2. Railroads—United
States—History—19th century.   3. Railroads—Confederate States
of America—History.   4. United States—Politics and
government—1861–1865.   5. Confederate States of
America—Politics and government.   6. United States.
Army—Management—History—19th century.   7. Confederate States
of America. Army—Management.   8. United States.
Army—Transportation—History—19th century.   9. Confederate
States of America. Army—Transportation.   I. Title.   II. Series
    E491.C58   2001
    973.7'42—dc21

    2001002452

*To the memory of Raymond E. Banta, who made it conceivable,
and with appreciation to James M. McPherson, who made it possible*

Contents

Illustrations

‡+++++++++++++++++++++++++++++++++++++

PREFACE

James M. McPherson, in his Pulitzer Prize–winning *Battle Cry of Freedom*, describes in two sentences the rail movement of the Union's 11th and 12th Corps from Virginia to Tennessee in the Fall of 1863. Both his citations were more than forty years old: George Edgar Turner's *Victory Rode the Rails* (1953) devotes seven pages to the subject; Thomas Weber's *The Northern Railroads in the Civil War* (1952) covers it in five pages. Both relied almost exclusively on telegrams found in the *Official Records of the War of the Rebellion*. They provided the first clues that I had a subject worth exploring.

The 11th and 12th Corps movement, although well known, has escaped in-depth study. As my research developed, I found myself increasingly admiring the confidence and expert skill with which John W. Garrett, Daniel C. McCallum, Thomas A. Scott, and William Prescott Smith so quickly organized and directed this massive undertaking. I decided to compare it with the movement of Confederate General

James Longstreet's corps to Chickamauga, which concluded as the 11th and 12th Corps commenced, partly in response to it. The Longstreet movement has also received little detailed attention. In researching the Confederate war economy as background for the Longstreet movement, I became increasingly disturbed by flawed Confederate organization and management decisions that frequently brought to mind the old saw, "It's a heck of a way to run a railroad." A heck of a way to fight a war, too, but the Confederate leadership never recognized or understood this truth. It never mobilized southern railroads for war, and its failure to do so limited its prospects for victory.

My focus thus evolved from my initial interest in a single rail movement to a comparison of Union and Confederate war management as revealed in each side's use of railroads. The Longstreet and 11th and 12th Corps movements provide case studies to illustrate the consequences of the differences in management.

Logistics as a modern discipline began its rise to prominence in the Civil War. Its transportation, or distribution, element, as demonstrated by each side's use of railroads, clearly emerged as a critical factor in each side's ability to wage war. Logistics occupies a central role in today's military planning. It now takes twelve support troops to sustain one combat soldier in the United States Army. In spite of the critical role of logistics in waging war, support functions remain largely unseen. Many Americans' memories of the Persian Gulf War, for example, include swept-wing F-14 Tomcat fighters blasting off carrier decks and M1A1 Abrams tanks racing across the desert trailing plumes of dust. They do not recall the lowly oilers and supply ships or water, fuel, and ammunition carriers without which the planes and tanks could neither blast nor plume. An out-of-ammunition Abrams with an empty fuel tank projects the technological sophistication of a sixty-ton club.

This book describes the approaches taken by the Union and Confederate governments to mobilize their railroads for war. It then tells the stories of the two rail movements as case studies that illustrate the success and failure of each side's war management. It provides a new perspective on the elements that determined victory and defeat in the Civil War. It does not attempt to study all aspects of Union and Confederate war management. I refer interested readers to Paul A. C. Koistinen's scholarly *Beating Plowshares into Swords: The Political Economy of American Warfare, 1606–1865* (Lawrence: University Press of Kansas, 1996). I commend Koistinen's book, including its excellent footnotes and bibliography, as an essential resource to anyone studying Civil War logistics. Another book that bears mentioning is Roger Pickenpaugh's *Rescue by Rail: Troop Transfer and the Civil War in the West, 1863*, recently published by the University of Nebraska Press. Readers will find some similarities in the descriptions of the troop movements, to which Mr. Pickenpaugh limits his study.

The present study considers some aspects of the larger issues of war management to the extent they affected northern and southern railroads. It does not attempt to assess, much less rank, all the components of victory and defeat in the Civil War. Other historians have studied this subject; readers will find many of them in the bibliography. The quality of railroad management, however, certainly contributed to Union victory and the failure of the Confederacy, and thus, to that extent, this work considers some elements relating to the war's outcome.

George Rogers Taylor describes the railroads' role in the economic development of the United States as a "transportation revolution." In 1861, however, railroads had not yet matured as a truly integrated transportation system; gaps between lines, incompatible track gauges, and other vexing impediments remained in both North and South. The skill with which Union and Confederate war leaders dealt with railroad operational problems and practices becomes clear in studying the Longstreet and 11th and 12th Corps movements. Examining how leaders on both sides identified, addressed, and solved problems, or avoided, tried to finesse, or simply botched them, enhances our understanding of the development of war management.

History is about people, the challenges they face in their lives, and how they meet them. The Union and Confederate soldiers' experiences on their way west reveal remarkably similar attitudes and outlooks, mirroring one another. Be they blue or gray, their observations and activities and the incidents that occurred on their journeys speak to their common heritage, a legacy that the Confederates could not escape by attempting to secede.

*   *   *

In June 1988, Peg Banta, a lovely lady from my hometown of Ridgewood, New Jersey, let me read a blanket box filled with letters that her
husband wrote to her from China during World War II. Raymond E.
Banta, M.D., commanded the 40th U.S. Army Portable Surgical Hospital. The Army sent the 40th and nine other portable surgical hospi-
tals to China specifically to treat Chinese soldiers as part of General
Joseph Stilwell's plan to liberate China from Japan. The letters, written
by a remarkable man, tell a powerful and moving story. My first experience with primary research, the letters redirected my life: they led me
to Princeton University for a doctorate in history.

Peg got upset with me for taking an eight-year side trip to Princeton
instead of completing the work on her husband's papers. I told her
that it was Ray's fault, that I was simply one more person whose life he
touched. *Military History Quarterly* published my Banta article in its
Autumn 1998 issue. I have returned to working on the letters.

I owe a great debt to Jim McPherson, who recognized my determination (and, I hope, some promise). His gracious comments in my first
course evaluation encouraged me to keep going. His classical questions
in our seminars, the simple force of his arguments, and the clarity of
his writing are examples I dream of someday approaching. His gra-
ciousness and humanity match his stature as a historian.

I've never met a historian I didn't like. Many people went out of
their way to help me, giving freely of their insights, direction, and suggestions. Michael Musick at the National Archives helped me find
Quartermaster Corps telegrams from the 11th and 12th Corps movement not found in the *Official Records;* they provided valuable insights
into the organization and management of the operation. Dr. Richard
Sommers and his staff at the U.S. Army Military History Institute, Carlisle Barracks, Pennsylvania, directed me to soldiers' letters and diaries
that added human interest and valuable information about the 11th
and 12th Corps movement.

Reid Mitchell advised me to fall in love with my subject because he
said that I would marry it. I did, and discovered that passion has another benefit. A writer learns that it helps to talk about his work with
anyone willing to listen, or unable to escape. As a result of my storytell-
ing, Dick Sommers introduced me to Frederick A. Eiserman. Rick let

me read his research files for his study of the Longstreet movement at the U.S. Army's Command and General Staff College. An unrelated phone call to West Point's History Department led me to Major Thomas G. Ziek Jr. Tom's master's thesis at Texas A&M University describes the southern railroads' deterioration during the Civil War.

Mary George, my research librarian and good friend at Princeton's Firestone Library found misplaced books and research material, read my early drafts, and offered ideas, thoughtful criticism, and constant and enthusiastic encouragement. She was the first person to tell me that I had a publishable manuscript. Nancy Blasberg of the Ridgewood Library read several drafts of the manuscript; her comments tightened the organization and improved my prose. My Dartmouth classmate Dan Tompkins served as my unofficial mentor. Chairman of Temple University's Classics Department, Dan interpreted and guided me through the academic thickets. He often sent me articles, book reviews, and books on teaching, constant reminders of his ongoing interest.

Many historians helped me. Alfred Chandler, Peter Cozzens, Mary DeCredico, Paul Escott, Richard Goff, Allen Trelease, and Frank Vandiver graciously spent time with me discussing their research and analyzing different aspects of the subject. Some material, especially railroad studies, though written more than thirty years ago, remain fresh, an ongoing tribute to the writers. As lonely a business as writing is, no one writes alone. John Murrin's and Russell Weigley's critiques helped me greatly to improve the final draft, as did Gary Gallagher's comments.

I want to add a special thanks to George Roupe, my editor at LSU Press. His eye for detail, attentiveness to my concerns for the flow of the study, spirit of partnership, and sense of humor helped to produce a better final product.

My wife, Norma, happily no longer shares her marriage with doctoral study. Son Rob and daughter Elizabeth and her husband Ralph are impressed with their father's mid-life doctorate as much as they wonder what Dad will become when he grows up. Son Tom, age thirteen, a great age for a baseball player, likes the fact that his Dad now has time to watch him play baseball instead of chasing footnotes.

Railroads in the Civil War

INTRODUCTION

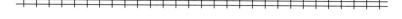

Development of an American Transportation System

> Logistics: The procurement, distribution, maintenance, and
> replacement of matériel and personnel.
> —*The American Heritage Dictionary of the English Language*

> Logistics: Beans, bullets, and bodies.
> —Soldier slang

In September 1863, Union General William S. Rosecrans' Army of the
Cumberland slashed through eastern Tennessee, captured Chattanooga, and continued marching straight toward Atlanta. Even as Rosecrans entered Chattanooga, however, thirteen thousand Confederate
soldiers in General James Longstreet's corps left Virginia, headed west
to stop him. Riding broken-down southern railroads, half reached
northwest Georgia in time to reinforce General Braxton Bragg's Army
of Tennessee, make a significant contribution to the victory at Chickamauga, and save Atlanta for the Confederacy for a year. Following a
failed attempt to recapture Knoxville, Longstreet's troops returned to
the Army of Northern Virginia in the spring of 1864.

Five days after Chickamauga, twenty-three thousand soldiers in the
11th and 12th Corps of the Union Army of the Potomac began boarding trains in Virginia. Northern railroads carried them and their artillery, horses and wagons, and equipment to Tennessee to reinforce the

hard-pressed Cumberlanders, now besieged in Chattanooga. They first guarded the Nashville & Chattanooga Railroad from Confederate raiders intent on breaking Rosecrans' supply line, helped to lift the siege, and then drove the Confederates from east Tennessee. They transformed Chattanooga into a gigantic warehouse, the forward supply depot that supported General William T. Sherman's decisive campaign for Atlanta in 1864. The 11th and 12th Corps, now consolidated into the 20th Corps of the Army of the Cumberland, marched with him to victory.

Dramatic logistics accomplishments, the two rail movements illustrate the great importance of railroads in the Civil War. Almost fifty years ago, Kenneth P. Williams wrote of the 11th and 12th Corps movement, "the fifty pages in the Official Records devoted to the move tell a thrilling story that can still be studied with profit by anyone interested in logistics."[1] They also provide a unique opportunity to compare and contrast the quality of war management exercised by Union and Confederate leaders.

Many elements contributed to the mosaics of victory and defeat. In his Second Inaugural Address, President Lincoln attributed victory to "the progress of our arms, on which all else chiefly depends." The armies' victories and defeats on the war's many battlefields certainly decided the outcome of the war. The competence with which each side managed the noncombat elements of its war effort, however, also emerges as an important factor.

Superior organization and management, as demonstrated by its skillful use of railroads, made a genuine contribution to Union victory. The Confederacy's leaders, in contrast, proved unable to recognize or adapt to the demands of an increasingly logistics-driven conflict. The failure of its war management, as seen in part by its inability to organize the southern railroads effectively to support the war effort, thus represents an important, if little studied, factor in Confederate defeat.

At the beginning of the expected short conflict, few Civil War leaders anticipated, or even dimly understood, war's management compo-

---

1. Kenneth P. Williams, *Lincoln Finds a General: A Military Study of the Civil War* (New York: Macmillan, 1950–1959), 2:765.

nent. When short turned long, however, their ability to adapt to new conditions became crucial. The Confederates began what Emory Thomas calls a "conservative" revolution. But, he adds, they did not use revolutionary means to fight it, while the Union "revolutionized the art of war."[2]

The Civil War affected every activity in the Union and Confederacy and required a total commitment of civilian and military effort. Starting as a traditional, Napoleonic-style conflict, it quickly evolved as a war of transition. New technology, such as the railroads, and the rising importance of logistics, combined with war's reckless waste and insatiable appetite for food, material and equipment, and especially human lives, advance the arguments of those who define the Civil War as the first modern war.

Frank E. Vandiver observes that "mass war meant mass logistics." The prominence of logistics as a prerequisite to war began in the Civil War and distinguishes it from earlier conflicts. The European armies of the eighteenth and nineteenth centuries generally limited their campaigns to populated areas because they depended on local food supplies for sustenance. They also had to keep moving (a tactic Martin van Creveld calls "flight forward,") lest they exhaust the area's resources and risk starvation themselves. Small ammunition issues lasted entire campaigns because infantrymen only fired their wildly inaccurate smoothbore muskets in the final steps of massed frontal assaults.[3]

The sparse population of the southern states forced both Union and Confederate armies, with notable exceptions, to abandon the traditional practice of living off the land. Railroads and steamboats sustained armies fighting again and again over exhausted Virginia terrain, and across hundreds of miles of thinly populated areas of Georgia, Mississippi, and Tennessee. Ammunition consumption soared in the Civil

2. Emory M. Thomas, *The Confederacy as a Revolutionary Experience* (Englewood Cliffs, N.J.: Prentice Hall, 1971; reprint Columbia: University of South Carolina Press, 1991), 1, 51.

3. Frank E. Vandiver, *Rebel Brass: The Confederate Command System* (Baton Rouge: Louisiana State University Press, 1956), 81; Martin L. van Creveld, *Supplying War: Logistics from Wallenstein to Patton* (Cambridge: Cambridge University Press, 1977), 7, 24–25, 35.

War because of the long-range accuracy of rifled muskets and the intro-
duction of repeating weapons. Infantrymen entered combat with a
standard issue of "forty rounds in the cartridge-box" and many put
another "twenty in the pocket." They rapidly used all their ammunition in heavy fighting even though the coarse black powder of the day
forced them to stop after every twelve to fifteen rounds to clean their
weapons.[4]

Both sides evacuated wounded and sick soldiers by rail in attempts
to improve their still-primitive medical service, another example of an
increasingly twitching logistical tail. Also, civilians by 1861 had come
to rely on products delivered by railroads. Allen Trelease, citing a newspaper editorial that excoriated the railroads for neglecting the delivery
of rosin for street lighting, observes that home-front morale suffered
when southern railroads failed to supply these "new dependencies."[5]

A nation must expertly manage its war effort in order to successfully
prosecute the type of conflict that evolved in the Civil War. A combatant must establish clear objectives and set sound priorities. It must efficiently marshal its manpower and resources and then skillfully employ
them for maximum effectiveness. General Josiah Gorgas, the Confederacy's brilliant chief of ordnance, prophetically identified in the Civil
War a singular characteristic of modern war. "The great struggle in
which we are engaged," he said, "disorganizes everything which is not
energetically supervised."[6]

Success in overcoming the logistical challenges contributed directly
to both victory and defeat. The emerging importance of logistics relates directly to the effective use of railroads. The Civil War was a railroad war. Iron rails became logistics and communications lifelines. The
armies' success or failure depended on the men and matériel provided
by their governments and carried to them by railroads. Archer Jones
attributes "an almost revolutionary importance" to the strategic deployment of troops by rail.

4. James M. McPherson, conversation with the author.
5. Allen W. Trelease, *The North Carolina Railroad, 1849–1871, and the Modernization of North Carolina* (Chapel Hill: University of North Carolina Press,
1991), 174.
6. Frank E. Vandiver, ed., *The Civil War Diary of General Josiah Gorgas* (Tuscaloosa: University of Alabama Press, 1947), 10.

Union strategists deliberately targeted rail junctions such as Corinth, Mississippi, Chattanooga, and Atlanta as campaign objectives. The armies fought along rail lines. Every major battle east of the Mississippi took place within twenty miles of a railroad or navigable river. Thomas Weber observes that General William T. Sherman could not have conducted his Atlanta campaign without first securing for his army adequate rail support as an absolute prerequisite; indeed railroads offered "the sole means of transporting supplies." Sherman adds, "and only then, because we had the men and means to maintain and defend them in addition to what were necessary to overcome the enemy." Sherman observed that sustaining his 100,000-man army and 35,000 animals for the 196-day campaign over a 473-mile supply line would have required 36,600 six-mule teams, each hauling 2 tons of freight 20 miles per day, "a simple impossibility on roads such as then existed in that region." Well aware of the railroad's value, when Sherman abandoned Atlanta to begin his March to the Sea, his railroad men pulled up all the rails back to Chattanooga to deny them to the Confederates.[7]

Both Union and Confederate governments faced similar challenges in establishing wartime political, military, and industrial policies. Securing the cooperation of their railroads became of utmost importance in order to fight a war of mobility. They had to arrange adequate rate agreements for both military passengers and freight, integrate the tracks and operations of separately owned and competing railroads, find ways to compensate for the war's drain on skilled manpower, and prioritize and allocate scarce resources. By examining the success with which each side met these challenges, as reflected in the Longstreet and 11th and 12th Corps movements, one sees that the Union superbly— and the Confederacy deplorably—managed its war effort.

Bruce Catton describes the United States in the Civil War as an "industrialized nation waging industrial warfare." He makes his point with a story about Herman Haupt, the great railroad engineer. Haupt managed General Ambrose E. Burnside's military railroad during the

7. Archer Jones, *Civil War Command and Strategy: The Process of Victory and Defeat* (New York: Free, 1992), 240; Thomas Weber, *The Northern Railroads in the Civil War* (New York: King's Crown, 1952), 200; William T. Sherman, *Memoirs of Gen. W. T. Sherman* (New York: Charles L. Webster, 1891), 2:398–99.

1862 Fredericksburg campaign. He doubted that he would need a reserve supply of rails to support Burnside's army, but just in case, he ordered an extra ten miles "as a form of insurance." Writing off ten miles of iron rails as "the small change" of a Civil War campaign demonstrates to Catton the enormous strength of the Union's industrial resources. Southern foundries, in contrast, did not roll a single new iron rail after 1861.[8]

The resources that America diverted to the business of war in 1861 reflected the nation's burgeoning economic growth. Improved transportation fueled manufacturing-financial-industrial synergies that help to explain the northern railroads' ability to contribute to Union victory. Americans' willingness to innovate, acceptance of new technology, genius at practical engineering, propensity for improving productivity, and relentless drive to achieve maximum efficiency from scarce manpower all merged in railroads to propel America's transition from a subsistence to a market economy. Iron rails bound the several states together as one nation, despite dire predictions to the contrary by such astute observers as Alexis de Tocqueville and John C. Calhoun and implicit even in the very attempt to rend the Union by secession.[9]

In 1816 it cost nine dollars in freight charges to ship one ton of cargo from Europe to America. It cost another nine dollars to haul it just thirty miles inland on primitive roads. Shipping upstate New York wheat to New York City cost three times its market value, corn six

8. Bruce Catton, *Glory Road* (Garden City, N.Y.: Doubleday, 1952), 29, citing U.S. War Department, *The War of the Rebellion: A Compilation of the Official Records of the Union and Confederate Armies* (hereinafter cited as *OR*), 21:832; Robert C. Black III, *The Railroads of the Confederacy* (Chapel Hill: University of North Carolina Press, 1952), 124. The Tredegar Iron Works of Richmond, Virginia, had stopped making rails in the 1850s because it could not compete with northern or English foundry prices. Charles B. Dew, *Ironmaker to the Confederacy: Joseph R. Anderson and the Tredegar Iron Works* (New Haven: Yale University Press, 1966), 14.

9. George Rogers Taylor, *The Transportation Revolution, 1815–1860* (New York: Holt, Rinehart and Winston, 1951), 221; James A. Ward, *Railroads and the Character of America, 1820–1877* (Knoxville: University of Tennessee Press, 1986), 13–14.

times. Steamboats, first on the Hudson River, then on western rivers, started America's economic transformation. The opening of the Erie Canal in 1825 accelerated the change by making low-value, high-volume bulk cargo, such as grain, commercially viable. The canal lowered the cost of inland freight from 19.12 cents per ton-mile in 1817 to 0.672 cents in 1859, a 96.5 percent reduction.[10]

Baltimore's terrain did not lend itself to canal building, so its civic leaders bet the city's future on the new railroad technology. They chartered what would become the first long-distance railroad in America, the Baltimore & Ohio, in 1827. Its tracks reached Harpers Ferry, Virginia, in 1835; Cumberland, Maryland, in 1844; and the Ohio River, 379 miles from Baltimore, in December 1852. It commenced sixteen-hour through-service in January 1853.[11] Ironically, in an example of changing technology, it ran alongside, and competed for riverbank space with, the Chesapeake & Ohio Canal to Harpers Ferry and beyond. Appalachian Trail hikers today walk the C&O towpath for four miles north of Harpers Ferry beside regularly passing coal trains operated by the B&O's successor, CSX Corporation.

One might imagine that railroads were conceived with America's huge size in mind. John F. Stover points out that by 1857 the United States, with 5 percent of the world's population, had built 24,500 rail miles, almost half of the world's 51,000-mile total. Railroads traveled faster and farther—all day, every day, and in all kinds of weather—than any other form of transportation then known to mankind. The boatman and his "mule named Sal, fifteen miles on the Erie Canal" might take three weeks to walk "every step of the way from Albany to Buf-

10. Albert Fishlow, *American Railroads and the Transformation of the Antebellum Economy* (Cambridge: Harvard University Press, 1965), 22, 132–33; Edward Countryman, *Americans: A Collision of Histories* (New York: Hill and Wang, 1996), 116.

11. The South Carolina Canal and Railroad Company (to be renamed the South Carolina Railroad) completed a 136-mile route from Charleston to Hamburg, South Carolina, across the Savannah River from Augusta, Georgia, in October 1833, the longest railroad in the world at the time, according to John F. Stover, *American Railroads*, 2nd. ed. (Chicago: University of Chicago Press, 1997), 13, 39.

falo" on the 360-mile canal. When Erastus Corning consolidated fourteen separate railroads into the New York Central system in 1853, their
joined tracks reduced the 290-rail-mile Albany-Buffalo trip to one day,
a reflection of the railroad's speed and ability to use a more direct
route. In October 1853 a special speed run between New York and
Buffalo completed the 444 miles in 14.5 hours.[12]

The railroads' high speed introduced time as a factor in business.
Passenger trains between Cincinnati and St. Louis took sixteen hours,
and freight trains thirty, compared with seventy hours by steamboat.
Cincinnati to Pittsburgh took fifteen hours by rail, three days by river.
When the Boston & Lowell extended its tracks to Concord, New
Hampshire, in 1842, it reduced travel time from five days north and
four days south via canals and the Merrimack River to four hours each
way.[13]

Railroads also carried exponentially more than competing modes of
transportation. A horse-drawn wagon carried an upper limit of 15,000
ton-miles per year, a railroad 3.5 million. By 1840, taking into account
weather, speed, and reliability, Stanley Lebergott estimates that railroads could potentially carry fifty times more freight per mile per year
than a canal, or three to five times more in terms of resource costs.[14]

12. John F. Stover, *Iron Road to the West: American Railroads in the 1850s*
(New York: Columbia University Press, 1978), 16; Ward, *Railroads and the Character of America,* 131, citing *American Railroad Journal,* October 22, 1853.

13. Alfred D. Chandler Jr., *The Visible Hand: The Managerial Revolution in
American Business* (Cambridge: Belknap, 1977), 86, citing Edward Chase Kirk-
land, *Men, Cities, and Transportation* (Cambridge: Harvard University Press,
1948), 261, 262.

14. G. Taylor, *Transportation Revolution,* 135; Fishlow, *American Railroads,*
23–24, 29, citing J. Edwin Holmstrom, *Railways and Roads in Pioneer Development Overseas* (London, 1934), 56; Chandler, *Visible Hand,* 86, citing Stanley
Lebergott, "United States Transport and Externalities," *Journal of Economic History* 26 (December 1966): 444–46. According to Albro Martin, although the trip
from Albany to Schenectady took ten hours by canal, one by railroad, New York
law prohibited head-to-head competition. Railroads could run a parallel route only
when weather closed the canal, a critical foot in the door. The legislature repealed
the law in 1851. *Railroads Triumphant* (New York: Oxford University Press,
1992), 247.

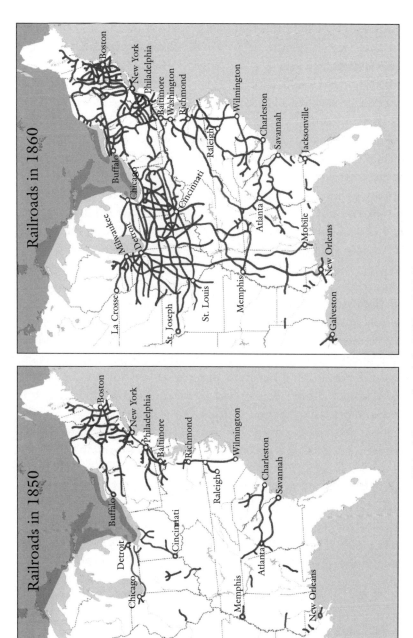

Railroads in 1850

Railroads in 1860

United States railroads in 1850 and 1860

Railroads propelled gains that would transform America into an industrial colossus. Their speed, regular and dependable scheduling, and direct routes reduced the cost of transportation in America by 95 percent between 1815 and 1860, freeing capital for other uses; the cost would decline another 50 percent by 1895.[15] The cost of mailing a letter decreased from fifty cents to three cents by 1850. Railroads, and the telegraph's instant communication, began to insinuate time as a factor into people's daily lives, and elevated time value to prominence in business thinking.

Much as water moves before it begins to boil, one senses, rather than sees, the emerging engineering sophistication, technological and agricultural discovery, and amassing of national wealth at the time of the Civil War. Walt W. Rostow designates 1843–1860 as the beginning of what he calls America's economic take-off, a "positive, sustained, and self-reinforcing response" to growth. Gains layered on gains prepared the nation for its "drive to maturity," as Rostow terms it, an explosion of economic activity driven by increasing contributions of science and technology in the last third of the nineteenth century. They reduced the cost of living by another 30 percent and made America the wealthiest nation in the world. In 1860, America produced less than either Great Britain, France, or Germany. In 1894, it produced more than the three combined.[16]

Railroads quickly cornered the market in passenger traffic and began to erode the canals' and steamboats' monopoly in freight. The railroads contributed to the reduction of New Orleans' share of western shipping traffic from 58 percent in 1820 to 23 percent, albeit of much greater volume, by 1860. Brokers shipped cotton by steamboat from Memphis to Cincinnati, then by rail to Boston. Railroad fares cost less, and shipments arrived thirty days faster than by the sea route. The Erie Canal and east-west railroads also shifted westerners' economic, and

15. G. Taylor, *Transportation Revolution*, 135, 149–50; John F. Stover, *The Life and Decline of the American Railroad* (New York: Oxford University Press, 1970), 88.

16. Walt Whitman Rostow, *The Stages of Economic Growth: A Non-Communist Manifesto* (Cambridge: Cambridge University Press, 1971), 2:37, 59; G. Taylor, *Transportation Revolution*, 249.

thus political, orientation from south to east, a matter of profound significance for American history. The Pennsylvania Central Railroad's cotton shipments increased from 5.7 million pounds in 1858 to 17.9 million in 1859 to 28.7 million pounds in 1860.[17] The seceding states blithely discarded a distinct and valuable regional economic interdependence in 1861.

Railroads created Chicago: one railroad entered the village in 1850; fifteen, four with through routes to the East, served the city with one hundred daily trains in 1860. Railroads made Chicago the world's grain depot. Maury Klein argues that the increase in Old Northwest rail mileage from 1,350 to 11,000 during the 1850s gave the region "decisive political weight" by 1860.[18]

Alfred D. Chandler Jr. calls railroads America's first "big business." Charles Francis O'Connell argues that the United States Army deserves the title. He points out that the first railroads simply borrowed military management principles, such as span of control, standard operating procedures, and chain of command, devised by the army to ensure uniform decentralized administration of its far-flung outposts. Management principles certainly evolved from the earliest efforts of men to control and coordinate the movements and actions of other men, i.e., soldiers and sailors. One clearly sees the military's organizational legacy in the pyramidal corporate structures that Chandler describes in *The Visible Hand.* After all, the army *was* a big business—10,929 officers and men served in 1850, compared with 4,381 employed in railroading.[19]

17. Douglass C. North, *The Economic Growth of the United States, 1790–1860* (Englewood Cliffs, N.J.: Prentice Hall, 1961), 110; Alfred D. Chandler Jr., *The Railroads: The Nation's First Big Business* (New York: Harcourt, Brace & World, 1965), 22.

18. Maury Klein, *Unfinished Business: The Railroad in American Life* (Hanover, N.H.: University Press of New England, 1994), 10–11; Stover, *Iron Road,* 115.

19. Charles Francis O'Connell Jr., "The United States Army and the Origins of Modern Management, 1818–1860" (Ph.D. diss., Ohio State University, 1982); Russell F. Weigley, *The History of the United States Army* (Bloomington: Indiana University Press, 1967), 597–98; G. Taylor, *Transportation Revolution,* 291.

The importance of Chandler's scholarship, however, lies in his recognition that the railroads' phenomenal growth, starting in the late
1840s, presented managers with problems of entirely new dimensions.
Modern business management evolved to meet the requirements
emerging from the rapid growth, both in size and in a complexity
never before seen, of long-distance railroads. Railroad growth ex-
ploded in the late 1840s. By 1860, railroad employment had grown to
36,567, while 16,215 officers and men served in the army. Total track
miles in America increased from 8,879 to 30,626, two-thirds of them
in northern states. Southern rail miles increased from 2,006 to 8,947
between 1850 and 1860, of 22,000 total new miles built in the United
States during the decade. The Pennsylvania Central reached Pittsburgh
in 1854. The 1850s saw the birth of the combination called the New
York Central. Twenty-five American railroads operated two hundred or
more miles of tracks in 1860.[20] The ten such railroads in the southern
states, however, trailed significantly in revenue, reflecting more recent
construction, the process of growing the business, and the nature of
northern and southern economies. The four largest-revenue-produc-
ing northern railroads on average operated 80 percent more track miles
and generated 80 percent more revenue per mile than the four largest
southern railroads in 1860.

The railroads urgently needed to develop strong managers. Economies of scale promised greatly improved efficiency and profitability to
capital-intensive railroads, but only if they could overcome the obstacles to efficiency imposed by size itself. The expansion in track miles
changed traditional management understanding of mass, space,
money, and time. Railroads operated on a scale far greater than any
business endeavor ever before seen. Railroad management in 1860

20. Black, *Railroads of the Confederacy*, 2; G. Taylor, *Transportation Revolution*, 84–85; Stover, *Iron Road*, 116. Railroad mileage statistics are presented with
caution. John F. Stover says that southern rail miles increased in the 1850s from
2,080 to 9,167 in *The Railroads of the South 1865–1900: A Study in Control*
(Chapel Hill: University of North Carolina Press, 1955), 3, citing the Eighth Census of the United States, 1860, "Mortality and Property" (Washington, 1866),
333–34. The *American Railroad Journal* of January 1861 reports different rail
mileage in some states, suggesting inconsistent reporting methods.

thus differed from previous forms, not only in degree, but in kind. Baltimore & Ohio managers wrote one of the first business organization manuals and used financial reports as a management tool. The Pennsylvania Central separated line and staff management functions in the 1850s. Railroad managers did more than simply modify the army's management principles; they transformed them. Necessity, says Chandler, not managerial genius, led them to adopt modern practices in order to make "the machine" work efficiently.[21]

In 1856, Erie Railroad Superintendent Daniel McCallum set down "a few general principles" of management. They included "a proper division of responsibilities" with appropriate authority. A long-distance railroad could operate cost effectively only if it practiced a management system "perfect in its details, properly adapted and vigilantly enforced." Operational efficiency, McCallum said, results not from "*a difference in length*" (italics in original) but "in proportion to the perfection of the system adopted." Achieving perfection took hard work: "The enforcement of a rigid system of discipline in the government of works of great magnitude is indispensable to success." McCallum demanded "*personal accountability through every grade of service*" (italics in original) and stressed the importance of regular reports to permit fast response to problems so "evils may be at once corrected." In addition to early warning, reports "will also point out the delinquent." McCallum's principles recall Josiah Gorgas' description of modern war, which, Gorgas says, "disorganizes everything . . . not energetically supervised."[22]

Railroad management involved nearly constant travel to inspect the

21. Alfred D. Chandler Jr., "The Railroads: Pioneers in Modern Corporate Management," *Business History Review* 39 (1965): 17 (citing revenue comparisons taken from *American Railroad Journal* [January 1861]: 10–13), 21–23; Chandler, *Big Business*, 9. Market demand forced manufacturers to adopt mass-production techniques for similar reasons. See David Hounshell, *From the American System to Mass Production, 1800–1932* (Baltimore: Johns Hopkins University Press, 1984).

22. Chandler, *Big Business*, 9, 101, 102, citing Daniel C. McCallum, "Superintendent's Report," March 25, 1856, in *Annual Report of the New York and Erie Railroad Company for 1855* (New York, 1856), 33–37, 39–41, 50–54, 57–59; Vandiver, *Gorgas*, 10.

line and consult with and advise local employees. Recognizing the limits to an individual's span of control, railroads developed extremely decentralized but highly integrated management structures. Railroads appointed a general superintendent, normally a professional engineer, as the senior line officer, "the central focus of both authority and communication." Three managers reported to him. The master of the roads maintained tracks, bridges, and buildings. The master of machinery oversaw maintenance of rolling stock and locomotives, as well as maintenance and repair shops. The master of transportation supervised "all such as belong specially to the forwarding of passengers and tonnage over the road." As railroads grew, line management further decentralized as masters delegated duties to division superintendents who managed one-hundred mile sections, the perceived maximum control radius. Staff personnel took over finance and accounting functions.[23]

Decentralized management required unprecedented delegation of authority. Size and distance dictated that local managers had to master every aspect of their areas of responsibility. They alone would have to resolve whatever problems arose, to find solutions and make decisions regardless of the problem's nature or complexity. Railroads also introduced a new element into the management mix: speed of response became increasingly important, especially at the operational level. Subordinates not only had to make correct decisions on complicated and critical issues, but they had to make them fast.[24] Performance meant everything. The ability to improvise, to innovate, and to make good decisions quickly defines a strong manager.

An organization can accommodate a decentralized management structure only with firmly disciplined control. Top management maintained control with data, lots of it, the more detailed the better. Railroad managers analyzed reports stuffed with statistics—on-time percentages, passenger and freight manifests, speed, tonnage, traffic volume to and from specific destinations, rail life, fuel efficiency—"a complete daily history of details in all their minutiae." Modern cost accounting emerged from such attention to detail.[25]

23. Chandler, *Big Business*, 14, 25–26.
24. Ibid., 97–98.
25. Ibid., 102–8, 125.

Railroading, for all its dramatic growth, was still an emerging industry in 1861. Many major rivers remained unbridged because of the high cost of construction, limited prewar volume, and lack of control of the road on the other side. Travelers still forded or floated their wagons across rivers or crossed them on ferries. In every community in America, noon was when the sun was directly overhead. Self-taught mechanics tinkered with designs and custom built locomotives one-by-one by eyeball measurement; design standardization, with some creative exceptions, lay a generation away.

The Baltimore & Ohio built bridges at Benwood and Parkersburg, West Virginia, its Ohio River termini, between 1868 and 1871. The combined cost, $2,237,156.80, amounted to 15 percent of the total cost of the original road. Edward Hungerford implies, but does not state outright, that the war delayed construction. The bridge eliminated the B&O's competitive disadvantage with the Pennsylvania and New York Central railroads for Chicago and western business.[26]

The Louisville & Nashville completed an Albert Fink–designed bridge across the Ohio River to Jeffersonville in 1870. Thus the river was no longer a barrier, but the bridge did not resolve a gauge break with the standard-gauge Jeffersonville, Madisonville & Indianapolis on the other side. Local opposition prevented railroad bridges across the Hudson as far north as Albany until after the war. A Philadelphia, Wilmington & Baltimore bridge across the Susquehanna River at Havre de Grace, Maryland, collapsed during construction in 1863 because of bad weather.[27]

After the war the Illinois Central Railroad cooperated with three southern roads to connect Chicago to New Orleans. It used car ferries to cross the Ohio River, during which time it changed the cars' axle width to conform northbound trains to the Illinois Central's standard-gauge tracks and southbound trains to the southern roads' five-foot

26. Edward Hungerford, *Story of the Baltimore and Ohio Railroad* (New York: G. P. Putnam's Sons, 1928), 2:40, 109–10.

27. Maury Klein, *History of the Louisville and Nashville Railroad* (New York: Macmillan, 1972), 90; George Rogers Taylor and Irene D. Neu, *The American Railroad Network, 1861–1890* (Cambridge: Harvard University Press, 1956), 16.

width. On August 21, 1881, the southern roads changed their tracks to the Illinois Central's standard gauge in nine hours, an achievement other railroads studied before all nonconforming roads switched to standard gauge in 1886. The Illinois Central, however, did not complete a bridge over the Ohio River to replace the car ferry service until 1889.[28]

Differences in track gauges illustrate that despite the rapid growth of the railroads and development of new operating methods, acceptance of change was not universal. George Rogers Taylor notes that promoters had originally only imagined the first railroads as short-haul vehicles, a reasonable assumption considering the limited industrial base at the time. Time had eroded, but not yet changed, the old thinking. Northern railroads rolled on thirteen different gauges in 1861, although three predominated. More than half, including the Baltimore & Ohio and Pennsylvania Central, used the 4-foot 8½-inch "standard" gauge. The New York Central changed to standard gauge during the Civil War. The Erie, however, stayed with a six-foot gauge until 1880, when it finally realized that its "monopoly" kept it from sharing a much larger, if competitive, pie. Travelers between New York and Washington rode on 4-foot 10-inch "New Jersey" (or "Ohio") gauge tracks to Philadelphia, then standard gauge to Washington. Extra-wide wheels on "compromise cars" allowed some cars to ride on either gauge.[29] Most southern railroads ran on either standard gauge or five-foot gauge. Railroad managers worried about the wear and tear to their tracks from other lines' cars riding over them, and they feared the permanent loss of their cars if they let them roll on other roads' tracks.

Civic and business interests recognized that different gauges en-

28. Taylor and Neu, *American Railroad Network,* 16.

29. James A. Ward, *Railroads and the Character of America,* 43; Weber, *Northern Railroads,* 7–8; Stover, *Life and Decline,* 62. Albro Martin repeats a story ("it is claimed") that the great English locomotive experimenter Robert Stephenson measured the axle length of his manure cart to select what would become the 4-foot 8½-inch "standard" gauge (*Railroads Triumphant,* 13). Stover, however, calls the standard gauge "a figure long customary to English wagons" (*American Railroads,* 24).

sured local monopolies. Some cities and towns passed ordinances designed to protect local businesses and boost town pride by prohibiting railroads from connecting their tracks. These featherbedding laws provided employment for stevedores and liverymen who unloaded passengers and freight, hauled them to forwarding stations, and reloaded them.

Americans had long foreseen the important role that railroads could take in national defense. Boosters invariably played the defense angle when soliciting construction capital. Experimentation and self-interest do not explain why the federal government never demanded an integrated national rail system.[30] The federal government's absence from the track-gauge debate may have stemmed from lack of expertise and the period's widely held belief that the government had no right to intrude in private business. Assigning soldiers to survey and supervise early railroad construction, however, belies this argument.

Antebellum railroads, for all their contributions to American economic development, however, offered mixed blessings; progress had a price. A contemporary described an early locomotive as a "mad dragon of an engine . . . scattering in all directions a shower of burning sparks . . . screeching, hissing, yelling, panting, until at last the thirsty monster stops beneath a covered way to drink." City fathers relegated railroads to the edges of town, their terminals blocks apart to minimize the noise, clouds of choking smoke, and sparks that posed genuine fire hazards.[31]

A few "union" stations in the North served several lines. Jersey City's handled as many as 112 trains a day for 6 different railroads. Three railroads served Philadelphia (and the Camden & Amboy ended just across the Delaware River), but none of their tracks connected, and each had separate terminals. Horse-drawn wagons and liveries carried freight and passengers through city streets from one terminal to another. The obstacles to rapid and efficient shipments produced annoying transshipment bottlenecks, even in peacetime. In Baltimore,

30. Ward, *Railroads and the Character of America,* 43.
31. Stover, *Life and Decline,* 21, citing Charles Dickens in *American Notes;* Taylor and Neu, *American Railroad Network,* 45.

the B&O; Philadelphia, Wilmington & Baltimore; and Northern Central each had its own terminal, unconnected with the others. Unconnected terminals would increase security problems in wartime. A secessionist Baltimore mob brawled with the Washington-bound 6th Masssachusetts Regiment marching between the PW&B and B&O stations on April 19, 1861.[32]

The small and widely dispersed population, modest manufacturing base, and predominance of seasonal agriculture generated limited demand for rail service in most of the southern United States. Southern railroads had less capital invested, compared to northern railroads, and many southern roads' condition reflected the cheap construction techniques associated with early railroad development. Investment in Georgia's railroads, for example, averaged $19,709 per track mile, compared with Pennsylvania's $50,509. Land acquisition costs were greater in the North, but most of the difference in expenditure reflects ongoing capital improvements to the northern roads.[33]

By 1861, many railroad leaders, particularly in the northern states, had begun to see distinct advantages to joining their tracks and adopting a single "standard" gauge to speed long-distance passengers and freight, much as a later generation would ignite a technology explosion with a comparable discovery of the advantages of being "IBM compatible." Expanding markets and cost-conscious businessmen demanded faster operating methods. According to Taylor and Neu, as late as 1869 transshipment costs between the Mississippi River and New York increased total shipping costs by twenty percent. Merchants and manufacturers became intolerant of gauge breaks and other impediments, however good for local business, when they realized the high price they paid for them. And as railroad financing became less local, "it was possible to ignore local pressures."[34]

Capital-intensive industries tend to pursue cost efficiency vigor-

32. Taylor and Neu, *American Railroad Network*, 13, 66; Weber, *Northern Railroads*, 8–9, 30–31; James M. McPherson, *Battle Cry of Freedom: The Civil War Era* (Oxford: Oxford University Press, 1988), 285.
33. Black, *Railroads of the Confederacy*, 4.
34. Taylor and Neu, *American Railroad Network*, 52, 53, 67.

ously. As railroad leaders came to appreciate the time value of money, they recognized the benefits of standard gauge and union terminals. Shipping freight to its destination in one car avoided breaking bulk at each railroad terminus. Through-shipping reduced waste and pilferage and saved time and money. Faster shipments and reduced costs increased profits. In the end, the financial bottom line overrode northern railroads' fears of losing cars to other roads' tracks, and the wear and tear from other railroads' cars running on their tracks. The huge increase in, and urgency of, wartime traffic would provide additional incentives, although, according to Taylor and Neu, "military requirements merely reinforced a movement which was gathering momentum in any case." Regardless, complete conversion to a single gauge across America would not occur until 1886, almost three years after the railroads had adopted standard timekeeping.[35]

Thomas Weber describes northern railroads in 1861 as "an articulate national network," if not a completely integrated system. Southern railroads, just as they were, also adequately served the antebellum region's needs. Robert Black says that, in spite of rough edges, the southern railroads represented "an imperfect skeleton of interior lines" at the start of the Civil War. He argues that they could have enabled the Confederacy to sustain the fighting until a war-weary Union gave up, but he adds an important qualification—the Confederacy had to make "sophisticated use" of its railroads to overcome shortages of manpower, matériel, and equipment.[36]

The Civil War made unprecedented demands that required fundamental changes from antebellum railroad practices in both the North and the South. Rail gaps, incompatible gauges, unconnected stations, local featherbedding ordinances, and arrogance that societies tolerated

---

35. Ibid., 6; Oliver Jensen, *American Heritage History of American Railroads* (New York: American Heritage, 1975), 144.

36. Weber, *Northern Railroads*, 4–5; W. Kirk Wood, "U. B. Phillips and Antebellum Southern Rail Inferiority: The Origins of the Myth," *Southern Studies* 26 (1987): 173–87; Robert C. Black, "The War on Rails," in William C. Davis and Bell I. Wiley, eds., *Civil War Times Illustrated Photographic History of the Civil War* (National Historical Society, 1981–1982; reprint, New York: Black Dog & Leventhal, 1994), 855.

Confederate railroads in 1861

PRINCIPAL INTERSTATE RAILROAD
LINKS OF THE CONFEDERATE STATES

SPRING 1861

SCALE IN MILES

Lines in operation
Lines under construction
Steamboat routes

Key to Railroads

1. Mobile & Ohio
2. Memphis & Charleston
3. Mississippi Central
4. New Orleans, Jackson
   & Great Northern
5. Southern of Mississippi
6. Northeast & Southwest
7. Alabama & Miss. Rivers
8. Mobile & Great Northern
9. Alabama & Florida of Ala.
10. Alabama & West Point
11. Atlanta & West Point
12. Western & Atlantic
13. Nashville & Chattanooga
14. Louisville & Nashville
15. E. Tennessee & Georgia
16. E. Tennessee & Virginia
17. Virginia & Tennessee
18. Orange & Alexandria
19. Virginia Central
20. South Side
21. Richmond & Danville
22. Richmond, Fredericksburg
    & Potomac
23. Richmond & Petersburg
24. Petersburg
25. Raleigh & Goston
26. North Carolina
27. Charlotte & S. Carolina
28. South Carolina
29. Georgia
30. Macon & Western
31. Central of Georgia
32. Charleston & Savannah
33. Northeastern
34. Wilmington & Monchester
35. Wilmington & Weldon

in peacetime would exert an unacceptable drag in prosecuting a war. The degree to which the Union and Confederate governments recognized and addressed these impediments would have profound consequences on the success of their war efforts.

Excellent management of its war-making resources became critically important when the smaller, weaker Confederacy recognized that it faced a long struggle for independence. Though hardly the first people to find themselves unprepared for the war they found themselves fighting, the Jefferson Davis administration proved inflexible and incapable of rising to the challenge. The Confederate leaders did not adjust to the unfamiliar and seemed unable to improvise to meet the unexpected. The Davis administration never took charge. It overlooked obvious problems, responded slowly and timidly to others, and bungled still others. It never adopted central planning, which would have enabled it to establish priorities and allocate its scarce resources for maximum benefit. This meant that it squandered part of its war production. It performed hardly better in allocating skilled manpower. The would-be nation thus left itself ill equipped to meet the relentless grind and endless confusions that Clausewitz called the "friction" of war. The Confederacy's flawed management emerges clearly in its failure to effectively mobilize southern railroads to achieve its war objectives. It allowed "badly conducted" railroads, as Josiah Gorgas described them, to deteriorate, then collapse.[37] The Confederate armies followed.

As case studies, the Longstreet and 11th and 12th Corps movements contrast a sophisticated and expertly managed northern rail system with uncoordinated and poorly maintained southern railroads. The Longstreet movement shows the consequences of the Jefferson Davis administration's wretched war management and contributes to understanding the growing importance of logistics in war.

The United States faced formidable obstacles in the Civil War. Victory proved an extremely difficult, and at times seemingly insurmountable, challenge. The federal government called on America's great industrial and manufacturing resources and rapidly improving trans-

37. Vandiver, *Gorgas*, 10.

portation system to fight this new type of conflict. It enjoyed, to be sure, tremendous natural, industrial, and human resources. More significantly, it applied them effectively to overcome the Confederacy's advantages.

Russell F. Weigley, in his fine biography of Union Quartermaster General Montgomery C. Meigs, notes that the Union's allegedly vast war-making capacity existed only as a potential advantage at the start of the war. The successful marshaling of its assets converted that potential into a genuine advantage, as the North's use of its railroads demonstrates.[38] The railroads' enormous lift capacity and round-the-clock operating capability sustained Union armies as they invaded the southern states. They helped Union armies exploit interior lines in terms of time as collapsing southern railroads cost the Confederacy its advantage of interior lines in terms of space. The Union's successful use of railroads neutralized a determined Confederacy's vast land mass. They changed the nature of warfare by enabling the Union to shrink the Confederacy to a manageable—and vulnerable—size.

One can easily overstate the importance of the North's industrial advantage. The Union could outproduce the Confederacy and replace its losses, to be sure; these advantages conferred staying power and numerical superiority but not technological superiority. Further, the Union could not always provide superior resources, as the near-starvation of the Cumberlanders in Chattanooga attests.

Union war managers had to surmount unforeseen, changing, and ever-increasing challenges to meet the armies' logistical requirements. Union forces operated over the Union's southern perimeter, which extended more than eight hundred miles from Washington to the junction of the Mississippi and Ohio Rivers, as well as along two thousand miles of Confederate coastline; railroads and waterborne transportation supplied them. Retreating Confederate armies fell back toward their bases of supply as Yankees advancing into the Confederate heart-

38. Russell F. Weigley, *Quartermaster General of the Union Army: A Biography of M. C. Meigs* (New York: Columbia University Press, 1959), 5. Weigley attributes no small part of Meigs's success to his broad experience in dealing with private businessmen and in supervising large contracts, having overseen the Great Falls aqueduct project that serves Washington, D.C., and the extension of the Capitol, 162.

land marched away from theirs. According to Herman Hattaway and Archer Jones, the Union soldiers diverted to defending lengthening lines of communication consumed as much as 30 percent of the Union's manpower advantage. Approximately 112,000 Union soldiers guarded railroads and other rear areas against 22,000 Confederate raiders.[39] The Confederacy also assigned large numbers of soldiers to defend its perimeter, a necessary concession to states' rights, but it did not have to bear the burden of total victory.

The Union correctly identified and addressed its major problems, carefully evaluated its options, and skillfully exploited its advantages. Outstanding management allowed the federal government to marshal its resources successfully to meet the test. Securing the cooperation of northern railroads enabled Union armies to fight a war of mobility by sustaining the Union armies in the field. Railroads and ships enabled the fighting forces to win the war on the battlefields, overwhelm the Confederacy, and preserve the Union.

The modern management principles and procedures developed by antebellum northern railroads produced outstanding managers whose ability and experience proved invaluable to the Union war effort. They enabled America's emerging transportation and communications systems to play critical roles in preserving the Union, as the 11th and 12th Corps movement surely demonstrates.

Talented and experienced railroad men provided a great service to the United States in the Civil War. John Garrett, Daniel McCallum, Tom Scott, and Prescott Smith, architects of the 11th and 12th Corps movement, exercised exceptional management skill. Their subordinates showed similar ability, clear evidence of the northern railroads' management depth. Their service contrasts with southern railroad executives who, according to Frank Vandiver, seemed to lack the ability to think on their feet.[40] Excepting a few men, such as Josiah Gorgas, the Confederacy neither identified nor promoted the strong managers necessary to help it conduct a successful war.

The federal government adopted strong policies to mobilize the

---

39. Herman Hattaway and Archer Jones, *How the North Won: A Military History of the Civil War* (Urbana: University of Illinois Press, 1983), 491, 721.
40. Frank E. Vandiver, telephone conversation with the author, April 4, 1996.

northern railroads. It raised the velvet fist of national police power to ensure the cooperation of independent-minded railroad executives. At the same time, however, it negotiated rate schedules that ensured profits to efficient railroads. It otherwise left the railroads free to operate according to their own business practices, and it specifically insulated them from military interference.

Northern railroads faced rising prices and shortages of manpower, matériel, and equipment, but strains and shortages define wartime economies. Struggling with these problems forced the northern railroads to adopt still more efficient operating methods. Necessity, Thomas Weber says, also pushed them into greater cooperation with each other.[41] The lessons learned by northern railroad managers in the Civil War had profound implications for the postwar development of a national rail system.

Confederate President Jefferson Davis worked very hard to create a strong central government; unfortunately for the Cause, he created an uncoordinated and inefficient one. The Confederacy absolutely had to have an adequate transportation system in order to fight a winning war. An early transcontinental railroad proponent, Davis certainly understood railroads' importance to the war effort. He asked for, and the Confederate Congress gave him, strong legislation that authorized the government to seize the railroads if necessary to ensure their cooperation. He had the authority but he did not use it.

The Confederate government imposed neither its will nor the law on railroad managers. With a cultivated arrogance that matched their ferocious capitalism-run-amok independence, some managers withheld the cooperation necessary to organize southern railroads into a workable Confederate rail system. The Confederacy's inability to secure the railroads' cooperation tends to support Paul Escott's argument that it never developed a strong sense of nationalism.[42]

Gary W. Gallagher asks how the rebellion survived for four years "if the Confederates so woefully mismanaged their war effort," as argued in this work. He raises a good question, an important question, because he shifts the focus to a new perspective. No one or two elements

41. Weber, *Northern Railroads,* 229.
42. Paul D. Escott, *After Secession: Jefferson Davis and the Failure of Confederate Nationalism* (Baton Rouge: Louisiana State University Press, 1978), 54.

in isolation determined the outcome of the Civil War. One finds exceptions to each reason given, and subpoints, counterarguments, and changing colorations within each of them, tendencies more often than carved-in-stone reasons, and all of them relative.[43]

The Longstreet and 11th and 12th Corps movements illustrate the importance and consequences of logistics management in the Civil War, from organizational and management skill to the speed and quality of decision making under pressure. The two movements provide a clear picture of the rail operations problems the Union and Confederate war managers faced and how effectively, or ineffectively, each side identified and solved or avoided those problems. An examination of the two movements enhances our understanding of the development of war management. Considering the emerging importance of logistics as an element in war, the Union recognized and responded to the new conditions that the Civil War brought forth. This enabled it to fight and win what some call a modern war. The Confederacy's failure to comprehend the changing landscape of war condemned it to fight and lose a war of the past.[44]

By studying the contributions of railroads to the Union and Confederacy war efforts, one gains insights into the elements of victory and defeat, an understanding of why the Union won a war that it could have lost, and why the Confederacy lost a war that it might have won.

43. Letter to the author from Gary W. Gallagher dated October 23, 1997. Gallagher brings into perspective many conflicting arguments about the causes of victory and defeat in *The Confederate War: How Popular Will, Nationalism, and Military Strategy Could Not Stave Off Defeat* (Cambridge: Harvard University Press, 1997). He makes a strong case for Confederate nationalism, at least as determined by a sustained popular will to keep fighting, and he refutes arguments that allege flawed Confederate military strategy. In the end, he says, the Union simply wore down the rebellion.

44. In Stig Förster and Jörg Nagler, eds., *On the Road to Total War: The American Civil War and the German Wars of Unification, 1861–1871* (Washington, D.C.: German Historical Institute; Cambridge: Cambridge University Press, 1997), James M. McPherson makes the argument in "From Limited War to Total War in America," 295–309, that the Civil War qualifies as a "modern" or "total" war, while Mark E. Neely Jr. takes the opposite position in "Was the Civil War a Total War?" 29–52.

1

THE CHALLENGE OF WAR MANAGEMENT

Union and Confederate Government Responses

> In a war for national existence . . . the whole mass of the nation
> must be engaged.
> —Josiah Gorgas

Neither the Confederacy nor the Union expected a long war, nor
could they have anticipated the scale to which it would grow. As its
harsh unfolding erased any expectations of a short and glorious war,
both Union and Confederate war governments faced the challenges of
establishing political, military, and industrial policies. They had to determine their objectives; marshal, prioritize, and allocate scarce resources; and then employ them effectively to achieve the final victory.

They needed the cooperation of their railroads in order to fight a
war governed by logistics and mobility. This meant arranging adequate
military passenger and freight rates, integrating separately owned and
competing railroads, compensating for the war's drain on skilled manpower, and insulating railroad operations from army interference. The
Union and Confederate governments took different paths to meet
these challenges. Comparing the Longstreet and 11th and 12th Corps

movements demonstrates the success with which each side achieved its goals.

A nation fighting for its existence ignores reality at its peril. As the weaker combatant, the Confederate government had to take bold steps to achieve maximum effectiveness with its war-making resources. Central planning and sound management policies would have provided essential guidance in determining how to win a long fight for independence. Planning would have enabled the Confederate government to assess its needs, identify obstacles to meeting them, and determine the most appropriate solutions. Carefully established priorities would have shown the Confederacy how to husband and allocate its scarce resources. The Confederacy could not satisfy every legitimate need. It had to decide who must have and who could not. It had to establish a system to coordinate and manage the timing of logistics procurement, transportation, and distribution functions. It did none of these things. In spite of having absolute control of all natural and manufacturing resources, the Confederate government never centralized procurement or established priorities for allocating its limited supplies. As a result, it squandered resources essential to its war economy, encouraged wasteful duplication of effort, and promoted destructive competition. The combination proved fatal to a weak combatant fighting a war increasingly dominated by logistics. Frank E. Vandiver describes a Confederacy "wrecked by decentralized centralization."[1]

Confederate departments scrambled for materials. Resourceful bureau chiefs hoarded supplies, thus denying them to other agencies in need. In July 1864, for example, Commissary General Northrop learned that Josiah Gorgas' ordnance officers had bypassed his office and cornered a six-month supply of wheat to feed Ordnance Department personnel. They purchased all they needed by simply ignoring Northrop's carefully established price schedules.[2]

1. Vandiver, *Rebel Brass,* 83–96, 126.
2. Jerrold Northrop Moore, *Confederate Commissary General: Lucius Bellinger Northrop and the Subsistence Bureau of the Southern Army* (Shippensburg, Penn.: White Mane, 1996), 260, citing *OR,* Ser. 4, 3: 533, 535.

The Confederacy believed at the start of the war that geography, specifically its huge size and interior lines of communication, gave it substantial advantages. The total Confederate land mass covered a map of Europe from the Bay of Biscay to east of Moscow. The military concept of interior lines presumes an advantage in an army's ability to reinforce or concentrate separated units from a central position more rapidly than its enemy; that is, an army can move between two points inside an area faster than an enemy moving around the perimeter, or invading its interior, at comparable speed. Soldiers before the Civil War thought of interior lines in terms of space, or distance, although geography sometimes conferred an additional advantage. The Civil War began to modify the concept, increasingly framing the advantage in terms of time, as railroads and steamboats improved travel speed and freight loads; today's soldiers call it "superior lateral communications." The air age has eroded the concept's significance, though it remains valid for such aspects of logistics planning as bulk cargo shipping.

General Pierre G. T. Beauregard used the Manassas Gap Railroad to shuttle General Joseph E. Johnston's troops from the Shenandoah Valley to the First Manassas battlefield in July 1861. Enough soldiers arrived just in time to reinforce Beauregard's army and contribute to winning the war's first battle. Beauregard's creative use of railroads, according to Archer Jones, caused a "paranoid Union overestimate of Confederate capacity for strategic troop movements by rail." The Yankees believed that railroads brought troops from as far away as Mississippi for the Seven Days' Battles near Richmond in July 1862.[3]

General Braxton Bragg also demonstrated the strategic value of railroad movements within interior lines. He shipped 31,193 troops from Tupelo, Mississippi, to Chattanooga, Tennessee, to meet a Yankee threat in July 1862. His soldiers linked up with General Nathan Bedford Forrest's cavalry, and the combined forces attacked Union General Don Carlos Buell's columns advancing toward Chattanooga. They threatened Buell's extended line of communication along the Nashville & Chattanooga Railroad and forced him to retreat. Bragg's timely

3. A. Jones, *Command and Strategy* (New York: Free, 1992), 100, 101.

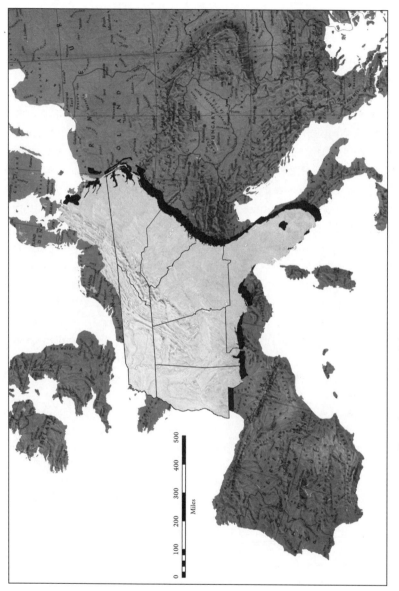

Size of eastern Confederacy compared with western Europe

movement saved Chattanooga and eastern Tennessee's invaluable copper and nitre reserves for the Confederacy for another year.

The Bragg movement, however, revealed the fragility of the interior
lines advantage. Union army planners, in order to break the Confederacy's lines of communication, shrewdly selected rail junctions as primary campaign objectives. They proved the strategy's soundness when
Union General Henry W. Halleck's army captured the rail junction at
Corinth, Mississippi, in May 1862. This blocked Bragg's most direct
route to Chattanooga, 225 rail miles, and forced him to send his army
by way of Mobile, Alabama, a 776-mile journey. The first three thousand troops completed the trip in six days over six railroad lines.
Bragg's cavalry, artillery, and other horse-drawn equipment, in contrast, took six exhausting weeks to march overland. Other deficiencies
further eroded the advantage. Rail gaps between Meridian, Mississippi,
and Selma, Alabama, and between Selma and Montgomery, Alabama,
turned the 150-mile distance between Meridian and Montgomery into
a 350-mile detour through Mobile, adding two days to the trip.[4]

The true advantage of interior lines, Robert Black argues, depended
on the Confederacy's ability to exploit it. It had to act decisively to
cobble together a railroad system capable of meeting its wartime needs.
It had to integrate the railroads by closing critical gaps between them
and connecting the same-gauge tracks of different railroad companies
in order to exploit the most direct routes and maximize the use of

4. George Edgar Turner, *Victory Rode the Rails* (New York: Bobbs-Merrill,
1953), 180–82; Black, *Railroads of the Confederacy,* 2–12, 181; Thomas Lawrence Connelly, *Army of the Heartland: The Army of Tennessee, 1861–1862* (Baton
Rouge: Louisiana State University Press, 1967), 202–4. See *OR,* Ser. 1, 17, pt.
2:648–60, and Ser. 1, 16, pt. 2:738–41. Connelly declares the movement "well
planned on short notice," 203; Thomas G. Ziek Jr. points out, however, that the
initial three-thousand-man movement followed two weeks of planning and organizing and only involved six ten-car trains ("The Effects of Southern Railroads on
Interior Lines in the Civil War" [master's thesis, Texas A&M University], 99 n).
The 30th Tennessee Regiment repeated Bragg's 1862 route to get to Chickamauga, described in Samuel Robert Simpson Papers, Tennessee State Library and
Archives, Nashville, and in Lowell H. Harrison, ed., "The Diary of an 'Average'
Confederate Soldier," *Tennessee Historical Quarterly* 29 (1970): 263.

available rolling stock.[5] It had to provide adequate maintenance, parts, and equipment by leasing, purchasing, or, if it must, seizing outright or cannibalizing the rails and rolling stock of less critical routes. Lucius B. Northrop, the Confederate commissary general, immediately recognized the need to centralize railroad operations for the efficient collection and distribution of food supplies, as well as to prevent food speculation and "venality."[6] But the Confederacy took none of these steps and overcame none of these challenges.

The antebellum United States government, a deliberately small and loosely organized institution, reflected the pedestrian tempo of peacetime administration. There were 36,106 civilian employees in 1860, 85 percent of whom worked for the Post Office Department. According to James Huston, the army went to war armed with administrative structures "more often the product of tradition and policies and diplomacy and leadership than of clear-cut logic." The Founding Fathers, however, had designed a government that could grow strong enough to defend itself. In spite of early missteps, the Union achieved the most rapid mobilization in American history. The army expanded by a factor of 62, from 16,000 soldiers in 1861 to 1,000,000 men by 1865 without, Huston notes, the benefit of a National Guard, as in World War I, or a growing army of draftees, as at the beginning of World War II. Federal spending increased from $22,981,000 in 1861 to $1,032,323,000 in 1865.[7]

In spite of having to overcome problems related to the sheer magnitude of the task, such as rejecting dishonest vendors' shoddy goods, the United States marshaled its industrial base to destroy the Confederacy, much as it would do to bury three totalitarian regimes in the twentieth century. Tailors created standard sizes to clothe Union soldiers; specialization of labor and sewing machines reduced shirt-making time by a factor of eleven. Wool production tripled, and new

5. Black, *Railroads of the Confederacy*, 295.

6. J. Moore, *Confederate Commissary General*, 53–54.

7. James A. Huston, *The Sinews of War: Army Logistics 1775–1953* (Washington, D.C.: Office of the Chief of Military History, U.S. Army, 1966), 175; Michael Lind, *The Next American Nation: The New Nationalism and the Fourth American Revolution* (New York: Free, 1995), 34.

manufacturing techniques quadrupled shoe production. Grain and meat packing output soared. The Springfield Arsenal, the earliest example of the "American System of Manufacture," produced 350,000 rifles a year by the war's end for less than $12 each.[8]

An inherent conflict exists between a ferociously independent free-enterprise economy and a democratic free-market government fighting a desperate war. Robert Weber finds this "strikingly brought out" in the relationships of both northern and southern railroad leaders with their respective governments.[9] The Davis administration had to mind southerners' stubborn arrogance, while both his and the Lincoln administration had to overcome resistance and suspicion by businessmen unused, and not amenable, to any kind of governmental regulations or constraints.

Railroad managers' and businessmen's attitudes reflected the laissez-faire business culture of the period. The mid-nineteenth century American executive owed his first duty to his company's best interests. All other obligations came second, including present-day notions of patriotism. John Garrett, president of the Baltimore & Ohio Railroad, for example, evidently subordinated his strong southern sympathies because Union army traffic generated most of the east-west B&O's wartime revenue. Loyalty to his railroad made Garrett loyal to the Union. Confederate General Stonewall Jackson's depredations to the B&O cooled the passions of many secessionist-leaning Baltimore residents because he threatened the value of their investments in the company's stock.[10]

Their companies' welfare guided both southern and northern busi-

8. Huston, *Sinews of War,* 177–78. Rapid growth led to boundless opportunities for the greedy. Shoddy (a cheap cloth that gave the word a new meaning during the Civil War) products and outright fraud led to regulations almost as onerous as the misconduct they aimed to prevent. Of one antifraud proposal, Q.M. Gen. Meigs observed, "if the conditions in regard to contracts imposed by this bill become law the country may as well at once yield to the Southern rebels all they ask." Huston, *Sinews of War,* 181, citing Meigs's letter to Senator Henry Wilson, *OR,* Ser. 3, 1:378–79.

9. Weber, *Northern Railroads,* 94.

10. Ibid., 28–29.

nessmen's conduct. They never lost sight of, or reduced their primary interest in, the bottom line. They rejected the government's claim to any right to interfere with their private enterprises. Mary DeCredico describes southern business executives' attitudes as "patriotism for profit." Their worship of the invisible hand led "ambitious individuals" to enter war production "for selfless and selfish reasons . . . fully alert to the prospect of personal gain."[11] To blame southern businessmen's less-than-total cooperation on greed and obstinacy, however, oversimplifies the matter; northern businessmen held precisely the same attitudes. Governmental intrusion into business conduct, such as the Interstate Commerce Commission and the Sherman Antitrust Act, lay a generation in the future. Most businessmen's familiarity with the federal government began and ended at the post office, federal court, and customs house. Their understanding of government did not include its encroachment into their domains. Federal and Confederate leaders alike shared the attitudes born of the same culture.

The antebellum business mentality, coupled with the railroad leaders' devotion to their companies' bottom lines, encouraged behavior that would horrify observers of today's supposedly modest business ethics. James Guthrie's Louisville & Nashville Railroad carried on a lively trade between neutral Louisville and Confederate Nashville for months after the war began. Both governments looked the other way. Most L&N freight rolled south to Confederates who needed the goods. President Lincoln abided the activity because he would do nothing to disturb Kentucky's declared neutrality.[12]

Lincoln's patience paid off. On September 3, 1861, Confederate General Leonidas Polk, a West Pointer who became an Episcopal bishop, committed one of the greatest geographic blunders in the history of warfare. Expecting to excite an outpouring of Confederate sympathy, he invaded Columbus, Kentucky. The Confederate "aggression" prompted a quick and powerful Union response. The Yankee

11. Mary A. DeCredico, *Patriotism for Profit: Georgia's Urban Entrepreneurs and the Confederate War Effort* (Chapel Hill: University of North Carolina Press, 1990), 31–32.
12. Weber, *Northern Railroads,* 28–29.

counterthrust invigorated the career of a failed drunk named Ulysses S. Grant, adding to the magnitude of Polk's miscalculation. By violating Kentucky's neutrality Polk opened what had been an impenetrable Confederate sanctuary. The Cumberland and Tennessee rivers flow from Tennessee through Kentucky to the Ohio River and, with the Louisville & Nashville Railroad, became transportation daggers into the Confederate heartland, as the Yankees quickly demonstrated. They captured Nashville on February 23, 1862. Its significance as the first Confederate state capital to fall pales besides its importance as an industrial city—it produced all the Confederate gunpowder fired at First Manassas. The Yankees' taking Nashville also ripped the Tennessee breadbasket from the Confederacy. President Lincoln once said that he hoped to have God on his side, but he absolutely had to have Kentucky. It appears that he got both.[13]

A war for national survival aside, business was business. Fealty to that mind-set produced behavior that many twentieth-century Americans might find bizarre. Northern railroads participating in the 11th and 12th Corps movement, for example, maintained their regular schedules before moving the troop trains. The War Department knew it and, in spite of the mission's urgency, accepted the practice without question. When asked about the L&N's capacity to support the movement, General Boyle in Louisville advised Secretary Stanton that "Passenger trains occupy twelve hours between Louisville and Nashville; for trains with troops, about sixteen hours" for the 185-mile trip. The 150th New York spent many idle hours on side tracks, cooking bacon and boiling coffee because they "were not making schedule time." For this reason, and because of frequent stops for water, according to General Oliver Howard, they "did well to average fifteen [miles per hour]."[14]

13. For a first-rate study of Tennessee's strategic significance, see Connelly, *Army of the Heartland;* Polk's role at Columbus is discussed on pp. 52–55.

14. Boyle to Stanton, September 24, 1863, *OR*, Ser. 1, 29, pt. 1:149; Stephen W. Cook and Charles E. Benton, eds., *The Dutchess County Regiment: The 150th Regiment of New York Volunteer Infantry in the Civil War* (Danbury, Conn.: Danbury Medical, 1907), 52; *Autobiography of Oliver Otis Howard, Major General, United States Army* (New York: Baker & Taylor, 1907), 1:452.

The Civil War, however, demanded entirely new relationships between business and government. The federal government put itself in a position to receive excellent cooperation from the northern railroads throughout the war. Both President Lincoln and Secretary of War Edwin M. Stanton had represented railroads as lawyers before the war. They understood the technical sophistication needed to operate these complex systems, and they preferred to leave the railroads in civilian hands.[15] Lincoln, as a war president, proved an excellent delegator. No one in America understood more clearly the war's objective, shared his strategic vision for winning it, or felt deeper anguish about its cost. But he possessed the personal confidence and self-restraint to refrain from meddling and let others do their jobs. During the 11th and 12th Corps movement, for example, he stayed informed, but otherwise kept out of the way.

The northern railroads in 1861 also had a powerful ally in Assistant Secretary of War Thomas A. Scott. A former vice president of the Pennsylvania Central Railroad, he argued convincingly that the War Department should leave the northern railroads under civilian management. He made it quite clear to railroad managers, however, that he expected them to act as "direct adjuncts" of the War Department. He also assured them that cooperation served their interests better than otherwise certain coercion.[16]

Stanton and Scott helped placate the railroads by arranging a uniform shipping rate agreement. The government paid two cents per mile per man for military passengers. A sliding scale covered other government freight based on the type of cargo, weight, and distance. General cargo, for example, cost ten cents per hundred pounds for thirty miles, ninety cents for four hundred miles. A fair, actually generous, arrangement, the accord made good practical business sense. The government gained cost stability, and adequate payments gave the railroads the operating capital they needed to maintain their roads. Quartermaster General Montgomery Meigs later conceded that the

15. Turner, *Victory Rode the Rails,* 247.
16. Samuel Richey Kamm, *The Civil War Career of Thomas A. Scott* (Philadelphia: University of Pennsylvania, 1940), 38, 136, 68.

NET EARNINGS OF THE
BALTIMORE & OHIO RAILROAD, 1856–1864,
AND THE LOUISVILLE & NASHVILLE RAILROAD, 1861–1865

	B&O ($)	L&N ($)
1856	2,237,166	
1857	2,140,744	
1858	1,587,006	
1859	2,244,061	
1860	2,670,041	
1861	2,182,665	461,970[a]
1862	3,776,593	508,591
1863	5,016,113	1,062,165
1864	5,692,681	1,803,953
1865		2,172,515

Sources: Data for B&O from Peter Harold Jaynes, "The Civil War and Northern Railroads: A Test of the Cochran Thesis" (Ph.D. diss., Boston University, 1973), 265, citing Henry M. Flint, *The Railroads of the United States: Their History and Statistics* (Philadelphia: John E. Potter, 1868), 70; data for L&N from Klein, *Louisville & Nashville,* 42. Net earnings defined as revenue less operations and maintenance, debt service, and taxes, but not depreciation (Jaynes, 258).

[a] L&N profits for ten months of 1861.

government paid premium rates to the railroads but argued that it received outstanding, and therefore economical, rail service during the war.[17]

Capitalism measures success at the bottom line. Well-managed northern railroads made money hauling troops at the 2-cent rate; their prewar passenger costs averaged only 1.8 cents per mile. Once the railroads passed the break-even point, large volume guaranteed huge profits to their high-fixed, low-operating-cost businesses. A well-run railroad reached optimum operating efficiency as it approached maximum capacity, as the B&O's and L&N's wartime net earnings confirm.[18]

17. Weber, *Northern Railroads,* 127–30; *OR,* Ser. 3, 2:795.

18. Credit for recognizing the association of volume to profitability goes to either Herman Haupt or Tom Scott, depending on the biographer. Kamm, *Scott,* 68; James A. Ward, *That Man Haupt: A Biography of Herman Haupt* (Baton Rouge: Louisiana State University Press, 1973), 31.

The magnitude of the B&O's profits gains in significance when one considers the frequency and enthusiasm with which Confederate soldiers wrecked the road. Stonewall Jackson seized the B&O near Harpers Ferry shortly after the war began and literally held it hostage. When he withdrew in June 1861, he took as much B&O property as he could with him, including 14 locomotives and 36 miles of rails, and smashed an impressive amount of what he could not. His men destroyed 42 locomotives and 386 cars, burned 23 bridges, and pulled down 102 miles of telegraph line. Nine months passed before the B&O restored train service to the Ohio River.[19]

Robert E. Lee's Army of Northern Virginia tore up the B&O during the Antietam and Gettysburg campaigns, and cavalry raiders broke sections of the road at other times. The railroad enjoyed unhampered operations for only four and one-half months in 1862 and six months and six days in 1863. John Garrett would report that the road absorbed three million dollars in uncompensated war damage. Giving the devil his due, after the war Garrett hired former Confederate Captain Thomas R. Sharp, the man who removed the B&O property for Jackson.[20]

The war made the Louisville & Nashville Railroad a reluctant ally of the federal government, a military railroad in all but name. It supplied Union General Don Carlos Buell's columns when they invaded the Confederate heartland and captured Nashville in 1862 and during the campaigns for Chattanooga. Louisville became the northern terminus of General Sherman's supply line during the Atlanta campaign. The L&N's earnings show that war was good for business. Maury Klein reports that the L&N paid off all its debt by 1863, a remarkable accomplishment considering that it made its maiden run on October 27,

19. Weber, *Northern Railroads*, 77.
20. Ibid., 78–80; Hungerford, *Baltimore and Ohio*, 2:7–12, 15. Garrett told Sharp at his employment interview, "A man who can steal a fifty-mile section of a railroad, not to mention a lot of rolling stock, move the plunder across the country on a dirt road and place it in another fellow's line ought to be pretty well up on the transportation business." Sharp served the B&O from 1872 to 1877 (Hungerford, *Baltimore and Ohio*, 2:135ff).

1859. It also paid 10.25% stock and 14% cash dividends to its stock-holders during the war.[21]

The L&N's strategic location brought it into repeated friction with the army. Union officers accused the road of shipping civilian goods before military traffic on several occasions. A strong Kentucky Union-ist, L&N President James Guthrie accepted the government's demand for complete cooperation in theory, but rejected the "uncritical appli-cation of it in fact." Secretary of the Treasury in the Franklin Pierce administration, Guthrie argued that operating in a war zone posed unique problems for the L&N. In addition, as a newly completed road, it did not, he said, have the funds to develop both civilian and military traffic.[22]

The federal government paid the L&N a 25 percent premium on top of the standard rate agreement, and the road almost exclusively carried military traffic in the winter of 1863. Complaints of poor ser-vice, however, persisted amid accusations and denials that the railroad continued to give priority to civilian goods. At the beginning of the September–November 1863 Chickamauga-Chattanooga campaign, a time when the army needed sixty-five cars for its own needs, only six-teen freight cars a day rolled down L&N tracks.

The L&N's general superintendent, Albert Fink, an outstanding en-gineer who earlier had built many of the B&O's bridges, argued that the L&N's inability to carry all the freight the army needed did not automatically convict it of poor management. Maury Klein points out that the L&N's civilian business included a great deal of heavy but sea-sonal agricultural cargo. More than 80 percent of its traffic traveled south, meaning that many northbound cars deadheaded, or returned empty, to Louisville. The "peculiar traffic" thus led to an inefficient use of equipment.[23] The fact remains that the L&N made a fortune during the Civil War.

Profits rose dramatically for railroads swamped with war traffic. The Erie paid its first dividend, 8 percent, in 1863. The New York Central

21. Klein, *Louisville and Nashville,* 42.
22. Ibid., 16, 42.
23. Ibid., 37–39, 24.

increased its dividends from 6 percent to 9 percent between 1860 and 1864. The Northern Central's $1,476,889.68 net earnings in 1865 exceeded its 1861 gross of $1,417,977.06, even though, as a north-south road, many cars deadheaded on northbound legs.[24]

Robert Weber says that the railroads' wartime profits reinforced their leaders' faith in laissez-faire capitalism, as they conveniently over-looked the source of the business that produced those profits. They resented the government's intrusions and considered the War Department a nuisance. It ordered unscheduled shipments on short notice, supposedly in the name of secrecy, and sometimes under "crisis" con-ditions. Special shipments took longer to organize because managers could not plan them in advance; executives argued that the extra time outweighed the alleged benefits of secrecy. Unscheduled shipments, regardless of their profitability, upset the railroads' schedules and their executives' preference for regular and dependable business.[25] Business executives, then and now, relish their labels as risk takers and entrepreneurs, but many in fact prefer predictability and stable outcomes—in other words, level playing fields with favorable slopes.

In the war's glorious springtime, patriotic southern railroad executives offered to carry Confederate soldiers at no charge. When they recovered their senses, they too reached an agreement that called for the government to pay the railroads two cents per man per mile for troops, with a sliding schedule for freight. These rates, unfortunately, covered less than half of southern railroads' prewar operating costs. The cash-starved Confederacy also convinced the railroads to accept payment in Confederate bonds that devalued rapidly as the government financed the war with printing presses. The runaway inflation that naturally followed had the effect, as Paul Gates says, of "unhinging the machinery of trade." More important, the bonds deprived the railroads of cash revenue needed to pay for inflation-priced operating costs, mainte-nance, and replacement parts and equipment. The Georgia Railroad closed its books for 1864 showing its second straight deficit; Georgia Senator John B. King said of the railroad, "The more business it does,

24. Weber, *Northern Railroads,* 43, 54.
25. Ibid., 43, 94.

the more money it loses, and the greatest favor that could be conferred upon it—if public wants permitted—would be the privilege of quitting business until the end of the war!"[26] By paying the railroads poorly, either in cash or in kind, the Confederate government created a fundamental obstacle to securing their cooperation.

Southern railroads risked financial ruin with the two-cent arrangement. They improved cash flow by shipping civilian passengers and goods—their paying customers—before handling government traffic, even during military emergencies, with predictable effect on Confederate armies. The government resisted adjusting the rate schedule, but in the end cut separate deals with different railroads, making a mockery of standard rates. As uncontrolled inflation progressively made cash or bond payments irrelevant, businesses and railroads took part in extensive bartering schemes, often using cotton as the medium of exchange. Some ambitious railroad employees made fortunes by speculating in food and other sought-after items. They sometimes shipped their own goods before those of other railroad customers and often neglected to pay shipping charges. The North Carolina Railroad's superintendent, T. J. Summer, once shipped nine cars of flour to Richmond for sale on his personal account. NCRR president Thomas Webb knew about Summer's speculating in food. Allen Trelease wonders what else he knew.[27]

Mary DeCredico believes that southern railroad executives' narrow focus on profits caused them to withhold complete cooperation. As she puts it, "their conception of the managerial function was at variance

26. Robert Black, citing various lines' annual reports, states that southern railroads' costs ranged from less than 3 cents to 5.5 cents per mile (*Railroads of the Confederacy*, 21); Richard Goff reports antebellum civilian fares at 4.5 cents per mile (*Confederate Supply*, 17); Allen W. Trelease describes one railroad's calamitous experience with the Confederate payment system in "A Southern Railroad at War: The North Carolina Railroad and the Confederacy," *Railroad History* 164 (1991): 16; Paul W. Gates, *Agriculture and the Civil War* (New York: Alfred A. Knopf, 1965), 52; Senator John P. King quoted in Stover, *Life and Decline*, 42–43. For an overview of the inflationary impact of Union and Confederate fiscal policies, see McPherson, *Battle Cry of Freedom*, 437–50.

27. Trelease, "Southern Railroad," 5–41.

with military needs." They opposed centralized controls as an "anathema . . . a radical deviation from accepted notions of government-business relations." This, she maintains, prevented them from gaining a broader national focus "that could relate railroad strategy and decision making to Confederate national wants." She faults both government officials and railroad executives for committing a "cardinal sin" by failing to adopt central controls.[28] A cataclysm such as the Civil War epitomizes the definition of "radical deviation." Abraham Lincoln understood that perfectly. Jefferson Davis did not.

Southern railroad men did not refuse to cooperate out of hand, but they rejected outright the legitimacy of any governmental interference, and they absolutely expected to get paid. Capable of conduct that would make today's most unprincipled businessmen blush, they practiced outrageously unfettered capitalism. The Richmond & Petersburg Railroad's management, for example, demanded a fare increase before boarding Longstreet's soldiers en route to Chickamauga.[29] All societies have pigs and free riders. The Confederacy, while fighting for its life, however, allowed self-interest, blind pride, and individual objections to override national needs.

Focusing on profits to the exclusion of other concerns is ultimately an unprofitable exercise. Capitalism is the only economic philosophy that does not pretend to embrace any noble ideals; it relies on self-interest, call it greed, to serve the greater good. Profits line plutocrats' pockets, to be sure, but profits also provide capital for maintenance and expansion and investment in plant and equipment. Southern railroads lost revenue during the Civil War. This impaired their ability to maintain efficient operations and, finally, any operations at all. The federal government certainly paid the northern railroads well. Large profits indeed encouraged them to cooperate, but the profits also meant that they could *afford* to cooperate.

Other factors also limited the necessary cooperation between the

28. DeCredico, *Patriotism for Profit*, 102.
29. Ibid., 31–32, 104; Frederick Sims reports the R&P fare increase to H. M. Drane, J. R. Sharp, and H. J. Peake, September 11, 1863, Sims Letterbook, Huntington Library, San Marino, Calif.; Black, *Railroads of the Confederacy*, 186.

Confederate government and the railroads. Maury Klein reminds us that antebellum southern railroads were "local roads built with local capital to serve local needs under local management." W. Kirk Wood describes them as "very limited, local, and conservative enterprises that were not built with any system or larger socio-economic purposes in mind." He argues that it is presentist to criticize their managers' failure to consider larger national issues. Mary DeCredico suggests that the entrepreneurial spirit that drove early railroad management had matured to an administrative focus on profits, dividends, and stockholder interests, and thus "not all of the South's railroad men were able to respond creatively to the challenge of wartime mobilization."[30]

One struggles with these arguments. Good managers educate and motivate constituencies to help them understand why they want to, or must, follow management's or, in this case, the government's, direction. Northern railroads as well shared a local orientation in the early stages of their development. The peacetime southern railroad conditions and management attitudes described by Klein and Wood meant nothing once the war began. Wood's argument ignores the reality of the Confederacy's absolute need to have the railroads' strong cooperation to help it win its independence. This required forward thinking. DeCredico's observation seems doubtful as well. No American railroad, north or south, had reached a maturity consistent with a ministerial form of management by 1861. Further, many railroad managers must have had sons or brothers serving in the Confederate army. One would think that awareness of and concern for their sacrifices might have inspired greater cooperation with the Cause. If Wood and DeCredico accurately describe southern rail managers' thinking, they reveal attitudes of businessmen too long insulated from market competition. Similarly, the Davis administration's inability to enlist southern railroad leaders to serve its war objectives reflects weak management.

30. Maury Klein, *The Great Richmond Terminal: A Study of Businessmen and Business Strategy* (Charlottesville: University Press of Virginia, 1970), 11; Wood, "Phillips and Antebellum Southern Rail Inferiority," 181; DeCredico, *Patriotism for Profit*, 72.

The Lincoln administration underscored Thomas Scott's threat of enforced cooperation with a convincing display of the federal government's willingness to exercise its war powers. In January 1862 Congress authorized the president to take military control of the railroads in time of national emergency. Secretary Stanton applied that law during the 11th and 12th Corps movement.[31]

Food riots erupted in Richmond in late March and early April 1863 when railroads failed to deliver shipments for several days following a snowstorm. The Confederate Congress then authorized the quartermaster general to set through-freight schedules, to combine rolling stock from several roads and, to the horror of states' rights advocates, even to seize and operate uncooperative railroads. The Congress had earlier approved legislation authorizing the cannibalizing of secondary lines in order to maintain primary routes. The two Congresses' actions revealed the importance each accorded the issue: the United States Congress gave the authority to the president of the United States, the commander in chief; the Confederate Congress gave it to the quartermaster general. Appalled states' righters had denounced less draconian steps as "usurpation." Railroad managers stoutly resisted sharing their cars or their tracks with other roads. The state-owned or -controlled Georgia and North Carolina railroads refused to give up their cars under any circumstances, claiming higher state authority. "A thousand grievances" rose from executives who believed that their railroads met the definition of "primary." To Robert Black's thinking, their successful objections demonstrated "with pitiless clarity a fatal weakness" of the Confederacy. The legislation did not matter in any event—the Davis government could never bring itself to enforce the law.[32]

Northern railroad leaders shared the same opinions about governmental intervention as their southern cousins. Correspondence during the 11th and 12th Corps movement hints at some roads' reluctance to cooperate. A significant difference between northern and southern

31. Weber, *Northern Railroads,* 103–5.
32. Black, *Railroads of the Confederacy,* 95, 101, 119–22; Charles W. Ramsdell, "The Confederate Government and the Railroads," *American Historical Review* 22 (1917): 796–98, 807.

railroads, however, lay in the fact that the federal War Department combined the carrot of reasonable compensation with the stick of national police power. It paid the railroads well but made clear that it would compel their cooperation by seizing them, if it must. Absent carrot and stick, one suspects that northern railroads might have resisted as vigorously as the southern ones did. The secessionists, however, had started a revolution by creating the Confederacy. They had to take revolutionary steps if they expected to win the war. They did not take them.

The Confederacy never closed strategic gaps in order to improve the efficiency of its rail service. The failure to correct the problem impaired its interior lines advantage, though this did not affect the Longstreet movement. The Meridian-Selma-Montgomery gap, as noted earlier, added two hundred miles to Braxton Bragg's movement to Chattanooga in 1862. The gap remained throughout the war. It delayed the transfer of Confederate troops sent to reinforce Vicksburg in May 1863 and Joseph Johnston's troops en route to Chickamauga that September.

Florida became the Confederacy's primary source of red meat after the loss of the trans-Mississippi and most of Tennessee. The Confederate Congress failed to approve a proposed loan to build a connection between Florida and Georgia railroads. Cattle shipments to Atlanta took an extra day and additional toll on the animals due to the need to detour around a fifty-mile gap between Albany and Thomasville, Georgia. By the fall of 1863, commissary agents foraged ever deeper into Florida to find beef. Drovers sometimes walked the cattle all the way to Atlanta or Savannah, exhausting the animals, because broken-down railroads could not carry them. A devastating outbreak of hog cholera led a grim Commissary General Northrop to tell his superiors that the Confederacy could feed civilians or soldiers, but not both—one or the other must go hungry.[33]

A fifty-five-mile rail spur from Rome, Georgia, to Blue Mountain,

33. J. Moore, *Confederate Commissary General,* 222, 235; Ramsdell, "Confederate Government and the Railroads," 802, citing *Journal of the Congress of the Confederacy,* Statutes, I, 819.

Alabama, would have opened the region's vast iron reserves; its mines outproduced Virginia's by a factor of four. It takes two and one-half tons of refined ore to produce one ton of pig iron. By processing the ore in Alabama and at Rome foundries, the Confederacy could have avoided the wasteful practice of shipping unrefined ore to Virginia, one-fourth of which vanished en route on months-long trips over roundabout routes. A lack of rails, other equipment, and rolling stock delayed construction of the spur. It remained a work in progress when the war ended.[34]

The link that closed the Danville, Virginia–Greensboro, North Carolina, gap epitomizes the Confederacy's imbalanced attempts to improve its railroad service. The North Carolina Railroad demanded that the Confederate government construct the forty-mile link with standard-gauge tracks compatible with the NCRR's, even as it refused to connect its tracks with the link. This meant offloading and reloading all shipments at both ends because the Richmond & Danville's five-foot tracks created a gauge barrier at the northern end. The link opened in May 1864 after two years of planning and construction— Jefferson Davis himself delayed construction two months by insisting on personally reviewing the route survey. Better late, however, than never: six weeks after the link opened, the Yankees cut the Petersburg Railroad when General Grant laid siege to the city. The Greensboro-Danville link, such as it was, became Richmond's primary lifeline from the south for the rest of the war.[35]

The Union enjoyed an expanding northern rail net that provided connected rail service to all parts of the eastern states. The soldiers in the 11th and 12th Corps movement only had to make one train change due to a gauge barrier. Planners did have to work around the

34. Turner, *Victory Rode the Rails*, 338–45.
35. Ibid., 345; Trelease, *North Carolina Railroad*, 187–88. Trelease reports that southern lines began to change to five-foot gauge in April 1865 ("Southern Railroad," 31). Taylor and Neu point out, however, that the change was subject to the requirement that it revert to standard gauge within six months of the end of the war (*American Railroad Network*, 44–45). According to James McPherson, Confederate wagon trains detoured around the sections of the Petersburg Railroad held by Union forces (conversation with author).

fact that no railroad bridges spanned the Ohio River at the time of the Civil War, but two railroad companies had participated in building a railroad bridge across the Mississippi at Rock Island, Illinois, as early as 1854.

Gauge differences did not significantly delay either the Longstreet or 11th and 12th Corps movements. The Virginia railroads south of Richmond and the North Carolina railroads used standard gauge. South Carolina and Georgia railroads ran on five-foot gauge. Longstreet's brigades only had to change trains once because of differences in track gauge. The Confederacy had a more obvious problem, though one seemingly easy to solve. The railroads, supported by the communities where they terminated, refused to connect their tracks with other lines of the same gauge. Unconnected tracks, although tolerable for the leisurely pace of the antebellum southern economy, carried the seeds of disaster in war. Transferring a single regiment with its baggage from one railroad to another took five hours.[36] Connecting the tracks of different railroads would have eliminated most transfer delays, especially for transferring freight. Joined tracks would have permitted maximum use of available equipment and enhanced strategic flexibility by allowing the Confederacy to shift locomotives and cars rapidly to different sectors as needed. Joined tracks would also have made it easier to cannibalize rolling stock to overcome the lack of replacement parts. The Davis government, however, never demanded that railroads join their same-gauge tracks.

Railroads and communities joined together to defend the status quo vigorously, in spite of clear wartime necessity. Petersburg, Virginia, officials firmly declined a request made by no less than General Robert E. Lee himself to connect the tracks of the Petersburg to the Richmond & Petersburg, "and the congestion continued" with predictable results for wartime transportation efficiency. The railroads protested that they would never see their cars again if they released them to roll on another road's tracks. Richmond authorities refused to permit any of its five railroads to extend their tracks across the city throughout the war. They could have connected the tracks of three of four north-south

36. Black, *Railroads of the Confederacy,* 74.

roads by building a single half-mile link (the fifth road ran to the Peninsula). As a concession, the city fathers allowed mule teams to pull freight cars across the city on a single authorized spur.[37]

Neither the Confederate government nor the southern railroads or local communities seemed conscious of the need to connect same-gauge tracks to speed transportation or the consequences of failing to do so. Unconnected tracks meant that regiments waited at each railroad's terminus, sometimes for extended periods, until the forwarding road produced a train. Troop movements could proceed no faster than permitted by the capacity of each railroad's rolling stock. The effect of these artificially imposed delays, as we shall see, became clear in the Longstreet movement. They added days to the journey for some of his soldiers.

The huge increase in wartime traffic created grinding bottlenecks at transshipment points. Freight on the North Carolina Railroad, for example, piled up faster than laborers could offload, transfer, and reload, thus holding up deliveries to the armies. Inadequate warehousing left cargo stored in the open, exposed to pilferage and contamination and destruction by the elements. North Carolina Governor Zebulon Vance finally recommended that the partly state-owned North Carolina Railroad allow neighboring railroads to run on its tracks to relieve the bottleneck. William Sheppard Ashe, president of the Wilmington & Weldon Railroad and assistant quartermaster of transportation in Virginia, recommended linking southern railroads in December 1861. Jefferson Davis rejected the proposal, citing lack of funds.[38] One grants the delicate diplomacy involved in securing railroads' and municipalities' cooperation to meet the war's challenges, but the difficulty did not diminish the necessity.

Philadelphia, and its three railroads with their unconnected tracks and terminals, also seemed indifferent to the federal government's need for rapid wartime transit through the city. The government finally got everyone's attention with a congressional proposal to build a gov-

37. Ibid., 9; Ramsdell, "Confederate Government and the Railroads," 797.
38. Trelease, "Southern Railroad," 26–27; DeCredico, *Patriotism for Profit*, 78.

ernment-owned and subsidized railroad between New York and Washington. Proving responsive to market forces, if not the government's war needs, the Philadelphians completed a rail connection around the city in 1863 that joined the three roads' tracks. The Camden & Amboy opened car ferry service across the Delaware River in 1862.[39]

Northern cities also used featherbedding laws to pump up local employment. Assistant Secretary of War Tom Scott visited a Pittsburgh foundry during a February 1862 fact-finding inspection. A city ordinance required the foundry, which made mortars and armor plate for river gunboats, to haul finished work to the Allegheny River by horse-drawn wagon. War mocks the status quo. Citing "wartime necessity," Scott ordered a railroad siding built directly from the foundry to the river. The one-thousand-dollar expense reduced the government's drayage costs by 90 percent. Scott used the same device to outflank a Pittsburgh law that prohibited railroads from connecting their rails.[40]

Scott's decisiveness marks a significant difference between Union and Confederate management styles. Union managers addressed and overcame problems by simply overriding objections. Confederate leaders never demonstrated the force of will required to secure needed cooperation. A manager unwilling to assert his authority cannot succeed, especially in cases of hard or unpopular decisions. Men like Tom Scott did not have that reluctance.

Railroads of the Civil War era required constant maintenance. Many southern roads had upgraded to thirty-five-pound "T" rail, but some still ran on primitive "strap rails," iron strips nailed to wooden stringers. Many northern railroads, in contrast, had changed to sixty-seven-pound "T" rail by 1861 to carry larger locomotives and longer trains. Even before the war, rails fashioned from the relatively soft iron of the day wore away or broke, and wheels wore out of round. Minerals in undistilled stream water corroded locomotive boiler plate. Untreated wooden ties rotted from lying on bare ground. Although they tolerated the wear of once-a-day prewar trains, the pounding of heavy wartime volume ground down the "overburdened and underequipped"

39. Taylor and Neu, *American Railroad Network*, 28, 53.
40. Kamm, *Scott*, 89–90.

roads of the South. Northern railroads, facing similar maintenance problems, began to experiment with the stronger and more durable products of the new steel technology, but the infrastructure of the southern rails, lacking diligent upkeep, gradually crumbled.[41]

The southern railroads had to find a way to obtain enough replacement locomotives, rolling stock, rails, and equipment to continue operating. Most had purchased these items from northern foundries and mills before the war. They bought locomotives built in Paterson, New Jersey, boiler tubes from Pittsburgh, and whale-oil lubricants from New Bedford. Many imported rails from England or bought them from northern foundries. When the war shut down their access to northern suppliers, they turned to Europe, a source that a determined Union navy vigorously strove to deny them.[42]

Many railroads had also relied on northern foundries for maintenance services. Even railroads that operated their own maintenance facilities had contracted some work to a large network of foundries and machine shops in the North. Now lacking parts and raw material, they leased their shops to the Confederate government for war work and appealed to Richmond for maintenance support, but it never materialized. Combining or sharing maintenance facilities seems a simple solution to the problem but it "involved practical difficulties of management" that railroad executives proved incapable of resolving.[43] Perhaps, in the absence of parts and matériel, they saw no practical reason to seek solutions, but if so, especially in the face of dire necessity, this reveals a passivity suggestive of dulled management instincts.

The maintenance problem relates directly to the Confederacy's failure to overcome fundamental obstacles to a workable rail transportation system. In spite of the popular conception of its limited manufacturing capacity, the fact remains that the Confederacy did not make the most of what it had. The Tredegar Iron Works never operated

41. Black, *Railroads of the Confederacy*, 13–16, 22–24; Dew, *Ironmaker*, 177–78.

42. Ramsdell, "Confederate Government and the Railroads," 798; Black, *Railroads of the Confederacy*, 22; Dew, *Ironmaker*, 14.

43. Ramsdell, "Confederate Government and the Railroads," 803.

at more than one-third of its capacity throughout the war, according to Charles Dew. Its cannon barrel production, for example, dropped from 351 to 213 between 1862 and 1864. Dew argues that the inability of the southern raw materials sector to feed manufacturing's appetite represented a more significant limiting factor than the Confederacy's modest manufacturing capacity.[44]

The Rome–Blue Mountain link project, which would have addressed, and might have solved, the South's inability to supply its factories, exposes a larger problem: the lack of coordination between the raw materials, transportation, and manufacturing sectors. Planning would have identified and solved the obvious problems that the project had to overcome. The Confederacy did not seem to recognize the problem or the benefits of correcting it; thus it could neither establish priorities nor craft solutions. If the Confederates had recognized that completing the link would have enabled them to produce most or all of the rails and other iron products they needed, they might have tried more diligently to find a way to complete it. They could have forged rails locally with Alabama ore to build the link but did not. The failure to complete the link, in spite of self-imposed difficulties, shows a Confederacy incapable of rising above its problems.

One pays for maintenance whether it is performed or not. The Confederacy paid with declining railroad efficiency. By October 1863, an estimated fifty locomotives stood idle for want of nonexistent replacement wheels. Corroded boiler tubes increased fuel consumption: the Central of Georgia's average miles-per-cord-of-wood declined from 79 in 1861 to 60 in 1863; the Southern Railroad's fell from 84.5 to 67.1 in one year. By 1864, deteriorated tracks between Georgia and Virginia limited traffic to two or three trains a day. Accidents occurred with increasing frequency, even with speeds reduced to a walk.[45]

Excessive use, abuse, and lack of maintenance of the Petersburg Railroad, according to Howard Dozier, "played a far more important

44. Dew, *Ironmaker,* 103, 177–78.
45. Black, *Railroads of the Confederacy,* 125; Turner, *Victory Rode the Rails,* 316.

part in its undoing than the destruction wrought by the enemy." The Petersburg operated "with little attention to upkeep" for the first two years of the war, thanks to excellent prewar maintenance and ample supplies of parts. It then began to decline, even though it acquired the use of the Seaboard & Roanoke's rolling stock when the Confederates evacuated Norfolk.[46]

A newspaper reporter drily described a week-long journey to Clayton, Alabama, from Richmond in September 1863. Just months earlier, he reported, the trip could be "accomplished in three days." He attributed the slower speed "to the practice of economy, else with very rapid traveling our resources in this regard [i.e., rails] would soon be exhausted." The reporter also suspected "that the slow progress and frequent and unnecessary delays were prompted by the collusion of one of the conductors with certain railroad hotels," especially after his Wilmington & Manchester train reached Kingsville, "that delectable caravansary," thirteen hours late. He bemoaned the "great annoyance to the passenger on urgent business, and especially to the hundreds of furloughed soldiers that daily crowd the trains on their way southward to snatch a brief interval of peace and quiet with loved ones."[47] One imagines the "great annoyance" to military shipments.

Deferred maintenance "taxed to the utmost" the Richmond, Fredericksburg & Potomac Railroad's efforts to supply General Lee's army in Virginia. The line's president wrote to Secretary of War Seddon:

> The severe and constant use of that machinery, with little or no opportunity for repairs, greatly deteriorated and disabled it, and has since made some of it temporarily or permanently useless . . . the very great scarcity of mechanics have prevented repairs which otherwise might have been made. And if all the machinery . . . were in good repair . . . the want of adequate space and accommodations at the Richmond terminus . . . would render it im-

46. Howard D. Dozier, *A History of the Atlantic Coast Line Railroad* (Boston: Houghton Mifflin, 1920; reprint, New York: Augustus M. Kelly, 1971), 106–8.
47. Richmond *Daily Dispatch*, September 21, 1863, p. 1.

possible to perform the transportation exclusively on this road
and from its depot in Richmond required by such an army. This
is no theory, but the practical result of six months' experience.[48]

High volume aggravated poor maintenance. When the war ended,
the North Carolina Railroad had only 5 passenger cars still running on
its 233 miles of tracks. The Virginia Central had less than one hundred
dollars in gold. Charles Ramsdell concludes that, because of the collapse of the southern railroads, starvation would have driven General
Lee from northern Virginia, "even if Grant had been content to watch
him peaceably from a distance."[49]

The war also severely strained the Union's rail capacity. It increased
the demand for trains as it stripped the railroads of skilled trainmen and
mechanics. Less experienced replacement workers produced poorer
quality rolling stock, rails, and parts. Iron rails wore out in as few as six
months of hard use, driving railroads to experiment with steel rails in
high traffic areas. Stronger than iron but considered more brittle, steel
would not enter into widespread use until after the war. Roads had
difficulty keeping up with the increased maintenance made necessary
by the surge in war traffic. The Pennsylvania Central, for example, lost
ground in 1863 in spite of spending $1.5 million on maintenance and
an additional $1.6 million for new rolling stock and second track. De-
ferred maintenance caused an increase in accidents, although greater
volume clearly played a role. In 1861, 63 accidents killed 101 people
and injured 459; in 1864, 140 accidents killed 404 and injured another
1,846.[50]

Inflation made a mockery of financial projections. The war increased

48. Peter V. Daniel, president of the Richmond, Fredericksburg & Potomac
Railroad, to Secretary of War James Seddon, August 1, 1863, *OR,* Ser. 1, 51, pt.
2:747.

49. Graham A. Barringer, "Influence of Railroad Transportation," citing John
C. Schwab, *The Confederate States of America* (New York: 1901), 274; Ramsdell,
"Confederate Railroads," 809–10. Ramsdell denies that the railroads' problems
constituted a principal element in the Confederacy's defeat. He admits, however,
that solving those problems was central to victory.

50. Weber, *Northern Railroads,* 44, 62–65.

prices faster than profits and also produced shortages. Rising prices proved the biggest damper on profits. New-rail prices rose from $57.50 per ton in 1860 to $120 per ton by 1865; rerolled rails increased from $22 to $52 per ton, car wheels from $16 to $25 each. Fuel wood rose from $2.25 to $6 per cord, hard wood from $4.25 per cord to $6.75, and spikes from 3.5 cents per pound to 9.5 cents. The New York & New Haven's fuel costs per mile increased from $12.53 to $14.43 between 1861 and 1862 and to $20.50 in 1864.[51] The northern railroads coped with higher prices, lower quality, and shortages. They adapted their operations and became stronger as a result. Regardless of their difficulties, the northern railroads could at least obtain necessary parts and equipment. Southern railroads could rarely get new or replacement items at any price.

Thomas C. Cochran argues that the war stifled the railroads' growth and dampened the surging economy emerging from the Panic of 1857. He bases his argument on the modest 4,076 rail miles built by northern railroads during the Civil War, compared with the 16,714-mile explosion of rail construction in the ensuing 5 years.[52] One wonders how a cataclysm of the Civil War's magnitude could affect the economy otherwise. It redirected 10 percent of its labor force from productive efforts to the task of killing their countrymen and invested the nation's treasure in the tools with which to do the killing.

Peter Harold Jaynes rejects Cochran's argument. He finds track-miles constructed, taken in isolation, a poor growth indicator. Jaynes paints a fascinating picture of a rapidly improving northern railroad system. He points to the increase in "supportive track" that improved traffic management. This included adequate side tracks for loading and unloading trains, which kept the main lines open for through traffic. Along with additional terminal and yard track, these investments in logistical infrastructure improved a line's "sorting, storing, loading,

51. Ibid., 45, 48, 61, 75.
52. Thomas C. Cochran, "Did the Civil War Retard Industrialization?" in *The Economic Impact of the American Civil War*, ed. Ralph Andreano (Cambridge, Mass.: Schenkman, 1967), 167–79, citing U.S. Census Bureau, *Historical Statistics of the United States: Colonial Times to 1957* (Washington, D.C., 1960), 427–28.

hauling, and delivery of passenger and freight cars, to a degree out of proportion to its length." Jaynes says that Cochran also slights the impact of double-tracking existing routes. Although not considered new mileage, they increased capacity and safety at a fraction of the cost of new roads. The Pennsylvania Central began to double-track its entire route before the war as the only way to keep up with volume. It completed all but thirty-three miles between Harrisburg and Pittsburgh by 1862. War volume strained capacity, but improved infrastructure enhanced "the operating capacity, efficiency, and flexibility" of northern railroads. Jaynes's arguments support Thomas Weber's observation that wartime pressures forced the railroads to adopt more efficient practices.[53]

The Baltimore & Ohio voluntarily connected the Northern Central's tracks to its Washington branch, the only rail connection to Washington south of Baltimore. It did not, however, complete double-tracking the thirty-one miles to Washington until December 1864. It claimed that Confederate raids on the main line delayed its plan to double-track the branch. John Garrett strenuously fought proposals to allow a competitor to build a second railroad to the capital. Double-tracking helped to thwart the competition's threat to its monopoly.[54]

As the war consumed men, first the Confederacy and then the Union turned to conscription to fill their armies. Neither side at first gave much thought to the need to retain farm and factory workers,

53. Peter Harold Jaynes, "The Civil War and Northern Railroads: A Test of the Cochran Thesis" (Ph.D. diss., Boston University, 1973), 190–91; Weber, *Northern Railroads,* 61. In his fine study, Jaynes concentrates on New England railroads, many of which had completed their routes by 1861. Studying the developing railroads of the Old Northwest states, such as Illinois and Ohio, probably would have strengthened his argument. Jaynes also slightly contradicts his thesis that the war did not interfere with railroad development. He notes, for example, that "war demands" delayed construction of a Hartford & New Haven Railroad bridge over the Connecticut River (359, citing *Connecticut 13th Annual Report,* 10–11).

54. Festus P. Summers, *The Baltimore and Ohio in the Civil War* (New York: G. P. Putnam's Sons, 1939; reprint, Gettysburg: Stan Clark Military, 1993), 208, 217–18.

the people necessary to feed, clothe, arm, and sustain the armies. The perceptive Josiah Gorgas observed that in a "war for national existence . . . the whole mass of the nation must be engaged." Not everyone could bear arms, however. "Some must labor," Gorgas wrote, "or all will starve." The Confederate leadership did not understand the "new dimension of manpower," according to Frank Vandiver. It drafted workers with irreplaceable skills along with everyone else until "manpower failed to sustain the war."[55]

The Confederate Congress, hoping to spur voluntary enlistments, passed the first of three conscription acts on April 16, 1862, a week after the battle of Shiloh. A source of ongoing mischief, the law and its successors exposed the Confederacy to the charge of conducting a rich man's war but a poor man's fight. It exempted government workers and large slaveholders, as well as those in critical occupations, for which legions believed they qualified. General Lee opposed exemptions for any reason, quite reasonably considering them legalized draft dodging.

Confederate conscription laws initially exempted five in seven railroad jobs. Southern roads, however, still lost valuable employees to the army. Overused locomotives, lacking mechanics to maintain them, broke down under heavier loads. A shortage of track maintainers contributed to more frequent derailments and other accidents on failing tracks. Woodcutters who supplied fuel and ties disappeared into the army as more frequent trains and declining fuel efficiency increased the demand for wood. As the war drained the pool of military-age men, the Confederate government considered drafting all railroad employees under age forty-five and replacing them with older men, but it never put the plan into effect.[56]

Southern railroads faced an additional dimension to their manpower problems. Southern disdain for "mudsill" labor meant that northerners and railroad-owned slaves filled many skilled positions, such as locomotive engineers. Some, but not all, northerners left at the start of the war; as it continued, railroad-owned slaves became increasingly unreliable. Planters in a sellers' market often refused to lease their slaves

55. Vandiver, *Gorgas,* 77–78; Vandiver, *Rebel Brass,* 11.
56. Trelease, *North Carolina Railroad,* 14–17.

for railroad maintenance work, especially if Union forces operated nearby. The railroads also had to compete with the army for the limited supply of slave labor. Confederate officers generally declined to detail soldiers for railroad work, arguing that they could not spare combat troops. The North Carolina Railroad solved part of its labor shortage by purchasing twenty-eight slaves in December 1864 for "about $138,000 in depreciated end-of-the-war currency."[57]

The Confederacy never understood the need to husband its scarce manpower, including the skilled laborers at the Tredegar Iron Works, the Confederacy's principal—and at one time only—cannon factory. Caught up in the war's exciting blooming, managing partner Joseph Anderson founded the Tredegar Battalion and encouraged his employees to enlist. A cadet captain who graduated fourth in his West Point class of 1836, Anderson served but briefly in the army before starting his career at Tredegar. The Confederate War Department promoted him to brigadier general when it called up the battalion for the Seven Days' Battles. Anderson proved an able commander until he went down with a serious head wound. On recovering, he resigned his commission and returned to Tredegar.[58] The nonfatal injury may thus have been fortunate for the Confederate cause; the cost would have been great if the senior officer of the South's largest foundry had fallen to a Yankee missile. One can only wonder about the cost to the Confederacy of the loss of Anderson's skilled—and irreplaceable—workmen who died in the Tredegar Battalion.

As the war soured, a failing Confederacy began devouring its human resources. Once the army drafted skilled workers, employers found it very difficult to get them back. The Supply Bureau arranged to have skilled draftees detailed to its office. Amended regulations in October 1864, however, forced the bureau to return 20 percent of them to the army. Charles Dew believes that a reasonable policy would have detailed drafted railroad workers back to their railroads. He acknowledges, however, that unrelenting wartime demands overwhelmed local

57. Black, *Railroads of the Confederacy*, 215.
58. Dew, *Ironmaker*, 6, 150. Union Q.M. Gen. Montgomery C. Meigs graduated fifth in the class of 1836.

labor pools. Perhaps, but because the Confederacy never clearly understood the need to conserve its skilled labor force, it never seriously tried to address the problem. Secretary of War Seddon remained unaware that the Confederacy faced any manpower problems at all until the second year of the war.[59]

Northern railroads also faced severe manpower problems. The federal government's Conscription Act, which took effect in July 1863, specifically exempted telegraph operators and locomotive engineers. Railroad executives led by Tom Scott, however, pleaded for an across-the-board exemption for all railroad workers, citing their critical skills. As the harried Secretary of War Stanton considered their request, the adjutant general's office preempted him by issuing General Order 99, Draft Regulations, on August 9, 1863. It exempted only engineers. The outcries suggest that a reluctance to serve competed with one's definition of critical occupation. Stanton compromised. He said that if the loss of conscripted men hurt the railroads and thus the war effort, the army would release them. He stood firm, however, in limiting railroad exemptions to locomotive engineers. Tom Scott suggested that railroads buy substitutes for critical employees drafted by the army. Stanton approved the scheme, but the war ended before the railroads put it into effect.[60]

The use of railroads in the Civil War provides an excellent example of the application of new technology in warfare. Thomas Weber says that railroads "materially affected the character" of the war. Many officers, Union and Confederate, recognized the strategic potential of the railroads' rapid heavy-lift capacity. Some, however, mistook their smooth efficiency for simplicity of operation and tried to command the railroads personally, often with disastrous results. Railroads are highly

59. Ibid., 249; Vandiver, *Rebel Brass,* 11, 98–99. The loss of farm labor to the armies had a severe impact on southern agricultural yields. The southern states were already net food importers from the "western" states before the war, but the Confederacy's food problems ballooned as farmers entered the ranks and as Union forces conquered food-growing areas. The Union faced similar problems but overcame them with increased use of labor-saving farm machinery (Gates, *Agriculture,* 23).

60. Weber, *Northern Railroads,* 130–33.

sophisticated systems, hardly spontaneous instruments. What appears as operating simplicity comes from careful advance planning by expert managers. Frederick W. Sims, chief of the Confederate Railroad Bureau, complained that officers failed to recognize that railroads represented "a specialty differing from any element heretofore entering into military operations." Great difficulty awaited those who tried to command railroads without proper training and experience, specifically a clear understanding of "the difficulties arising from a want of control of the movement of trains." Sims disdainfully noted a correlation between untrained officers' attempts to run railroads and unsuccessful results.[61]

Confederate War Department regulations prohibited officers from disrupting the railroads' private business operations, but they were enforced with a familiar lack of firmness. Officers from the commander in chief down busied themselves with rail operations throughout the war. Many seemed indifferent to the most rudimentary railroad practices. Quartermasters used boxcars as warehouses on wheels; some ordered their own rail movements. W. D. Whitcomb of the Virginia Central pointed out the "absolute necessity" of the army's immediately unloading military freight so that the precious rolling stock could quickly return to service. Neither the government nor the army responded, which further reduced the efficiency of the roads' limited supply of available cars.[62]

Confederate quartermasters apparently received inadequate training relative to their responsibilities. Few understood the need to work with the railroads that supplied their armies. General Lee complained to the War Department about delays in receiving supplies on the Richmond, Fredericksburg & Potomac during the Fredericksburg campaign. Peter V. Daniel Jr., President of the RF&P, "with great respect," responded: "Until the last two days for more than a week two daily freight trains have gone to Gen Lee's army with only one half to one third as much

61. Ibid., Foreword; Sims to Lewis Cruger [of the Treasury], January 8, 1864, Sims Papers, National Archives, quoted in Black, *Railroads of the Confederacy*, 174, 199.

62. Black, *Railroads of the Confederacy*, 67.

commissary stores as they could carry because no more had been ordered by the Commissaries or Quartermasters of the army. That army can be kept supplied by continuous & regular transportation over this [railroad] but not by fitful efforts to do in a day the work omitted in ten."[63] The absence of central control led to other embarrassments. Quartermasters in Macon shipped twenty thousand bushels of corn to General Beauregard in Savannah while their counterparts in Savannah shipped twenty thousand bushels of corn to General Bragg in Macon, both on the Central of Georgia Railroad.[64] Mistakes occur in life; war cruelly exaggerates them. Caesar's centurions, Hannibal's elephant drivers, Wellington's "scum of the earth," and Civil War soldiers all would have instantly understood the acronym SNAFU (situation normal, all fouled up) coined by an anonymous GI in World War II. A hard put Confederacy, however, could not afford the luxury of costly mistakes.

Longstreet's soldiers rode to Georgia in hastily assembled boxcars. They cut holes in the sides to let in air and light; in their enthusiasm, some removed all but the roof supports. At other times rowdy soldiers on leave, sometimes in the presence of indifferent officers, vandalized passenger cars. They broke lamps and seats, stole cushions, and fouled drinking water by dipping dirty canteens into the barrels. Howard Dozier claims that soldiers did more damage in one trip than prewar railroads experienced in a year.[65] They blithely wrecked cars that southern railroads could ill afford to lose, especially absent parts or manpower to repair them. Union soldiers also damaged cars during the 11th and 12th Corps movement. They caused inconvenience and expense, but the northern railroads had the means to repair the damage.

Jeffrey Lash, a student of railroads and the Confederate armies,

63. Stuart, "Samuel Ruth and General R. E. Lee: Disloyalty and the Line of Supply to Fredericksburg, 1862–1863," *Virginia Magazine of History and Biography* 71, no. 1: 70–71, citing Daniel to Secretary of War Seddon, January 24, 1863, in Letters Sent, Secretary of War, vol. 10, Jan.–Mar. 1863, National Archives, Record Group 109.

64. Gates, *Agriculture,* 37, citing the Sumter, S.C., *Watchman* in the Mobile *Advertiser and Register,* February 3, 1864.

65. Dozier, *Atlantic Coast Line Railroad,* 106–9.

holds up General Joseph E. Johnston as a prime example of how officers misused railroads. Johnston commanded Confederate forces in
Northern Virginia in January 1862. Anticipating a Union offensive, he
planned an orderly withdrawal and asked Orange & Alexandria officials
to remove his food reserves to safety. Because of an unexplained failure
of communications, Johnston's chief quartermaster also began to evacuate supplies. Inexperienced officers innocently seized control of the
railroad, disrupted the O&A managers' work, and overloaded the
tracks. A six-hour trip on a sixty-one-mile route turned into a thirty-
six-hour nightmare. In the end, Johnston destroyed more than a million pounds of meat to keep it out of Yankee bellies.[66] The problem
resulted directly from the absence of clear lines of authority between
the army and the railroads, the type of coordination that planning per-
mits. Lash holds Johnston responsible for the fiasco, arguing that he
"conspicuously failed to appreciate" the critical importance of close
cooperation with the railroads. He adds that Johnston wanted to take
military control of the Virginia railroads.[67]

Lash also faults Johnston for allowing General Sherman to destroy
tracks and burn the bridge over the Pearl River near Jackson, Mississippi, during the Vicksburg campaign. He further criticizes Johnston
for suspending repairs to the bridge after Vicksburg fell, even though
he did so to deny it to the Yankees. Unfortunately, Johnston left seventy-five locomotives and more than six hundred cars on the far side
of the bridge, trapped in Grenada, Mississippi, and lost forever to the
Confederacy. Lash additionally blames Johnston for refusing local railroads' requests to detail soldiers for maintenance work. The general
expected railroads to take care of their own repairs. Lash finds this "a
disastrously inflexible and unenterprising policy in view of the military
necessity of the work." He also charges Johnston with failing to remove rails during withdrawals. These decisions, he claims, were signs
of the general's "culpable unfamiliarity with War Department railway

66. Jeffrey N. Lash, "Joseph E. Johnston and the Virginia Railroads, 1861–
62," *Civil War History* 35 (1989): 18–19.
67. Ibid., 24.

policy, his indifference to commercial interests of railroad managers, and his lack of strategic imagination and professional enterprise."[68]

Johnston commanded an army, not a railroad. He may have had a limited grasp of railroad operations but he hardly stands alone among Confederate, or Union, officers in that respect. As General Sherman descended on Atlanta in August 1864, General John Bell Hood's quartermasters waited too long before evacuating two trains loaded with ammunition, weapons, and supplies. The Yankees cut the track, forcing Hood to destroy five irreplaceable locomotives and eighty-one cars and their cargo.[69] Union photographers dramatically captured the aftermath of the event so vividly depicted in *Gone with the Wind*.

T. Harry Williams attributes Confederate defeat in part to its commanders' failure to learn or adapt to the changes that took place during the war. He argues that "they never freed themselves from the influence of traditional doctrine."[70] The flawed experiences of some officers with southern railroads support Williams' argument. One cautiously admits to some correlation between long army careers and misuse of railroads. Career officers, such as Johnston, Robert E. Lee, and John Pope fumbled railroad operations, in contrast with formerly civilian officers such as Braxton Bragg, Ulysses S. Grant, and Henry Halleck, who demonstrated sound understanding and use of railroads. On the other hand, Pierre Beauregard, a career officer, creatively used Virginia railroads to achieve the Confederate victory at First Manassas. William Rosecrans, however, who had left the antebellum army to enter business, allowed Braxton Bragg to interdict his railroad supply line after Chickamauga and brought his army to the edge of starvation. The

68. Jeffrey N. Lash, *Destroyer of the Iron Horse* (Kent: Kent State University Press, 1991), 59, 74–77, 99, 105–6.

69. James G. Bogle, "The Western and Atlantic Railroad in the Campaign for Atlanta," in *The Campaign for Atlanta and Sherman's March to the Sea*, ed. Theodore P. Savas and David A. Woodbury (Campbell, Calif.: Savas Woodbury, 1994), 335.

70. T. Harry Williams, "The Military Leadership of North and South," in *Why the North Won the Civil War*, ed. David Donald (Baton Rouge: Louisiana State University Press, 1960), 41.

quality of railroad results probably correlated closely with local commanders' and their quartermasters' abilities to collaborate with their civilian counterparts. Officers who worked well with railroad managers tended to get good rail service. Those who could not did not.

Lash might better have directed his legitimate criticism at the shortcomings of the Confederate Quartermaster Department and the railroad men with whom the quartermasters worked rather than Joe Johnston, even though the commander bears the ultimate responsibility. Their poor working relationship was the result of the Confederate government's neglecting to design and implement a coherent railroad policy. It should have insulated railroads from military interference and arranged for railroad managers to work closely with army quartermasters. Instead, the absence of planning led to interference and gaps in performance. John B. Jones bemoaned the loss of the Richmond, Fredericksburg & Potomac's "fine iron" rails during a Confederate withdrawal. "Mr. Seddon's subordinates must answer for this," he insisted. "The iron was wanted more than anything else but men." Jones described not "the want of men" but the want of management and planning.[71]

The federal War Department recognized early in the war that army engineers could not manage the railroads or telegraph operations as efficiently as civilians. Secretary Stanton quickly turned to the professionals. He recruited railroad men into the army, the first of many successful wartime collaborations between the government and the American business community. According to Robert Weber, this collaboration showed that highly skilled civilians could contribute to winning the war and, he believes, taught a "valuable lesson" to the soldiers.[72]

Daniel McCallum and Herman Haupt, the brilliant, if touchy, engineer, managed the U.S. Military Railroad. Authorized on January 31, 1862, the USMRR built or rebuilt and operated railroads in Union-controlled southern territory. By the war's end, McCallum com-

71. John B. Jones, *A Rebel War Clerk's Diary,* ed. Howard Swiggert (New York: Old Hickory Bookshop, 1935), August 10, 1862, 2:10.

72. Weber, *Northern Railroads,* 24.

manded the largest railroad in the world with 24,965 men serving in the USMRR. They drove 419 engines and 6,330 cars over 2,105 miles of track. The USMRR's Construction Corps laid or relaid 642 miles of track and built or rebuilt 26 miles of bridges. The total operation cost the War Department less than $30 million.[73]

A hands-on field operator, Haupt took charge of construction and transportation while McCallum applied his great administrative talent in the office. The two men worked well, if not comfortably, together. Supremely goal-oriented, they solved problems by trying any number of ideas until they found one that worked. Their freewheeling optimizing occasionally brought them into conflict with army officers' rigid mentality; the railroad men simply ignored them. By the time of the 1862 Fredericksburg campaign, Haupt had turned untrained laborers into an experienced construction corps. They built an eighty-foot high, four-hundred-foot long bridge over Potomac Creek that looked to President Lincoln as if Haupt had made it with "beanpoles and cornstalks."[74]

No one felt neutral about Haupt. One contemporary described him as "pugnaciously efficient." Entering West Point at age fourteen, too small to handle his musket in the manual of arms, Haupt resigned his commission three months after graduating in 1835. A creative and resourceful thinker, he reasoned out a formula for measuring stress on bridge trusses by 1840. His engineering brilliance carried him rapidly upward in Pennsylvania Central Railroad management. He also recognized young Tom Scott's talent and nurtured his career. Haupt accumulated a net worth of $500,000 by 1860, a fortune for that era. His

73. McCallum's Final Report, May 26, 1865, *OR*, Ser. 3, 5:999–1004. McCallum indicated that the USMRR spent $42,462,142.55 but sold rolling stock and other equipment to southern railroads after the war for $12,623,965.83, a $29,838,176.72 net cost. Because of the financial distress of postwar southern railroads and many defaults, one should consider the $12 million sales figure a soft number, though exemplary for war surplus.

74. Ward, *That Man Haupt*, 114, 119; Francis A. Lord, *Lincoln's Railroad Man: Herman Haupt* (Teaneck, N.J.: Fairleigh Dickinson University Press, 1969), 77; Weber, *Northern Railroads*, 152; Herman Haupt, *Reminiscences of General Herman Haupt* . . . (Milwaukee: Wright & Joys, 1901), 47–49.

arrogance, however, led him to financial ruin in the bowels of the un-forgiving Hoosac Tunnel through Massachusetts' Berkshire Mountains.[75]

Haupt refused to accept any compensation other than expenses from the War Department. He explained to General Halleck that this arrangement allowed him absolute control of his time; he wanted to return to digging his tunnel as soon as possible. He declined to wear a uniform and refused to work on the Sabbath "unless necessity imperatively requires it." He carried the honorary title of "general" but never held a commission during the Civil War.[76]

Army officers routinely commandeered the USMRR's scarce railroad cars for mobile offices and warehouses. The take-charge Haupt stopped the practice. Finding a boxcar set up as a paymaster's office, Haupt physically threw the man, his strong boxes, and paper work off the train. On another occasion, an officer's wife stopped a train so she could inquire about accommodations. A stern Haupt persuaded her not to do it again. He stopped soldiers from pilfering wood intended for locomotive fuel and relocated the army's bathing areas to prevent soapy water from contaminating locomotive boilers.[77]

Strong management held the key to operating an efficient military railroad. Haupt asserted bluntly, "A single track road in good order and properly equipped may supply an army of 200,000 men, when, if these conditions were not complied with, the same road would not support 30,000." He determined that quartermasters wasted supplies. They ordered too much, distributed them too slowly, and too readily abandoned them when the army withdrew. Haupt imposed strict standard operating procedures that allowed nothing to delay his trains. Quartermasters would fill supply orders only as needed and in amounts that receiving units could unload promptly in order to return the cars rapidly. If necessary, officers in the receiving units must assign extra

75. Ward, *That Man Haupt*, 7, 18–19, 30–31, 107, 169. Scott could also pick talent. He hired seventeen-year-old telegrapher Andrew Carnegie as his personal secretary.

76. Lord, *Lincoln's Railroad Man*, 23–24, 54–56, 58, 76–77.

77. Weber, *Northern Railroads*, 144; Lord, *Lincoln's Railroad Man*, 108, 112, citing *Report of the Committee of the Conduct of the War*, Part I (1863), 682–87.

laborers to ensure rapid turnaround. He set cargo priorities as well: subsistence, forage, ammunition, hospital supplies, veteran troops, and finally, raw troops.[78]

Then there was John Pope. General Pope came east to lead the Army of Virginia in June 1862. A blowhard who grandly told his new command that his western troops had only seen the backs of their retreating enemies, he announced that inquirers would find his headquarters in the saddle. This inspired wags to observe that Pope made his headquarters where his hindquarters ought to be. Unimpressed with the need for good rail management, Pope delegated his railroad operations to the Quartermaster Department. Haupt promptly wrote off John Pope. He resigned and went home to go broke digging his tunnel.[79]

Pope belatedly discovered the chaotic condition of his "most wretched and inefficient" railroads and humbly asked Haupt to return. Haupt acidly observed that Pope had "at last discovered that a railroad could not be run successfully with more than one person to give orders." General Halleck put Haupt in complete charge of Pope's railroads on August 24, 1862, but it was too late. On August 26, Stonewall Jackson's foot cavalry, having marched fifty miles in two days, fell upon Pope's supply trains at Manassas Junction. They stuffed themselves with fruit, canned goods, whiskey, and other Yankee delicacies. Experts at the train-wrecking business by now, they destroyed several locomotives and hundreds of loaded boxcars before leaving Manassas. The War Department at last grasped the importance of insulating railroads from interference by officers. It removed railroads from all but the USMRR's control. Civilian experts, some in uniform, would exclusively control even military railroads for the rest of the war.[80]

---

78. Lord, *Lincoln's Railroad Man,* 108–10, 120, citing General Orders, June 2, 1862, in *Military Railroads 1861–67: General Orders, Instructions and Reports* (n.p., n.d.), Association of General Railroads Library, Washington, D.C.; Weber, *Northern Railroads,* 152.

79. Ward, *That Man Haupt,* 122.

80. Haupt, *Reminiscences,* August 19, 1862, p. 73; Weber, *Northern Railroads,* 150. Lord says that Pope lost three hundred freight cars and seven locomotives at Second Manassas because of Pope's failure to remove the exposed trains

The Confederate government paid a high price for its failure to plan. It did not establish clear priorities for allocating scarce resources such as iron. Its posture toward blockade running reveals its inability to recognize and exploit opportunities.

Rails began to wear out in large numbers just as the Civil War began, an unfortunate quirk of the timing of southern railroad development. Charles B. Dew estimates that southern railroads needed fifty thousand tons of replacement rails each year, in addition to wheels, axles, and other iron products. Southern mills in 1860, however, only produced 16,072 tons of "bar and railroad iron," according to the 1860 Census. They would not produce more than twenty thousand tons of iron in any of the war years. In contrast, Pennsylvania foundries alone produced 266,253 tons of iron in 1860.[81]

Weapons production consumed the bulk of available iron. Most southern iron, however, had metallurgical properties that made it unsuitable for gun iron. Southern-cast artillery tubes tended to explode when fired. Some cautious artillerymen understandably refused to fire them.[82] This wasted both the iron and the manpower used to forge the defective cannons. Southern railroads desperately needed iron for rails and other products. Instead of directing iron to this use, however, the government diverted one-quarter of the Confederacy's iron production to the navy's imaginative but flawed ironclad ship program.

An analysis of Confederate naval strategy exceeds the scope of this study. One neither dismisses the potential impact of an effective Confederate ironclad fleet nor slights the genius of Navy Secretary Stephen R. Mallory's conception of it. One can, however, assess the merits of

---

(*Lincoln's Railroad Man,* 124–27, 146, citing Special Order 248, November 10, 1862, and Special Order 337, signed by Secretary of War Stanton). George Edgar Turner puts the numbers at eleven locomotives and four hundred cars and cites the incident as a good example of northern industry's ability to replace damage of this type (*Victory Rode the Rails,* 254).

81. Dew, *Ironmaker,* 268–69 and census table 3, p. 88. Dew says that iron rails lasted an average of ten years. Southern iron statistics do not include the output of the border states, to which the Union denied the Confederacy access.

82. Ibid., 180. According to Dew, Josiah Gorgas denied any weakness in southern-made cannon, 278.

allocating scarce iron to this program in terms of its actual contribution to the Cause. The Confederate navy started construction of twenty-six ironclads during the war, beginning with the famous USS *Merrimack,* renamed the CSS *Virginia.* Ironically, tracks torn up from local railroads provided the vessel's armor.

The USS *Monitor* and the *Virginia* changed naval warfare and made wooden warships obsolete overnight. The Confederate program, however, never lived up to its promise. Its ironclads sank a total of three Union warships during the Civil War, including two wooden ships in the *Virginia*'s debut. Often underpowered, most struggled to make headway against tidal or river currents. Design flaws rendered many unseaworthy and limited their combat efficiency. Only half saw action. The few that entered into service attracted Union warships like magnets. The Confederate navy destroyed many of its ironclads, including the *Virginia,* to prevent Union forces from capturing them. This inspired Josiah Gorgas to call the navy "that unfortunate branch of the service . . . always foremost in misfortune." Secretary Mallory reportedly once took a group of young ladies to inspect his beloved ironclads. When the tour ended, a Miss Maggie Howell "demurely" asked to see "the place where you blow them up." Southern shipyards continued to build ironclads in spite of disappointing results. As late as November 1864, those under construction waited for 4,230 tons of iron armor plate.[83]

His critics accused Secretary Mallory of wasting iron by persisting with the ironclad program in spite of its dismal performance. Mallory does not deserve to bear the sole blame, but he did remain singularly blind to the program's lack of accomplishment. Ironclads consumed scarce iron better used elsewhere. Planning could have assessed their progress and identified and allocated iron to more profitable uses, such

83. Joseph T. Durkin, S.J., *Stephen R. Mallory: Confederate Navy Chief* (Chapel Hill: University of North Carolina Press, 1954), 312, 324; Rembert W. Patrick, *Jefferson Davis and His Cabinet* (Baton Rouge: Louisiana State University Press, 1944), 260, citing Thomas Cooper DeLeon, *Belles, Beaux, and Brains of the '60s* (New York, 1909), 415–16; Vandiver, *Gorgas,* 156, 132; Bern Anderson, *By Sea and by River: The Naval History of the Civil War* (New York: Alfred A. Knopf, 1962), 300–301.

as railroad hardware. Planning would also have recognized the great potential offered by blockade running.

Southerners purchased most of their consumer and industrial products from northern or European sources before the war. The Confederacy also planned to import weapons and other war supplies that it could not manufacture itself. Ordnance Chief Gorgas expected to make fifty to sixty thousand rifled muskets per year. By July 1863, however, southern factories had produced only forty thousand muskets, while Gorgas had imported 200,000 British Enfields. Two-thirds of all Confederate small arms came through the blockade during the war.[84]

The Union navy blockaded southern ports to keep European goods from reaching the Confederacy. In contrast to the Confederacy's inefficient response to the blockade, the U.S. War Department formed a Blockade Strategy Board composed of northern businessmen, shippers, and naval officers. A prototype of U.S. Army Air Corps's strategic bombing planners of World War II, the Blockade Strategy Board identified the most likely blockade-running ports: those with deep water channels and access to railroads, canals, and riverboats and those with adequate dockyards and banking institutions. Union ground and naval forces closed six of the Confederacy's eight best ports, including New Orleans, by the spring of 1862.[85]

The Lincoln administration waged a determined and effective diplomatic campaign to persuade Great Britain and France to honor the blockade. Charles Francis Adams, ambassador to the Court of St. James, repeatedly stressed the warmth of Anglo-American friendship in his meetings with Lord John Russell, the British foreign secretary. At the same time, Adams firmly reminded Russell of the substantial risks to Great Britain inherent in meddling in America's domestic problems. Faced with the choices of honoring the blockade or choosing certain

84. Stephen R. Wise, *Lifeline of the Confederacy: Blockade Running During the Civil War* (Columbia: University of South Carolina Press, 1988), 90. Grant liked the high-quality British-made weapons. He replaced the obsolete smoothbore muskets that some of his regiments still carried with the 30,000 Enfields captured at Vicksburg. *Personal Memoirs of U. S. Grant* (New York: Da Capo, 1982), 300.

85. Wise, *Lifeline*, 13, 24, 63.

war with the United States by trying to force it, the governments of Britain and France backed away from the Confederacy.[86]

The Davis government turned its back on blockade running's enormous potential contribution to the Cause. Southern manufacturers and railroad executives asked the government in 1862 to take part in a joint trading venture. They planned to run cotton through the then-leaky blockade to pay for machinery, equipment, and other imported goods. According to George Edgar Turner, the Confederate government refused to participate on the grounds that it was not a "proper function" of the government "to support private enterprise." Stephen Wise says that Davis feared dependence on profit-seeking blockade runners. Secretary of the Navy Mallory rejected cooperative ventures on the basis that they would require interdepartmental sharing of authority, apparently a bureaucratic impossibility. President Davis finally signed a law in February 1864 requiring blockade runners to set aside half their shipments for government cargo, but the runners evaded the restriction with near impunity.[87]

That it shrank from encouraging blockade running for fear that someone would make a profit speaks volumes about the Davis administration's ignorance of, and contempt for, business and about its distorted perception of the war's realities. Its posture supports George Edgar Turner's argument that the Confederate government's "temperament, disposition and capacity" and "its lack of industrial comprehension, and . . . inability to deal in a practical manner with the mechanics involved" left it incapable of understanding logistics in modern war. This lack of understanding stands in sharp contrast to Union Quartermaster General Meigs's justifying the generous fares the War Department paid northern railroads based on the excellent, and therefore economical, service they provided.[88]

Absent direction from Richmond regarding the blockade, everyone looked out for himself. The ubiquitous Josiah Gorgas supervised the

86. Norman A. Graebner, "Northern Diplomacy and European Neutrality," in Donald, *Why the North Won the Civil War*, 54–64, 70.

87. Turner, *Victory Rode the Rails*, 242; Wise, *Lifeline*, 53, 56, 145.

88. Turner, *Victory Rode the Rails*, 71; Weber, *Northern Railroads*, 129–30.

"clandestine trade" for the Ordnance Department. North Carolina and Georgia, both with large investments in their states' railroads, went into the blockade running business. The North Carolina Railroad ordered locomotive boiler plate, flange wheels, and plush carpeting from a British exporter. As a result, it reported its rolling stock in good condition as late as 1863.[89]

Shipyards built light, fast steamers especially designed to run the blockade. They traded reduced cargo capacity for increased speed. Between September 1861 and December 1862, 77 of 105 attempts to run the blockade succeeded. The Union navy, however, eventually captured, sank, or ran aground twenty-eight of the thirty-six ships involved. Over the course of the war three hundred steamers successfully ran the blockade one thousand times in thirteen hundred attempts during the war. They carried 350,000 bales of cotton through the blockade, a pittance, however, compared to the three million bales exported in 1860 alone. The United States Navy captured 136 ships and destroyed 85 more.[90]

A blockade runner had a life expectancy of two round trips. Fantastic profits, as high as 650 percent, however, compensated for the high risk; a successful 1300-bale shipment brought a $200,000 profit. The business attracted the ambitious and the bold. Daring and highly paid sailors brought in cloth, food, weapons, iron products, locomotive parts, marine engines, and raw materials such as lead and saltpeter to sustain the fighting Confederacy. Huge profits and the discovery that civilian goods earned larger profits than military shipments corrupted even the best-intentioned patriots. Joseph Anderson's Tredegar Iron Works bought into a cotton running venture to pay for manufacturing machinery and tools. The first successful attempt brought in wire rope, but the rest of the cargo consisted of such items as "ten dozen ladies'

89. Wise, *Lifeline*, 53, 105, 158–59; Frank E. Vandiver, *Ploughshares into Swords: Josiah Gorgas and Confederate Ordnance* (Austin: University of Texas Press, 1952), 84; Trelease, "Southern Railroad," 12–13.

90. J. Moore, *Confederate Commissary General*, 265; Wise, *Lifeline*, 72, 221. The Union prohibited the export of nonsmoking northern anthracite coal to deny the blockade runners a preferred means of concealment (Anderson, *By Sea and by River*, 219).

hose" and "one thousand best segars." Charles Dew explains that Anderson hedged his bet to protect his company in the event the Cause went sour. Tredegar's London sterling account assured the firm's postwar survival, thus justifying Anderson's actions as "prudent as well as profitable."[91]

In their 1864 campaigns, Generals Sherman and Grant relentlessly pounded their opponents. Nonstop fighting gave Confederate armies no time to rest or refit, much less reinforce each other. Steady combat also dramatically increased their supply requirements. The blockade runners kept up. Between October 1864 and January 1865 they ran in 50,000 rifles, 400,000 pounds of lead as well as copper, tin, blankets, shoes, tinned beef, and saltpeter. Stephen Wise argues that blockade runners, no thanks to the Davis government, brought in enough goods to enable the Confederacy to sustain its armies adequately as long as ships could get through. Confederate forces aggressively defended the approaches to Wilmington, North Carolina, the last Atlantic blockade running port. Although not the most desirable port, Wilmington had unique advantages. Shore batteries covered the several passages in and out, forcing the Union navy to patrol a fifty-mile entrance. Further, its treacherous waters proved a graveyard for ships and offered the concealment of fog. A yellow fever epidemic shut down Wilmington port operations for several weeks in the summer of 1863, a more effective blockade than anything the Yankees could achieve. Combined Union army and navy operations finally closed Wilmington in January 1865. Its supply jugular choked off, a ragged, starving Confederacy died three months later.[92]

The Confederacy could quite possibly have overcome the blockade with a properly coordinated effort. Instead of ironclads, it might have built "flying squadrons" of fast warships to run interference for blockade runners, protecting and extending their flanks with fields of the newly invented, and psychologically intimidating, torpedoes, or sea mines. Blockade running offered an excellent offset to the Confederacy's industrial weakness, but the Davis administration squandered this

91. Wise, *Lifeline*, 115; Dew, *Ironmaker*, 205–9.
92. Wise, *Lifeline*, 165–66, 196.

genuine opportunity. No one so much as prepared lists of goods desired or available through blockade sources. Purchasing agents in Nassau, Bahamas, and Hamilton, Bermuda, therefore had to guess which items the Confederate armies might need. Blockade running ran aground on an absence of planning, petty interdepartmental posturing, and the refusal of private interests as well as state and national governments to cooperate for the greater good.[93]

Had the Confederacy concentrated its domestic production in areas that could make positive contributions to its war economy and relied on blockade runners for the balance of its needs, it might have bought enough time to wear down the Union's will. Instead of casting cannons that blew up, the Confederacy could have imported artillery from Europe. Instead of forging armor plate for a navy that sank, southern foundries could have made wheels and rails with domestic iron. But no one planned. The real potential of the blockade becomes clear from the fact that the supplies run through the blockade, in spite of the most casual management, kept the Confederacy in the fight until the Yankees closed the last port.

The federal government received excellent rail service from the northern railroads for several reasons. It left operational control in the hands of experts. It paid reasonable fares to the railroads, which removed money as a source of contention and encouraged cooperation. It passed a law giving it authority to take military control of the railroads in times of emergency, and it demonstrated its will to exercise that authority. Finally, it insulated railroads from military interference. Northern industry and superb railroad management did the rest.

The Confederacy, in contrast, did not pay responsible fares to the southern railroads, exposing them to financial ruin. The railroads in turn had to cope with practices that ran directly counter to the pressing needs of the Confederate war effort. Legislation enabled the Confederacy to take military control of the railroads, but the Davis administration never used it to force their cooperation, thus squandering an important element of control. Finally, it never insulated southern railroads from destructive meddling by army officers, however well in-

93. Ibid., 53, 75, 90.

tended. The Confederacy needed to exercise skillful management in order to prosecute its war for independence successfully. It needed intelligent, experienced leaders to draft sound, coordinated war plans. It needed confident managers to make firm, swift decisions. It did not pass the test. The Davis government took two weeks before making the decision to send Longstreet's divisions to Georgia. The complete absence of any sense of urgency suggests an air of unreality at the very top of the Confederate government. Perhaps it did not know what to do, and so it did nothing, a fatal management posture. The United States Army has a phrase, "Lead, Follow, or Get Out of the Way." The Confederacy did none of these. Charles Darwin foresaw a bleak future for creatures that could not adapt to a changed environment.

The Confederacy had to have effective railroads in order to exploit the advantage of interior lines and prolong the war until it wore out the Union. In spite of shortages and myriad other obstacles to creating and maintaining an effective rail system, the fact remains that the Confederate leadership did not take the most basic steps to achieve the crudest level of railroad efficiency. The consequences of prior decisions, or the failure to make them, would become clear in the movement of James Longstreet's divisions to a river of death.

The Union positioned itself to get the best results from northern railroads, its logistical distribution component. They delivered the services it needed. For reasons that can only be attributed to a failure of management, the Confederacy did not get the service it needed from its railroads. It failed the railroads and the railroads failed the Confederacy.

2

THE CONFEDERACY

┼┼┼

Crisis and Decision

> It was suddenly determined in Richmond to quietly withdraw
> Longstreet's corps from General Lee's army and send it to Bragg
> to stop the wild careening of our lively friend Rosecrans through
> Georgia.
>
> —Benjamin Abbott, Adjutant, Benning's Georgia Brigade

War weariness drained the Confederacy in the summer of 1863. The
would-be nation faced crises in all directions that tested its will to keep
on. The endless casualty lists from Gettysburg vied with the dreadful
news that General John Pemberton surrendered Vicksburg and thirty
thousand soldiers on the Fourth of July after a seven-week siege; seven
thousand more surrendered at Port Hudson five days later. Vicksburg's
loss gave the Union control of the entire Mississippi River. It ripped
the trans-Mississippi away, exposing the Confederacy's weakness and
opening "the whole Southwest to the enemy who now have two powerful armies opposed to two feeble ones."[1]

A young sergeant in the 7th South Carolina, recovering from a long

---

1. Edward Younger, ed., *Inside the Confederate Government: The Diary of Robert Garelick Kean, Head of the Bureau of War* (New York: Oxford University Press,
1957), 79.

siege of recurring fever, recalled the desperate fighting on Gettysburg's Little Round Top. "[M]y life was not worth a straw," James Suddath despairingly wrote to his brother. "I see no chance ahead of me I am tired of this war and it looks like it might last for years yet Oh for peace, peace." In Chattanooga, "the bright shining hopes of the citizens had evaporated under the pressures of the long war." John Jones, a government employee in Richmond felt that "the momentary gloom, hanging like the pall of death over our affairs, cannot be dispelled without a decisive victory somewhere, or news of speedy foreign intervention."[2]

Some Confederates still accentuated the positive aspects of the Cause's situation. The Memphis *Daily Appeal* (now publishing in Atlanta following several relocations inspired by advancing Union armies) proclaimed "No Cause for Despondency" on July 31, 1863. Success lay ahead because "He is more than doubly armed who fights in a righteous cause and," it added, "on the defensive." The Raleigh *Standard*, however, had editorialized for a year that the Confederacy should end a war that it could no longer win.[3]

Advancing Yankees seemed to attack everywhere, and they showed no signs of letting up. Federal cavalry and infantry raided deep into southwestern Virginia, threatening irreplaceable salt works and iron foundries and savaging the Virginia & East Tennessee Railroad. Union infantry columns approached Knoxville, raising the hopes of long-suffering North Carolina and Tennessee Unionists. The Union army's big guns pounded Charleston, the flash point of the rebellion. Al-

2. Frank B. Williams Jr., ed., "From Sumter to the Wilderness: Letters of Sergeant James Butler Suddath, Co F, 7th Regiment, S.C.V." *South Carolina Historical Magazine* 63 (1962): 98–99; Charles Stuart McGehee, "Wake of the Flood: A Southern City in the Civil War, Chattanooga, 1838–1873" (Ph.D. diss., University of Virginia, 1985), 109; J. Jones, *Rebel War Clerk's Diary*, August 2, 1863, 2:4.

3. R. A. Halley, "A Rebel Newspaper's War Story: Being a Narrative of the War History of the Memphis *Appeal*," *Tennessee Historical Society Quarterly* 8 (1903): 144; Robert Talley, *One Hundred Years of the "Commercial Appeal"* (Memphis: Memphis Publishing, 1940), 34; W. B. Yearns and John G. Barrett, eds., *North Carolina Civil War Documentary* (Chapel Hill: University of North Carolina Press, 1980), 292.

though combined army and navy operations could not capture the city, the navy closed it as a blockade-running port for months, and Major General William H. C. Whiting, commanding the Cape Fear District, advised Secretary of War James A. Seddon on Sept. 8, 1863, that Charleston "has well nigh ceased to belong to us." In addition, defending Charleston all but exhausted the Confederacy's pitifully depleted artillery ammunition reserves.[4]

The Yankee navy also inserted soldiers on the North Carolina coast. They landed dangerously close to Wilmington, the Confederacy's only other remaining major Atlantic blockade-running port. The raiders tore up railroad tracks and destroyed water tanks in an attempt to break the coastal railroad. General Whiting believed that the Federals would close the Cape Fear River, isolate Wilmington, and cut the Confederate logistical lifeline. "There are besides other lines of attack equally feasible," he warned. Whiting urged "the constant presence" of troops to defend the coastline. Assembling an army, however, would take time "in the present condition of our transportation and resources."[5]

The Yankees themselves took the pressure off. The Army of the Potomac, victors at Gettysburg, rested and refitted in blissful contentment in its camps along Virginia's Rappahannock River. The army's commander, General George G. Meade, patiently explained his limited prospects for a successful campaign against the Confederates to an increasingly impatient President Abraham Lincoln. The general told the president that an attacking army requires a three-to-two manpower advantage over an opponent. Confederate General Robert E. Lee's somewhat smaller Army of Northern Virginia thus neutralized Meade's numerical superiority. Lincoln noticed "an oddity in the military art," according to Bruce Catton, and asked General in Chief Henry W. Halleck, "If the enem[y']s sixty thousand are sufficient to keep our ninety thousand away from Richmond why, by the same rule, may not forty thousand of ours keep their sixty thousand away from Washington, leaving us fifty thousand to put to some other use?" Though "a civil-

---

4. *OR*, Ser. 1, 29, pt. 2:703–4, 716–28; Richard D. Goff, *Confederate Supply* (Durham: Duke University Press, 1969), 141.

5. *OR*, Ser. 1, 29, pt. 2:696–97, 700.

ian's question, awkward and somewhat innocent," Catton says, Lincoln's query was "hard to answer."[6]

Despite his impatience with Meade, Lincoln himself unwittingly gave the Confederacy some relief. The president believed that retired General in Chief Winfield Scott's strategy, the once-derided Anaconda Plan, held the key to victory. He had tried, with miserable success, to convince his generals to maintain simultaneous and constant pressure at several points in order to overwhelm the Confederacy.[7] In the late summer of 1863, however, he temporarily set aside that strategy in order to pursue his political goals for restoring the Union. General Ulysses S. Grant, the hero of Vicksburg, had proposed capturing Mobile, Alabama. Lincoln overruled him in favor of operations that he expected to result in the readmission to the Union of reconstructed Texas, Louisiana, and Arkansas. His plan made good political sense but dispersed Union forces that must necessarily first destroy the Confederate armies in order to crush the rebellion; victory alone could make restoration possible. Thousands of young men would pay a high price for the president's decision.

The Confederate leadership, however, struggling with endless demands on its strained resources, felt no letup in pressure. They saw instead still another crisis looming in Tennessee. Union General William S. Rosecrans' Army of the Cumberland, long dormant southeast of Nashville, now marched swiftly across Tennessee's forbidding terrain. Rosecrans advanced eighty miles in just eleven days in a series of masterful flanking maneuvers. The Cumberlanders suffered fewer than six hundred casualties as they drove General Braxton Bragg's Army of Tennessee from the Confederate heartland. Bragg, stunned by Rose-

6. Bruce Catton, *Never Call Retreat: The Centennial History of the Civil War* (Garden City, N.Y.: Doubleday, 1965) 3:271; Lincoln to Halleck, Sept. 19, 1863, *The Collected Works of Abraham Lincoln*, ed. Roy P. Basler (New Brunswick: Rutgers University Press, 1953) 6:466–67.

7. Joseph T. Glatthaar makes a strong and positive assessment of Lincoln as a war president, specifically the "genius" of his strategic vision. *Partners in Command: The Relationships between Leaders in the Civil War* (New York: Free, 1994), 230.

crans' new aggressiveness, stumbled back toward Chattanooga and its critical rail junction.[8]

President Jefferson Davis, in an attempt to buck up the wavering and faint of heart, declared August 21 a Day of National Fasting, Humiliation, and Prayer. A visitor from New Orleans, the Reverend B. M. Palmer, gave the invocation at Chattanooga's First Presbyterian Church on Market Street. As the faithful bowed their heads, Rosecrans' gunners obligingly punctuated the urgency of deliverance by lobbing cannon shells into the city. One round aimed at the steeple landed in front of the church, breaking a little girl's leg.[9]

The Confederate government in Richmond finally grasped a harsh reality—ignoring the heartland had opened the back door. If Rosecrans' Cumberlanders took Chattanooga, they opened the way to Atlanta. If Atlanta fell, the Yankees would again have split the Confederacy in two and almost surely have crushed the dream of independence. Someone had to stop Rosecrans. On August 24, 1863, President Davis asked General Robert E. Lee to come to Richmond to consult with him "on military questions of a general character." Davis had increasingly turned to General Lee for advice as the war progressed. The two men discussed the Rosecrans threat at length with Secretary of War James A. Seddon and other Confederate leaders. They reviewed fundamental strategic options: should the Confederacy shift troops to threatened positions, or attack the Union's "vital areas" to keep the Yankees off balance and force them to react? Lee argued forcefully for the latter course.[10] Lee knew that the Confederacy could lose the war in the West, but he firmly believed that it could only win it in the East. Victory, though, depended on his destroying the Army of the Potomac before the Yankees, with their limitless resources, inevitably

8. Peter Cozzens, *This Terrible Sound: The Battle of Chickamauga* (Urbana: University of Illinois Press, 1992), 21.

9. Cozzens, *This Terrible Sound,* 36, citing Chattanooga *Sunday Times* magazine section, August 2, 1936, 5. Colonel John T. Wilder's Union artillery fired the first rounds. A champion of mounted infantry armed with repeating rifles, Wilder became mayor of Chattanooga after the war.

10. *OR,* Ser. 1, 51, pt. 2:759; Steven E. Woodworth, *Davis and Lee at War* (Lawrence: University Press of Kansas, 1995), 254–55.

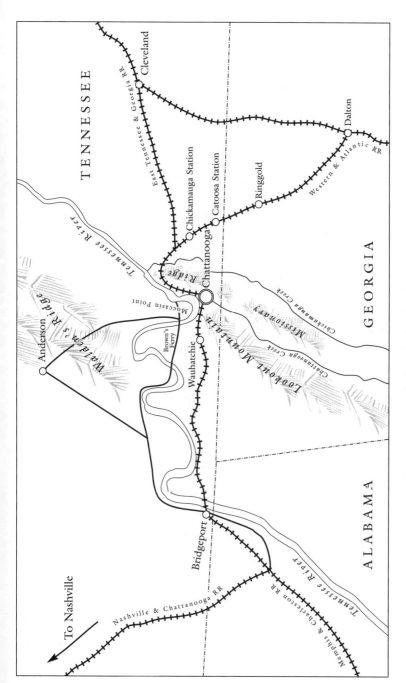

Chattanooga area before the Battle of Chickamauga

overwhelmed him. Not one to lack aggressiveness, Lee proposed send-
ing the Army of Northern Virginia north to invade Pennsylvania again.
This time he would deliver the knockout punch that Meade ducked at
Gettysburg.

After a full week of discussions, Lee believed that he had persuaded
President Davis to let him march north. Still in Richmond, and unable
to detach himself gracefully from the president, Lee ordered his First
Corps commander, General James Longstreet, to "use every exertion
to prepare the army for offensive operations and improve the condition
of [the] men and animals." Lee, however, had misjudged Davis, who
heard powerful voices urging a swift and powerful strike in the West.
By the end of the week, Davis bent to the pressure of those voices.
Sometime around September 1, Davis decided to send troops from
Virginia to reinforce Braxton Bragg. The president and his advisors,
however, demonstrating a casual sense of urgency, then spent another
week choosing whom to send and how to send them.[11]

The powerful voices came from an informal group of officers and
politicians called the Western Coalition. They believed that victory in
the West offered the Confederacy its only successful strategy for ending
"this exhausting war." According to General Pierre G. T. Beauregard,
the strategy needed only "a proper selection of the point of attack—
the Yankees themselves tell us where." Shortly after Lee's stunning victory at Chancellorsville in May, Louisiana's "Napoleon in Gray"
predicted that the Army of the Potomac would take no offensive action
for at least six months. For this reason he believed that Lee should shift
to a defensive posture in Virginia and send thirty thousand men to join
Braxton Bragg in Tennessee. The combined armies, under Bragg "or
whoever is put in his place," perhaps Beauregard, would then pounce
on Rosecrans and smash him. No small thinker, Beauregard planned
to exploit the victory by enlisting thirty thousand Kentucky and Tennessee volunteers to liberate their home states. They would then invade Ohio with help from friends of the Copperhead leader, Clement
Laird Vallandigham. His fertile imagination unleashed, Beauregard be-

11. Lee to Longstreet, August 31, 1863, *OR*, Ser. 1, 29, pt. 2:761; Woodworth, *Davis and Lee at War*, 255.

lieved that Indiana, Illinois, and Missouri would then "throw off the yoke of the accursed Yankee nation," forge a Northwestern alliance, and arrange treaties with the Confederacy.[12]

The fighting Episcopal bishop, General Leonidas Polk, also blessed the western strategy. He told Davis, his friend since their West Point days, that if Grant drove toward Mobile (precisely what Grant wanted to do), General Joseph E. Johnston could not stop him. "The consequence must be," Polk wrote, "that, sooner or later, Mobile will succumb, and Alabama, in spite of Johnston, be overrun." Polk recommended that Johnston leave a defensive screen in Alabama, join Bragg in Tennessee to form a massive concentration against Rosecrans, and "crush him." The combined forces would then retake Tennessee, break Grant's line of communication, and force him to abandon his campaign for Mobile. In Polk's opinion, the prospects for victory outweighed any short-term risk to Alabama.[13]

Virginia Senator G. A. Henry of Lexington also recommended combining Bragg's and Johnston's forces under the command of "fighting generals in the Army of Tennessee." Rosecrans' relentless advance toward Chattanooga convinced Henry that Bragg was not up to the job but, Henry wrote, "exhausts himself in organizing his army." The senator believed that the Army of Tennessee desperately needed stronger leadership "and you will see my statement verified if men of more nerve are put at its command." Suggesting that "the fate of Virginia depends upon the defense of East Tennessee," Henry presciently asked, "Can't Longstreet be sent out there?"[14]

General Longstreet also saw the benefits of a concentration in the West. Lee's "war horse" and most experienced senior officer, the South Carolinian had demonstrated his tactical genius by wrecking the Yankees, and General John Pope's career, with a well-timed bone-crunching counterattack at Second Manassas. He proved the futility of frontal assaults against entrenched positions when his dug-in troops

---

12. Beauregard to Charles J. Villerè, May 26, 1863, *OR*, Ser. 1, 14:955.

13. Polk to Davis, July 26, 1863, *OR*, Ser. 1, 23, pt. 2:932–33.

14. Senator G. A. Henry to Seddon, August 29, 1863, *OR*, Ser. 1, 51, pt. 2:760–61.

shattered repeated Yankee attacks at Fredericksburg. His First Corps bore the hardest fighting at Gettysburg, including the actions at the Peach Orchard, the Wheatfield, Little Round Top, and, over his bitter opposition, Pickett's Charge. He would almost die in the Wilderness, accidentally shot by his own troops in the confused fighting, but he would recover in time to stand at Lee's side at Appomattox.[15]

Longstreet had supported a proposal in the spring of 1863 to send troops to relieve Vicksburg until Lee's bold plan to invade Pennsylvania won him over. By September, however, he believed that the Confederacy faced very different tactical and strategic challenges than existed three months earlier. Although he promptly obeyed Lee's order to prepare the Army of Northern Virginia for another march north and alerted Generals Ewell and Hill to get ready, he questioned the likelihood of success. If Meade, as expected, stayed in his trenches, Longstreet saw no hope of victory unless Lee were "strong enough to cross the Potomac." He suggested a different approach. The Yankees had successfully defended selected positions while advancing elsewhere; the Confederacy should do the same. Convinced that the western theater offered "our best opportunity for great results," Longstreet believed that Lee should go over to the defensive, even if "it should become necessary to retire as far as Richmond temporarily," and send a corps to Tennessee. He warned his commander that "the enemy intends to confine his great operations to the west, and . . . it is time that we were shaping our movements to meet him. . . . I fear if it is put off any longer we shall be too late."[16]

Longstreet offered to command the reinforcements. If Lee could

---

15. After the war some officers blamed Longstreet for the failure at Gettysburg in order to protect Lee's and their own reputations. Longstreet's joining the Republican Party and urging reconciliation did not endear him to his former comrades. For a balanced biography, see Jeffry D. Wert, *General James Longstreet: The Confederacy's Most Controversial Soldier—A Biography* (New York: Simon & Schuster, 1993); for a more critical assessment, see William Garrett Piston, *Lee's Tarnished Lieutenant: James Longstreet and His Place in Southern History* (Athens: University of Georgia Press, 1987).

16. Longstreet to Lee, September 2, 1863, *OR*, Ser. 1, 29, pt. 2:693; Longstreet to Lee, September 5, 1863, ibid., 699.

not spare the First Corps, perhaps Longstreet could take other units. He suggested that "we might accomplish something" by his taking command of the Army of Tennessee "and giving [Bragg] my corps. We would surely make no great risk in such a change and we might gain a great deal." He doubted that "Bragg has confidence in his troops or himself either. He is not likely to do a great deal for us." Denying any "personal motive," Longstreet offered to "most cheerfully give up" the command after a Confederate victory stabilized the West.[17]

Some of Longstreet's detractors cite his seeking the job as proof of the man's appetite for self-promotion and grasping for command.[18] Perhaps, but Longstreet certainly qualified for the command as one of the Confederacy's most senior field generals. And he hardly stood alone in questioning Bragg's fitness for combat command. Further, his support of past proposals to reinforce the western armies indicates his interest in, and appreciation of, the region's strategic importance. His support at this time showed sound thinking. Finally, and perhaps most important, Jefferson Davis would most likely find Longstreet politically acceptable. If the president could have overcome his affliction of un-swerving loyalty to close but incompetent friends and given Longstreet command of Bragg's army, the Cause could hardly have fared worse than it did with Braxton Bragg.

On September 5, Davis made the decision. Longstreet would take John Bell Hood's division, now commanded by Evander McIver Law, and Lafayette McLaws' division to northwest Georgia. Longstreet's third division, George E. Pickett's, wrecked as a fighting force at Get-tysburg, would guard Richmond's defenses. This freed Micah Jenkins's brigade to go with Longstreet. Some thirteen thousand men would

---

17. Longstreet to Lee, September 5, 1863, ibid.

18. Thomas Lawrence Connelly says in *Autumn of Glory: The Army of Tennessee, 1862–1865* (Baton Rouge: Louisiana State University Press, 1971) that Longstreet's interest in the West "gives credence to the suspicion that Longstreet hungered for Bragg's command"(151). William Piston acknowledges the claims but discounts ambition as a major reason. He believes that Longstreet no longer wished to serve under Lee in the aftermath of Pickett's Charge (*Lee's Tarnished Lieutenant*, 66–67). Jeffrey Wert believes that Longstreet's critics oversimplify the man's thinking (*General James Longstreet*, 303).

travel to Georgia. Lee, fearing that two Georgia brigades in Hood's division might desert, sent them to defend Charleston. On September 6, Lee reported to Davis that he had given Longstreet his orders and arranged his transportation. He also said that he had made provisions for feeding the troops along the route.[19]

A great bear of a Kentuckian, and goat of his West Point class of 1853, the ferociously aggressive "Sam" Hood had proven an outstanding assault commander. A Yankee bullet shattered his left arm in the opening minutes of the Peach Orchard–Little Round Top fight. Doctors saved the arm but the now-useless appendage condemned him to a life of constant pain. Longstreet expected Hood to stay in Richmond to recuperate. Hood insisted on going to the train station to say farewell to his beloved Texas Brigade, self-described as "a great fighting machine, always ready and willing to fight." The Texans loudly demonstrated their great affection for their general as they boarded the trains. Hood, greatly moved, could not bring himself to leave them; his arm still in a sling, he decided on the spot to go with them.[20]

Evander Law, a brigadier general at age twenty-seven, had assumed command of the division when Hood fell. A South Carolinian and graduate of the South Carolina Military Academy (now the Citadel) in Charleston, he had become a respected officer. Micah Jenkins, another fine young officer, a popular leader, and an ardent secessionist, also graduated from the South Carolina Military Academy in the class before Law. Jefferson Davis preferred that Law continue to command the division in Hood's absence, but Longstreet wanted Jenkins. Hood's return obviated the decision but not the bad blood it caused between Longstreet and Law, nor the rivalry between Law and Jenkins.

19. Lee to Davis, September 6, 1863, *OR,* Ser. 1, 29, pt. 2:700–701; Lee to Davis, September 9, 1863, ibid., 706. Two of Pickett's three brigade commanders lay dead, the third gravely wounded, and every one of his thirteen regimental commanders was killed or wounded in the tragic charge of July 3, 1863.

20. Sgt. D. H. Hamilton, "History of Company M, First Texas Volunteer Infantry, Hood's Brigade," Groveton, Tex.: n.p., 1925. According to Hamilton, only 473 survivors of the Texas Brigade stood at Appomattox, less than 1 in 12 of those who originally formed the 3 regiments in 1861.

Longstreet's West Point classmate Lafayette McLaws commanded his second division. Although overshadowed by other generals in the Army of Northern Virginia, the Georgian enjoyed a reputation as a solid and dependable fighting general. Succumbing to the backbiting and acrimony that infected the Army of Tennessee before and after Chickamauga, Longstreet would ultimately relieve McLaws, and Law would resign, only to have Longstreet press charges against him. Nothing came of either matter. Both McLaws and Law served under Joseph Johnston until the end of the war. Micah Jenkins died in the rain of bullets that wounded Longstreet in the Wilderness.

Davis still hoped, as late as September 8, that Lee would agree to take command in the West, but the general skillfully resisted his efforts. Good Soldier Lee said that he would take the job if it served the Confederacy, but he doubted that he would be of much help. Lee's lack of enthusiasm disappointed Davis, but he needed the man in Virginia every bit as much as in Georgia. Some historians have criticized Lee for his alleged inability to see beyond the horizon of a theater commander. They point to his opposition to transferring Longstreet as a sign of a petty commander's "proprietary right" as well as his reluctance to take command in the West.[21]

Lee had good reason to worry. Meade had outnumbered him by half even with Longstreet's divisions. If the Army of the Potomac came at him with Longstreet gone, he might have to fall back as far as Richmond. The Yankees in fact appeared ready to do just that when they learned that Longstreet had left Virginia. Whatever Lee's motivation, he *was* a theater commander who had just given up almost one-quarter of his army for a doubtful mission that he opposed. As he wrote to Davis, "[W]e have lost the use of troops here, where they are much needed and . . . they have gone where they will do no good." Lee questioned whether Longstreet could reach Bragg "in time and condition

21. Woodworth, *Davis and Lee at War,* 254–57; Richard E. Beringer et al., *The Elements of Confederate Defeat* (Athens: University of Georgia Press, 1988), 135; see Thomas L. Connelly, "Robert E. Lee and the Western Confederacy: A Criticism of Lee's Strategic Ability" in *Lee the Soldier,* ed. Gary W. Gallagher (Lincoln: University of Nebraska Press, 1996), 189–207.

to be of any advantage to him." If Longstreet helped Bragg, then quickly returned to Virginia, well and good, but, he wrote, "should he be detained there without being able to do any good, it will result in evil." He then dumped the consequences on Davis' anxiety-ridden imagination, adding his confidence that his commander in chief would "have the means of judging this matter and of deciding correctly." Davis admitted to "vain regrets" about sending Longstreet, but if "successful, and rapidly followed up," he reasoned, "it may prove that the course adopted was, after all, the best."[22]

Meade's intentions did not worry Colonel G. Moxley Sorrel, Longstreet's chief of staff. Sorrel believed that once the Yankees learned of Longstreet's departure, they would send troops to Chattanooga to counter him, and they would have a longer route around the outside of the Confederacy's perimeter. Longstreet would beat the Yankees to Georgia, "hurrying by the short, straight cord of the circle." Sorrel believed that "This expectation proved correct."[23]

Its commanders' failures to support armies operating in other theaters had dogged the Union army from the beginning of the war. Had the Yankee forces in the Shenandoah Valley actively engaged Joe Johnston's Confederates at the beginning of the war, one questions whether he could have transferred his regiments to shore up Beauregard at First Manassas. Similarly, Rosecrans and his Cumberlanders sat out the spring and most of the summer of 1863. He ignored Lincoln's suggestion to march on Chattanooga as Grant closed in on Vicksburg, while the Army of the Potomac fought major battles at Chancellorsville and Gettysburg. Meanwhile, the Confederates sent men from Bragg's army facing Rosecrans in an effort, albeit unsuccessful, to help General John Pemberton's army besieged in Vicksburg. Rosecrans' inaction, in spite of President Lincoln's chiding, made the attempt possible.

Presuming continued passivity on the part of Meade's Army of the

22. Lee to Davis, September 14, 1863, *OR*, Ser. 1, 29, pt. 2:720–21; Davis to Lee, September 21, 1863, ibid., 738. True to form, Lee immediately shifted to the offensive when he confirmed the 11th and 12th Corps movement (Woodworth, *Davis and Lee at War*, 254–58).

23. Gen. G. Moxley Sorrel, *Recollections of a Confederate Staff Officer* (1917; reprint Dayton, Ohio: Morningside Bookshop, 1978), 188.

Potomac figured heavily in the Confederate decision to send Longstreet. It reflects the tragic consequences of the Union's inability to implement General Scott's Anaconda Plan. If, for example, the Army of the Potomac had actively campaigned in northern Virginia in the months following Gettysburg, the Davis administration would not have dared to detach Longstreet's brigades from the Army of Northern Virginia and send them to Chickamauga. Meade's passivity made the strategic Confederate move politically possible. Had Rosecrans' Cumberlanders faced Bragg and the Army of Tennessee alone, one can argue whether his lengthening supply lines would have allowed Rosecrans to take Atlanta in the fall of 1863. It seems less debatable, however, whether Bragg could have stopped him.

The orders cut, the men began moving out. A young officer wrote to a friend, "You will now discover that it was suddenly determined in Richmond to quietly withdraw Longstreet's corps from General Lee's army and send it to Bragg to stop the wild careening of our lively friend Rosecrans through Georgia. So the generals bundled us up in a lot of cars in a few minutes, said nothing about where we were going, and away we went for Georgia. We guessed first one thing and then another, but never paused until we pulled up at Ringgold about eight miles from Chickamauga."[24]

The advancing Rosecrans represented a genuine and immediate threat. It demanded that the Confederate leadership take prompt and decisive action to meet it. Taking two weeks to make a decision qualifies as neither prompt nor decisive. It fairly describes, however, dilatory Confederate leadership and substandard Confederate war management.

24. Benjamin Abbott, Gen. Benning's adjutant, to Green Haygood, Chickamauga, September 26, 1863, *"Dear Mother: Don't Grieve about Me. If I Get Killed, I'll Only be Dead": Letters from Georgia Soldiers in the Civil War,* ed. Mills Lane (Savannah: Beehive, 1972), 272.

3

SOUTHERN RAILROADS AND THE LONGSTREET
MOVEMENT

The Effect of Confederate Mismanagement

> Never before were such crazy cars . . . wabbling on the jumping
> strap iron—used for hauling good soldiers.
> —G. Moxley Sorrel, Longstreet's Chief of Staff

Quartermaster General Alexander R. Lawton arranged the movement.
"Everything turned on the question of transportation and supply," he
wrote, "and it all had to be decided and performed with telegraphic
haste." Lawton's "haste" addressed General Lee's fear that Rosecrans
would strike Bragg, and Meade attack Lee, while Longstreet's divisions
traveled between the two, unavailable to help either army.[1]

The most direct route to Chattanooga passed through Lynchburg,
Virginia, then south along the Holston and Tennessee Valleys. One
could get to Lynchburg by taking the Virginia Central and then the
Orange & Alexandria, or by taking the Richmond, Fredericksburg &
Potomac and then the Richmond & Danville and South Side railroads.
O&A passengers had to change trains in Lynchburg because the Vir-

---

1. *Life and Reminiscences of Jefferson Davis. By Distinguished Men of His Times*
(n.p.: Eastern, 1890), 197–98.

ginia & Tennessee's five-foot gauge tracks created a gauge barrier. The South Side tracks, though of compatible five-foot gauge, did not connect to the V&T. At Bristol, Virginia, the Virginia & Tennessee's tracks joined the East Tennessee & Virginia's, which terminated at Knoxville. The East Tennessee & Georgia Railroad covered the final leg to Chattanooga.

Major Frederick W. Sims, chief of the Confederate Railroad Bureau, telegraphed Thomas Dodamead, the superintendent of the Virginia & Tennessee Railroad, in Lynchburg, on September 5 to ask, "Will you need aid & how much to move twenty-thousand men & fifty pieces of Artillery to Bristol [Virginia] in five days." He later asked Dodamead how many locomotives and cars he would need, adding the hardly reassuring afterthought, "so as to send them to you if they are to be had. You shall be advised in time to prepare."[2]

Unfortunately for the Confederacy, the Yankees had just shut the door to Knoxville. Aggressive maneuvering by Union Major General Ambrose E. Burnside and his twenty-thousand-man army, as timely as it was rare, entered the undefended city on September 3. They seized such prizes as a nearly finished steamboat, two locomotives and several railroad cars, "and a very considerable amount of army stores." They also blocked Longstreet's route just as he intended to use it.[3]

For whatever reason, no one told either Longstreet or Sims that Knoxville had fallen. No one had given Braxton Bragg any particulars of the Longstreet movement, either, such as how many reinforcements he might expect, and when he might expect them. The incredible failure to pass on such important information, however, seems typical of Confederate communication lapses during this period. Longstreet and Sims continued to refine their plans for the Valley route, unaware that Burnside had taken it away, even though the Richmond *Daily Dispatch* reported Knoxville's fall on September 3 and confirmed it on September 4, albeit with sketchy details, and on September 8, Davis notified

2. Sims to Dodamead, September 5, 1863, Sims Letterbook.
3. Burnside to Halleck, September 3, 1863, *OR*, Ser. 1, 30, pt. 3:333. Sims later tersely advised Dodamead, "The contemplated movement has been changed" (Sims Letterbook).

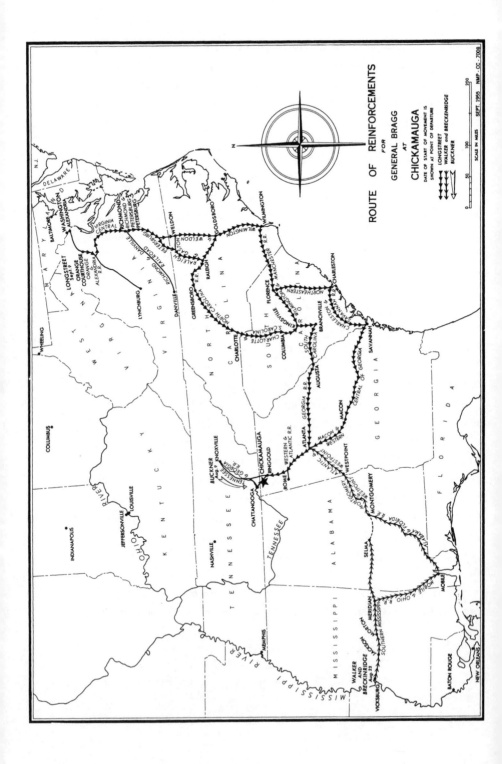

ROUTE OF REINFORCEMENTS

FOR

GENERAL BRAGG

AT

CHICKAMAUGA

DATE OF START OF MOVEMENT IS
SHOWN AT POINT OF DEPARTURE

LONGSTREET
WALKER and BRECKENRIDGE
BUCKNER

SCALE IN MILES

0   50   100   200

SEPT. 1955   NMP - CC - 7008

Lee that Braxton Bragg had reported Burnside in Knoxville.[4] A Union army in Knoxville posed a direct threat to Virginia's upper (southern) Shenandoah Valley. Had Lee known in time, he would certainly have argued to send Longstreet to dispose of Burnside before turning on Rosecrans.

The viability of the route through Knoxville, with or without Burnside's presence, seems questionable. The federal War Department had studied possible Confederate rail movements and routes. On New Year's Day, 1863, as Rosecrans and Bragg fought the battle of Murfreesboro, or Stones River, in Tennessee, a John Kimber advised Secretary Stanton that he "need have no undue apprehension" of the Virginia & East Tennessee Railroad's participating in any reinforcement of Bragg's army. Considering the distressed condition of the road's rolling stock and equipment and the delay caused by the gauge barrier at Lynchburg, the Confederates "could not, even if the bridges were not destroyed as reported, send 20,000 men in three weeks from Richmond to Murfreesborough." Nor, Kimber reported, could they complete an ammunition shipment in ten days under any circumstances.[5]

In June 1863, a Union man from east Tennessee, Dr. McGowan, assessed the condition of the southern railroads for General George Thomas. He counted 19 locomotives on the road between Chattanooga and Knoxville, "12 of which [were] unfit for service, and the balance considerably worn." Between Knoxville and Lynchburg, of twelve engines available, "three . . . [were] good and the others scarcely fit for use."[6] Attention to maintenance might have improved the railroad in the ensuing months; it seems most doubtful, however, considering the collapsing condition of other southern railroads by the fall of 1863.

With Knoxville no longer an option in any event, Major Sims patched together a circuitous 950-mile route to Chattanooga through

---

4. James Longstreet, *From Manassas to Appomattox: Memoirs of the Civil War in America* (Philadelphia: J. B. Lippincott, 1896), 436; *OR*, Ser. 1, 52, pt. 2:523.

5. Jno. Kimber Jr. to Stanton, January 5, 1863, *OR*, Ser. 1, 20, pt. 2:302–3.

6. McGowan to Thomas, June 24, 1863, *OR*, Ser. 1, 22, pt. 2:453–54.

Atlanta. He planned to split the traffic onto two routes at Gaston and Weldon, North Carolina, to increase capacity. Part of the movement would pass through Wilmington and Charleston, South Carolina, and Savannah, Georgia, en route to Atlanta. The second route passed through Raleigh and Charlotte, North Carolina; Columbia, South Carolina; and Augusta, Georgia. The new routes required eight separate transfers, with resulting delays because of unconnected or incompatible-gauge tracks, and impeded by deteriorated track and broken-down rolling stock. The expected two- to four-day trip via Knoxville became a seven- to eleven-day odyssey.[7]

George Edgar Turner describes Lawton's and Sims's mission as "an immense, laborious and vexatious piece of work." He says that their lack of authority to take military possession of the railroads made their task significantly more difficult. To the contrary, Quartermaster General Lawton did possess precisely the legal authority necessary to take military control of the railroads, but neither he nor his government asserted that authority, not even for an operation as complicated, strategically critical, and urgent as Longstreet's movement. As a result, Sims approached the railroads with hat-in-hand appeals. He asked the president of the Cheraw & Darlington, "Do you . . . need all your engines[?] I want two good ones for a month or so. Can you let me have them?" He told S. L. Fremont, superintendent of the Wilmington & Weldon in Wilmington that he would write to a Captain Ross "in your favor for cars." He informed J. R. Sharp in Columbia that he had no locomotives to give him but "You might get some from ET&Ga [East Tennessee and Georgia] Road." Somehow the scrambling Sims found twenty cars and arranged to send them to Wilmington.[8]

Sims's correspondence reveals a loosely organized and managed operation. He did not notify the managers of the affected railroads until September 7, although the troops would begin marching to northern Virginia railheads the next day. He then left them confused as to the

7. Sims to Drane, Sharp, and Peake, September 11, 1863, Sims Letterbook; Black, *Railroads of the Confederacy,* 186.

8. Turner, *Victory Rode the Rails,* 283–84; Sims Letterbook, September 9 and 11, 1863.

route and the numbers of men involved. John D. Whitford, president of the Atlantic & North Carolina Railroad, and recently appointed quartermaster for North Carolina, asked Sims if the troops would take the North Carolina Railroad, the Wilmington & Weldon, or both; he also asked whether Sims had notified the railroads participating in the movement. Sims replied that he would use both roads to avoid "overtasking" the Wilmington & Manchester Railroad. He also told Whitford that he had the authority to "order the Raleigh telegraph office to remain open when necessity requires it." Sims told H. M. Drane, the Wilmington & Manchester superintendent, to prepare for a "heavy movement of troops to Georgia, besides this there will be two brigades for Charleston." He could not, however, tell Drane "with any definity" when he might expect them.[9]

Sims did not know exactly how many soldiers would participate in the movement. He told the superintendent of the Georgia Railroad in Augusta, George Younge, to arrange transportation for "three-thousand troops per day for seven days in succession." Younge promptly closed the railroad to freight north of Rutledge "until further notice." On September 11, Sims informed Fremont of the Wilmington & Weldon that the movement would involve some 18,000 troops; he didn't know how many would pass through Wilmington but suggested, "Suppose about half." He advised H. J. Peake in Charleston that half would go by Kingsville and half by Columbia. On September 11, the South Carolina Railroad "temporarily discontinued" its night passenger train to accommodate the troop traffic.[10]

The other route branched at Weldon, the junction of the Petersburg Railroad and the Wilmington & Weldon, which ran to Wilmington, North Carolina. After a ferry ride across the unbridged Cape Fear River, the Wilmington & Manchester carried the soldiers west through Florence, South Carolina. The troops transferred at Manchester Junction to the South Carolina Railroad for the leg to Charleston. There they marched across the bridge over the Ashley River and took the

9. Sims Letterbook, September 7–8, 1863.

10. Ibid., September 11, 1863; Augusta *Constitution*, September 10–11, 1863.

Charleston & Savannah to Savannah, Georgia, where a recently completed bridge over the Savannah River avoided still another change. The C&S tracks connected to the Central of Georgia Railroad which, with the Macon & Western, led to Atlanta.

Longstreet's men had mixed emotions about leaving the state they had defended so well. Captain Joab Goodson of the 44th Alabama wrote that he and his troops "bade farewell to our old camps near Fredericksburg, I must say with regret, and started on our journey." He had "many regrets" on leaving, "perhaps forever, our noble Virginia army" and Virginia's "hospitable people."[11]

The soldiers traveled light. They could take only what they could fit into their haversacks or blanket rolls. According to Benjamin Abbott, General Henry Benning's adjutant, wrote, "Our troop[s] are so light now that it is nothing for them to be ready in thirty minutes to move a thousand miles." The officers took their personal mounts, but the brigades left their draft animals, wagons, and other equipment in Virginia. When the 15th Alabama arrived at Ringgold, Georgia, on September 16, it "encamped for the night, but without baggage and camp equipage, which had been left behind."[12]

Lawton reported to General Lee on September 7, "Arrangements all made." Sims sent trains to Hamilton's Crossing, four miles south of Fredericksburg on the Richmond, Fredericksburg & Potomac Railroad, until the last troops in Hood's division left for Georgia. He advised Lee that "Three-thousand troops a day is the utmost that can be transported South." He allowed that he could carry more troops to Richmond each day "but it will not result in any advantage to do so,"[13] probably because of the lack of capacity of the forwarding roads.

On September 8, Lawton told General Lafayette McLaws that his command would ship out on the evening of September 9 and that

11. W. Stanley Hoole, ed., "The Letters of Captain Joab Goodson," *Alabama Review* 10 (1957): 149–50.

12. Abbott to Green Haygood, Chickamauga, September 26, 1863, *"Dear Mother,"*, ed. Mills Lane, 272; William C. Oates, *The War Between the Union and the Confederacy and Its Lost Opportunities* (New York: Neale, 1905), 253.

13. Q.M. Gen. Alexander R. Lawton, Receipt Book, September 7, 1863; Sims to Lee, September 7, 1863, Sims Letterbook.

"Each train can bring about fifteen hundred." He soon reversed himself, however, and told McLaws that "to prevent confusion the Divisions are being moved separately." He would dispatch all of General Hood's division before starting to board McLaws' troops. Delays in shipping the last of Hood's men bumped McLaws to midday on the tenth. The first fifteen hundred soldiers left Richmond at 8:00 P.M. on September 8. On September 10, Sims reported to Major John D. Whitford in Raleigh that "Seventeen-hundred troops left [Richmond] last night and eighteen-hundred this morning."[14]

The experience of the 17th Mississippi, the "Confederate Guards" in McLaws' division, seems typical. The regiment, camped on the North Anna River, received orders on Monday evening, September 7, to march to Hanover Junction the next morning. Private Robert Moore wrote, "We are to march very early. Many are the conjectures as to where we will go." They hiked twenty miles, bivouacking near Hanover Junction, when Moore wrote, "It has become well settled with the soldiers that we go to Chattanooga." They turned in their wagons and draft animals and then spent a second night at Hanover Junction because of a delay in shipping the last of Hood's division.[15]

On Thursday, September 10, the regiment left Hanover Junction after midday and reached Richmond five hours later. The soldiers marched across the city, crossed the James River, and camped near Manchester Station. The next day, September 11, they rode twenty-three miles to Petersburg, Virginia, "a very nice & pleasant old city," arriving around noontime. They waited nine hours for a train.[16] Petersburg authorities had vigorously refused to allow anyone to connect the standard-gauge tracks of the Richmond & Petersburg to the Petersburg Railroad. It seems that the town fathers feared that joining the tracks would hurt the local economy and reduce the city to a back-

14. Lawton, Receipt Book, September 8, 1863; Sims Letterbook.

15. Robert A. Moore, *A Life for the Confederacy as Recorded in the Pocket Diaries of Pvt. Robert A. Moore,* ed. James W. Silver (Jackson, Tenn.: McCowat-Mercer, 1959), 164–66. For the recollections of Sylvester Cooper, also of the 17th Mississippi, see Norman Lee Cooper, *A Confederate Soldier and His Descendants* (Bowie, Md.: Norm Cooper Associates, 1982), 25–26.

16. R. Moore, *Diaries,* 164.

water. The practical effect of unjoined tracks, however, meant that forwarding Longstreet's troops depended on the timely availability of engines and cars at every transfer point. It also meant offloading freight, manhandling it to the adjoining line, and reloading, with more delays and damage. Further, unjoined tracks meant that other lines could not lend rolling stock to roads on the route. The Longstreet movement could proceed no faster than allowed by the railroad with the least rolling stock.

The Petersburg Railroad took the 17th Mississippi to Weldon, North Carolina, sixty-odd miles south of Petersburg. Other units took the branch line at Hicksford Junction directly to Gaston. The regiment arrived early in the morning of September 12, then spent three hours waiting for a Raleigh & Gaston train. The R&G also ran on standard gauge but, once again, the two roads' tracks did not connect. The Mississippians reached Raleigh, North Carolina, in the early morning of Sunday, September 13, having taken twenty hours to complete what Moore described as a ninety-eight-mile trip (fewer than eighty miles on today's highways). The Provost Guard barred the way to Raleigh and kept the traveling soldiers near the trains, "owing to the little difficulty between the 'Buffaloes' [peace-minded southerners] & the Ga. Troops a few days since." Moore considered Raleigh residents "very disloyal."[17]

The regiment headed toward Greensboro by day's end and reached Charlotte the next morning for a brief layover and a train change to the Charlotte & South Carolina's five-foot gauge tracks. It then took another 21 hours to travel the 110 miles between Charlotte and Columbia, South Carolina. Moore "with several friends proceeded from the depot to the City." They missed their train and "had to remain . . . all day . . . quite agreeably." The strays, with the encouragement of the Provost Guard, left Columbia for Augusta on the morning mail train. From Augusta they immediately pushed on to Atlanta, 170 miles away, arriving at sunrise on Thursday, September 17. They continued to Marietta where there was a long layover because of the proximity of

17. Ibid., 166.

the fighting and a traffic jam on the Western & Atlantic. Moore noted that Marietta "contains a great many exiles & refugees" and "a good many sick." The next day, the regiment passed through Dalton after a delay of several hours and on to Ringgold, Georgia, "which [was] as far as the cars run," a scant ten miles from the creek named Chickamauga. The regiment bivouacked in Ringgold for the next two nights. Moore reported, "Are cooking up 3 days rations. Cannonading in front all evening, suppose the cavalry are skirmishing."[18]

The 17th Mississippi spent eleven days traveling 950 miles between northern Virginia and northwest Georgia. Despite delays and layovers, the regiment arrived in time to fight at Chickamauga. Private Robert Moore arrived in time to die on Sunday, September 20.[19]

The strain on the railroads' capacity forced Lawton and Sims to press all available rolling stock into service. As Longstreet's Chief of Staff, Moxley Sorrel, lightly described it, "Never before were such crazy cars—passenger, baggage, mail, coal, box, platform, all and every sort wabbling on the jumping strap-iron—used for hauling good soldiers. But we got there nevertheless." Soldiers crammed into severely overloaded boxcars, dark and stuffy in the warm September weather. General Joseph B. Kershaw's brigade "loaded by one company being put inside and the next on top, so one-half of the corps made the long four days' journey on the top of boxcars." Some soldiers cut holes in the sides of the cars for light and air and to see the passing sights. In their enthusiasm, some cut away everything but the frame and the roof, leaving "little more than skeleton cars."[20]

A soldier in the 15th Alabama "rode the entire way to Atlanta on the top of a box car, the cars were jammed and packed inside and out." The 5th South Carolina squeezed itself into boxcars "packed in so tightly that there was no room to sit down and many stood from Virginia to Georgia with no chance to stretch cramped muscles except at

18. Ibid., 166–67.
19. Ibid.
20. Gen. G. Moxley Sorrel, *Recollections of a Confederate Staff Officer* (New York: Neale, 1917; reprint, Dayton, Ohio: Morningside Bookshop, 1978), 189–90; David A. Dickert, *History of Kershaw's Brigade* (Newberry, S.C.: Elbert H. Aull, 1899), 263, 266–67.

wayside stations, where the train stopped for a few minutes." Many climbed on the roofs to get air and stretch out. In the course of the journey, however, "many lost their lives by being swept off by over-hanging branches, road bridges, and other obstacles." One infantry-man wrote, however, "The trip was quite refreshing to us who were accustomed to travel on the 'gravel train' as the boys term the Virginia turnpike roads."[21]

In spite of cramped and uncomfortable cars, breakdowns, and de-lays, the Confederate soldiers would fondly remember their journey as "one grand ovation." Longstreet's trains passed through areas un-touched by war. Townspeople turned out in large numbers to greet their gray heroes. A man in Kershaw's brigade remembered, "The news of our coming had preceded us, and at every station and road crossing the people of the surrounding country, without regard to sex or age, crowded to see us pass, and gave us their blessings and God speed as we swept by with lightning speed." The outpouring of good-will touched the soldiers: "Old men slapped their hands in praise, boys threw up their hats in joy, while the ladies fanned the breeze with their flags and handkerchiefs." The soldiers atop the cars responded, "nor could those inside bear the idea of being shut up in a box car while their comrades on top were cheering and yelling themselves hoarse. . . . [T]he exuberant spirits of the Southern soldier were too great to allow him to hear the yelling going on and not yell himself."[22]

Each Confederate soldier expected an issue of four days' cooked ra-tions. According to Benjamin Abbott, however, combat capability came first. "If rations should 'by any accident' not be in the commis-sary," he wrote, "all that is necessary is to send around an ordnance Sergeant with forty rounds of cartridges to each man and start the army." The hungry soldier could hope to pass a cornfield, "provided

21. William C. Jordan, *Some Events and Incidents during the Civil War* (Mont-gomery, Ala.: Paragon, 1909), 50; Natalie Jenkins Bond and Osmun Latrobe Coward, eds., *The South Carolinians: Colonel Asbury Coward's Memoirs* (New York: Vantage Press, 1968), 83–84; Hoole, "Letters of Captain Joab Goodson," 149–50.

22. Dickert, *Kershaw's Brigade,* 263–64.

the horses haven't cleaned up the provender in advance"; if they had, he simply stayed hungry.[23]

When it comes to his stomach, a soldier leaves nothing to chance. An Alabama infantryman explained, "A soldier in active service will eat every time he can get it, for he never knows when he is going to be put on short rations, and he is generally in anticipation and eats accordingly." A man in the same soldier's regiment named Smith "always ate all his rations at the first halt on the march. It mattered not whether his rations were for one, two, or three days, he ate them all at once just the same, not because he was hungry; but, as he said, his rations were easier to carry that way than in his haversack." But the civilians knew the way to the soldiers' hearts—they fed them. According to Moxley Sorrel, Private Smith notwithstanding, "The journey through the States from Virginia was a continuous ovation to the troops. They were fed at every stopping place and must have hated the sight of food. Kisses and tokens of love and admiration for these war-torn heroes were ungrudgingly passed."[24]

The 17th Mississippi's Private Robert Moore recorded the many kind gestures from civilians during his regiment's journey south, especially in Charlotte. "The ladies are out to-night to welcome us," he wrote. "They have many nice viands which is very acceptable to the soldiers. God bless the ladies." En route to Augusta, Moore wrote, "The ladies at Orangeburg & other places on our route to-day were very kind."[25]

The 2nd South Carolina reached the rail junction at "Millen" (probably Milan, Georgia) for a meal stop. John Coxe recalled the enthusiasm: "Yes, supper! For immediately we were marched into a large, airy dining hall especially fitted up for just such hungry chaps as we. And such service and victuals we found in there! All things good to eat

23. Benjamin Abbott to Green Haygood, *"Dear Mother,"* 272.

24. Oates, *War Between the Union and the Confederacy*, 253; Sorrel, *Recollections*, 191. The Yankees had appetites, too. One described the adequacy of an issue of eight days' cooked rations, "enough, that is, for four days eating." Chaplain Alonzo Hall Quint, *The Record of the Second Massachusetts Infantry* (Boston: James P. Walker, 1867), 191.

25. R. Moore, *Diaries*, 164–66.

seemed to be there in great plenty, and at first some of us wondered whether we were still in our own beloved South."[26]

The Tom Green Rifles in the 4th Texas "found to [their] great joy and surprise a long table spread with goodies expressly for the Texas Brigade . . . prepared by the ladies of Sumterville [probably Sumter, South Carolina] and refugees from Charleston." The Texans made the most of the fifteen-minute stop. A late arrival wrote, "by the time I got to the table it was crowded to overflowing and I found myself completely cut off from a plate," so he watched his fellow Texans "act the hog." He accepted a cold sweet potato from a lady "with a very pretty smile," even though, he wrote, "if there is anything that I have a contempt for it is a cold sweet potato." He seemed happier with the cigar that a gentleman gave him.[27]

The soldiers basked in the townspeople's kindness. "Perhaps the best of all," one wrote, "was the galaxy of fine and beautiful young Southern women who served us." Fifty-nine years later, John Coxe, the 2nd South Carolinian, would remember the image, still fresh to him, of a pretty young lady with "a touching smile, large, laughing blue eyes, and, withal, an alluring personality that attracted ones attention as long as she was in sight. Where, O where is that Miss Mattie Wooding now?"[28]

Captain Joab Goodson of the 44th Alabama recalled that "Some of the boys amused themselves by writing billet deaux, and throwing them to some young ladies as they pas[sed]." Many wrote to them, the start of "a great deal of pleasure from the expected correspondence." Ladies also threw Texans "bouquets of flowers, and some of their written addresses place[d] in a small split stick, so it would be certain to make its landing, to correspond with anyone who desired to do so, to give them words of comfort and to cheer them on their way."[29]

26. John Coxe, "Chickamauga," *Confederate Veteran* 30 (1922): 291.

27. *Rags and Hope: The Recollections of Val C. Giles, Four Years with Hood's Brigade, Fourth Texas Infantry, 1861–1865,* ed. Mary Lasswell (New York: Coward-McCann, 1961), 196–97.

28. John Coxe, "Chickamauga," 291.

29. Hoole, "Letters of Captain Joab Goodson," 149–50; O. T. Hanks, "History of Captain B. F. Beton's Company, 1861–1865," Frederick A. Eiserman Research Collection, Carlisle, Pa., 25–26.

A South Carolinian found the warmest welcome from enthusiastic young ladies in Georgia, "showering boquets of flowers on us, and cheering our hearts with their winning smiles and graces, and, what is best of all, feeding our hungry souls with an abundance of every thing good." The ladies, he wrote, "entertained us in a more kind and hospitable manner than we were received anywhere on our route," and he wished that his home state had given them as warm a welcome.[30]

The soldiers praised the legendary grace and kindness of the southern woman. It seemed that every time the trains stopped to take on water or wood, the soldiers found "great tables were stretched, filled with the bounties of the land, while the fairest and best women on earth stood by and ministered to every wish or want." David Dickert asked, "Was there ever a purer devotion, a more passionate patriotism, a more sincere loyalty, than that displayed by the women of the South toward the soldier boys and the cause for which they fought? Was there ever elsewhere on earth such women?" The South Carolinian pondered America's tragedy: "Will there ever again exist circumstances and conditions that will require such heroism, fortitude, and suffering?" The soldiers imagined the sacrifices that the civilians made to feed them so well. A Texan marveled at their generosity: "No tongue can tell, no mind can conceive, no history can describe the devotion, the hardships and heroism of the women of the Southern Confederacy. . . . They would divide the last bite."[31]

Lieutenant Francis W. Dawson, a naval officer detailed to Longstreet's ordnance staff, believed that the civilians' greetings stemmed in part from the soldiers' novelty: "When we reached South Carolina we received attentions which had long ceased to be common in Virginia, where the passage of large bodies of troops was an everyday occurrence. . . . Our men were rather unaccustomed to so much kindness, in these days, but they enjoyed it thoroughly. At Augusta, and at Atlanta, also, we were most hospitably received." A Virginian noticed another difference: "The people here show no signs of the war and

30. Lt. Richard Lewis, Bratton's Brigade, Longstreet's Corps, to his mother, September 30, 1863, *Camp Life of a Confederate Boy* (News and Courier Book Presses, 1883), 56.

31. Dickert, *Kershaw's Brigade*, 264; Hanks, "B. F. Beton's Company," 25–26.

there is no sign of that worn-out and dingy appearance which tells the story of dear old Virginia's sufferings."[32]

Warm receptions and generous meals could not erase the war. Its mood covered the Longstreet movement like a shroud. Mary Chesnut, the perceptive southern diarist, wrote that she "caught a glimpse of our army. Longstreet's corps going west. God bless the gallant fellows." The soldiers sleeping on the flatcars struck her as "a strange sight. . . . In their grey blankets, packed in regular order, they looked like swathed mummies." The grim purpose of their journey gave her "a feeling of awful depression . . . All these fine fellows going to kill or be killed. Why? And a word got to beating about my head like an old song—'the unreturning brave.'" The troops rolled toward an inevitable, unstoppable tragedy. "When a knot of boyish, laughing young creatures passed me," she wrote, "a queer thrill of sympathy shook me. Ah, I know how your home folks feel, poor children."[33]

Many soldiers had not seen their families since they left to go to war, some for as long as two years. Trains passed near some men's homes without stopping. "Sometimes the mood was tempered," one wrote. "[M]any a mother dropped a silent tear or felt a heart-ache as she saw her long absent soldier boy flying pass without a word or kiss." When the 5th South Carolina passed Smith's Turnout, "William Isom's wife was out at the train to see him with a baby that he never had seen. He kissed her and the baby and got back on the train." His lieutenant, John McConnell, "shoved him off with [his] foot and told him to spend the night and come on the next train." Isom did, and later "got up with [the regiment] all right." The 5th paid a terrible price at Chickamauga; of the forty men in McConnell's company, twelve were killed and twenty-six wounded. Isom and McConnell survived.[34]

32. Francis W. Dawson, *Reminiscences of Confederate Service, 1861–1865,* ed. Bell I. Wiley (Baton Rouge: Louisiana State University Press, 1981), 100–101; Susan Leigh Blackford, comp., *Memoirs of Life in and out of the Army in Virginia during the War between the States* (Lynchburg, Va.: J. P. Bell, 1894–1896), 146–48.

33. C. Vann Woodward, ed., *Mary Chesnut's Civil War* (New Haven: Yale University Press, 1981), 470.

34. Dickert, *Kershaw's Brigade,* 264; John Daniel McConnell Family Papers, Winthrop University Manuscript Collection, Rock Hill, S.C.

A young South Carolinian rumbled through Columbia, his hometown, vainly hoping to see his parents. Deeply disappointed, he reconciled himself with the reflection that "after thinking of the short time I would have had to have stayed with you, it is better that we did not meet, as it would have been more trying for me to have torn myself from the embraces of my mother State." Moxley Sorrel, on the other hand, believed that the journey inspired the soldiers. Many of Longstreet's regiments came from the southern Confederacy and, "it was good for the men to show up in this fashion even for a few minutes with their home people. Many of the companies were carried through their own towns and villages and surrounded by the eager faces of kinsfolk and neighbors. But there were no desertions or stops. The brave fellows pressed stoutly on with comrades to meet the foe."[35]

Some of Longstreet's regiments came from areas occupied or threatened by Union armies. A few Arkansas men deserted and went home when they learned that the Yankees had captured Little Rock. However, "The majority, hardened veterans, vowed to fight even harder to lessen the pressure on the home folks." Joab Goodson wrote that "The possibility of my own dear native state being over run by the ruthless invaders" made him feel "more than ever like doing all in my power to defend our country."[36]

The journey made painfully clear the price that Americans paid in the Civil War. As they passed through towns along the way, O. T. Hanks of Company K in the 1st Texas saw "not a man among them save an old grandsire or wounded soldier, his arm in a sling, or hopping on his crutches, at home on a furlough." The patriotic outpourings moved Longstreet's veterans. The civilians reminded them that a serious fight waited at the end of the railroad line. As one wrote, "Some kind hearted old ladies, weeping, exhorted us to fight nobly for our common cause."[37]

General Henry A. Wise angrily assailed "the utter deficiency and ne-

35. Lewis, *Camp Life*, 55–56; Sorrel, *Recollections*, 191.

36. Calvin L. Collier, *"They'll Do to Tie To": The Story of the Third Regiment, Arkansas Infantry, C.S.A.* (Little Rock: Pioneer, 1959), 154–55; Hoole, "Letters of Captain Joab Goodson," 149–50.

37. Hanks, "B. F. Beton's Company," 25–26; Hoole, "Letters of Captain Joab Goodson," 149.

glect of transportation" on the Wilmington & Weldon Railroad. Wise, formerly governor of Virginia, had orders to ship his twenty-five-hundred-man brigade and sixty-seven horses from Richmond to bolster Charleston's defenses. He expected to depart Richmond at 4:00 P.M. on September 14, but only enough cars arrived to carry 1200 men; the rest of his command did not reach Petersburg until 5:00 the next morning. The brigade encountered the same obstacle in Petersburg and finally arrived in Weldon at 5:00 A.M. on September 16, having taken a day and one-half to move eighty miles.[38]

The brigade left Weldon after a five-hour layover, but the train broke down forty-five miles down the line, "owing to willful and very culpable neglect on the part of the chief machinist," as Wise reported the engineer's story. "The tire of one of the driving wheels of the locomotive bursted entirely off and all the wheels are in a condition unfit for use." The engineer said that he had "duly" reported the poor condition of the locomotive "and yet the locomotive was sent to Weldon without repairs to take on troops." In addition, "horses or cattle had just been taken" from the brigade's cars, leaving them in "very filthy condition." The fuming general "could find neither conductor nor R. R. Superintendent to have the matter remedied."[39]

Wise's description of the Wilmington & Weldon, "in bad condition, not superintended or conducted with any system or arrangement," summarizes the condition of most southern railroads bluntly but not unfairly. He thought it "shamefully out of time with its appointments" and predicted it would, "in case of serious emergency, demanding prompt, precise & sufficient transportation, disappoint & defeat the operations of our armies." He got precious little satisfaction, however. He confronted the Wilmington & Weldon superintendent, but "He, Fremont, behaved very badly, replying with insolence, showing a guiltiness of dereliction of duty and bad temper for making it known. He defied all interference from the Secy. of War even." Fremont then left

38. Wise to Samuel Cooper, adjutant and inspector general of the Confederate armies, intended for Secretary of War James Seddon, September 16, 1863, John D. Whitford Papers, North Carolina State Archives, Raleigh.

39. Ibid.

with the damaged locomotive, "leaving [Wise] with the 59th [Regiment], the baggage and the horses in the road, with an engine too small to draw the train." Wise boarded as many of his soldiers as he could, leaving another officer in charge of the rest. The superintendent did not hasten to produce a second locomotive, "and the train with the baggage and horses arrived here [in Wilmington] yesterday [September 17] at 4 p.m., taking three days to come 226 miles."[40]

Wise acknowledged the "deficiency" of replacement parts for rolling stock, the labor shortages, and the railroads' other problems, but found "no excuse for the present condition of things on this R. R." He then put his finger on the root issue: "The R. R. is either under the charge of the Govt. or of the Companies; if of the former *its* officers and agents ought to be held to strict responsibility; if of the latter, the Company is a contractor with the Govt. and ought to be made to meet the conditions of its contract."[41]

He believed, incorrectly considering the sad circumstances of other railroads, that "these conditions can't possibly be as bad as the condition & superintendence of the road now are." Wise would solve the problem by assigning a government representative to each railroad. "The delays at Junctions could easily be avoided, the cars & locomotives could be kept in order, and negligent employees & officers be *held accountable*" [emphasis added].[42]

Greater accountability would certainly have helped to correct the railroads' shortcomings. The Confederate government had appointed William Wadley to the Railroad Bureau precisely to provide that oversight. But it would give neither Wadley nor anyone else authority to match the responsibility. Even had Wadley possessed the authority, by September 1863, he could not have created parts and equipment out of the air. Wise made good suggestions but the problems by that time defied solution. Had he made them two years earlier—and had the government heeded him—it might have made a difference.

Worn-out equipment broke down. Repeated delays created a sig-

40. Ibid.
41. Ibid.
42. Ibid.

nificant drag on the movement's time line. John Coxe of the 2nd South Carolina recalled his regiment's "lively excursion." After leaving Wilmington, "bad luck overtook us," he wrote. The locomotive "was in bad order, and slow progress and many stops to allow the engineer to 'tinker' with his machine greatly delayed us." They went only forty miles that night, and then the engineer sidetracked the train.[43]

The replacement engine did not arrive until midafternoon; Coxe's account reminds one of a children's story: "But, dear me! Our new machine seemed in worse condition than that hooked to our train. It was old, wheezy, and leaked steam in many places, while the water gushed from the tender in several streams. We laughed, but had little hope of better conditions. However, that old rattletrap of an engine surprised us. . . . [I]t struck the main track with a blatant snort and then astonished us by the high speed it made, stopping only, but a little frequently, for water." Thus the Confederacy carried its warriors to battle.

The little engine changed the 2nd's luck. They heard the booming of siege cannon when they transferred at Charleston, and made good time to Savannah. Their "train on the Georgia Central being already made up and ready," they "got on and started for Macon." The "straight as a shingle" route and high-quality, state-owned rolling stock, well maintained by purchases run through the blockade, sped them toward Atlanta "through a beautiful country of fine old homes and numerous herds and flocks of fat cattle and sheep."[44]

The movement proceeded amid some confusion due to chronically flawed communications. Lawton did not order his quartermaster in Augusta, Georgia, to organize the South Carolina and Georgia railroads "for the prompt and uninterrupted transportation of the troops" until September 11. Those roads provided the main route between Kingsville, South Carolina, and Atlanta.[45]

On Sunday, September 12, the first troops, part of McNair's and Gregg's brigades, Hood's division, arrived in Atlanta. They immedi-

43. John Coxe, "Chickamauga," 291.
44. Ibid.
45. Lawton, Receipt Book.

ately boarded a Western & Atlantic train for Resaca. On Monday, September 13, two trains carrying 488 and 610 men each left Columbia for Augusta. A regiment from General Robertson's command passed through Kingsville. On Tuesday, September 14, agents in Columbia shipped one 14-car train of 123 men, 60 horses, and 6 cars of baggage to Augusta, followed by a 19-car train carrying a thousand soldiers. They also shipped a 15-car train carrying 550 "state troops" to Charleston and a second 15-car train with "700 Nigroes to work on fortifications at Charleston S.C." Agents in Kingsville forwarded one of Benning's and two more of Jerome B. Robertson's regiments, followed by two more regiments belonging to Robertson and Kershaw. Wilmington agents shipped George T. Anderson's 1,900-man brigade and a 350-man regiment of Kershaw's brigade. Drane reported having trains in Wilmington ready to carry 2,600 men from William T. Wofford's brigade and "some four-hundred scattering from various commands together with stragglers."[46]

On the same day, September 14, seventeen-hundred troops passed through Charlotte. Benning's last troops reached Atlanta, where they were "compelled to stop to ration and get shoes for barefooted men." The first of Robertson's thirteen-hundred-man brigade left Atlanta for Resaca.[47] And Longstreet and his staff boarded a train in Richmond.

Self-inflicted problems aggravated the difficulty of coordinating arrivals and departures. Layovers increased travel times. Unconnected tracks greatly increased the number of locomotives and cars needed for the movement, calling for rolling stock that the railroads did not have. Coordination also proved extremely difficult because the railroad men had never dealt with anything approaching the Longstreet movement's magnitude. Whitford reported a bottleneck in Raleigh: "troops arriving & departing with dispatch have over[?] run everything with cars here. I fear I have been too fast with transportation." His counterparts in Weldon and Gaston could not keep up with the flow. Sims suggested

46. Col. M. H. Wright to Col. George W. Brent, Sept. 12, 1863, *OR*, Ser. 1, 30, pt. 4:643; Sims Letterbook, September 13–14, 1863.

47. Col. M. H. Wright to Col. George W. Brent, September 15, 1863, *OR*, Ser. 1, 30, pt. 4:652.

that Whitford ask "the Atlantic road" to lend two trains "till the rush is relieved."[48]

Northbound traffic all but stopped. Dr. J. F. Shaffner left his home near High Point, North Carolina, to return to duty in Virginia. Starting "about 12 hours behind schedule time," he missed his connection at Raleigh "in consequence of the continued trains of troops passing Southward." It took him three days to travel from High Point to Richmond, where he "found that a train from Orange C. H. [Court House] would not leave before the next morning, so [he was] compelled to remain in Richmond during the day."[49]

On Wednesday, September 15, seven hundred of Kershaw's men left Kingsville. General Longstreet and his staff left Wilmington. With all troops shipped and only a few horses left, Agent Drane reported, "I have trains idle waiting." Fifteen hundred troops and twelve carloads of horses and baggage passed through Charlotte; Sharp advised that "all troops go off promptly from Columbia." Sims told Whitford, "Jenkins Brigade closed the movement." He later told him, "Advise all the roads in North Carolina that there are no more troops." Benning's thirteen hundred soldiers and Law's two thousand left Atlanta.[50]

On Thursday, September 16, Longstreet and 179 troops passed through Kingsville with 8 cars of baggage and horses. Another com-

48. Trelease, *North Carolina Railroad*, 74; Sims Letterbook, September 14–15, 1863. Sims probably referred to the Atlantic & North Carolina Railroad. The railroad men could not have done it at all without the telegraph, a technological advance resisted by some southern railroads. The Charlotte & South Carolina Railroad completed a telegraph line between Charlotte and Columbia in 1854, but the North Carolina Railroad had telegraph service only between Goldsboro and Raleigh at the start of the Civil War and extended wires to connect Charlotte and Raleigh only in 1862 (Trelease, *North Carolina Railroad*, 74). Trelease notes that in 1855 Daniel C. McCallum, then superintendent of the Erie Railroad, observed that a single-track railroad with telegraph service was safer than a double-track railroad without it.

49. Diary of Dr. J. F. Shaffner Sr., September 13–15, 1863, North Carolina State Archives, 3–4.

50. Sims Letterbook, September 15, 1863.

munications glitch occurred on the South Carolina Railroad. Superintendent H. J. Peake had stopped all scheduled trains, except for the mail and day passenger trains, and sent "all our trains" to assist the troop shipments at Kingsville and Columbia. Then Peake received a telegram from the quartermaster in Charleston requesting "transportation from Charleston for twelve hundred (1200) men." Peake had to move two trains back from Kingsville. Peake found the order "rather an embarrassment than relief" because his South Carolina Railroad had forwarded its troops promptly and without incident. Sims denied "any knowledge or consent" of the telegram from Charleston.[51]

The movement began to wind down. On Friday, September 17, agents in Columbia forwarded a train with one thousand men, followed by two trains carrying 872 and 470 men on the eighteenth, and 570 men and 6 baggage cars on the nineteenth. Thomas R. Shash(?) reported shipping two thousand troops from Manchester on the seventeenth, eight hundred on the eighteenth, and twenty cars of baggage and horses on the nineteenth, "which will be all that we have notice of." Wofford's brigade left Atlanta on the morning of September 19, and Jenkins' brigade followed the next evening. On September 21, Kingsville reported sending three hundred men and baggage to Augusta.[52]

Combat's violence and extraordinarily casual waste tends to desensitize men; some combat veterans internalize war's excesses. Paul Fussell argues that an infantryman's specific objective is his and his comrades' survival. Many, therefore, become indifferent to anything not directly related to their survival. Union and Confederate soldiers in both movements shared these characteristics.

When they reached Wilmington, North Carolina, Texans in Robertson's brigade proceeded to Paddy's Hollow, "an unsavory waterfront section," and promptly got very drunk and disorderly. Patrons called the night constabulary, "a half dozen elderly citizens," to restore order. The Texans, fighting drunk and completely unrestrained, at-

51. Ibid., J. H. Bowen report, H. J. Peake to Sims, September 16, 1863.
52. Ibid., September 17–19, 21, 1863.

tacked the old men. They knifed one and injured several others. No one filed charges before the brigade left the presumably relieved town in the morning.[53]

Georgia troops provoked a serious incident in Raleigh. War weariness had sapped the determination of Americans in both the Union and the Confederacy. The Raleigh *Standard*'s publisher, William W. Holden, had editorially questioned the likelihood of Confederate victory since the battle of Antietam in September 1862. Some readers agreed with Holden, but soldiers, who expressed their opinions of the war with their bodies, felt threatened by the editorials and damned the peace movement as treason. Georgians in General Henry Benning's brigade dealt with Holden's "disloyal" editorials by smashing the *Standard* office when they reached Raleigh on September 10. A civilian mob retaliated by wrecking the "loyal" *State Journal*.[54]

A critical test of states' rights ensued. North Carolina Governor Zebulon B. Vance had commanded the 26th North Carolina in the Seven Days' Battles before resigning his commission to seek the governor's seat. A strong states' righter, although a moderate prewar Unionist, Vance marched to his own drummer. "[T]he most frightful consequences may ensue," he warned President Davis, insisting that Davis forbid troops from entering Raleigh. North Carolina stood second only to Virginia in providing soldiers to the Cause. The president, mindful of the state's great importance, apologized to Vance and gave the order.[55]

Davis' best efforts, however, seemed timid to Vance, and the army's indifference to the soldiers' lawlessness infuriated the governor. He lectured the president, "The distance is quite short to either anarchy or despotism when armed soldiers, led by their officers, can with impunity outrage the laws of a State." He warned, "A few more such exhibitions

53. Roger J. Spiller, "The Real War," *American Heritage* 40, no. 7 (November 1989): 126–38; Harold B. Simpson, *Gaines' Mill to Appomattox: Waco and McLennan County in Hood's Texas Brigade* (Waco: Texian, 1963), 153–54.

54. Yearns and Barrett, *North Carolina Civil War Documentary*, 291–98.

55. Vance to Davis, Davis to Vance, September 10, 1863, *OR*, Ser. 1, 29, pt. 2:710.

will bring the North Carolina troops home to the defense of their own State and her institutions."[56]

Some 4th Alabamians, unaware that the Georgians had beaten them to it, also planned to wreck the *Standard,* but "No one could tell them where the 'Standard' office was." Undaunted, they "entered the city and spread terror in their path by threatening murder and conflagration." Some officers helped Vance "restrain them before they had done any damage." Vance claimed, "[they] threatened my life if I interfered with them. This thing is becoming intolerable." Vance put his foot down. He bluntly told the president, "If you wish to save North Carolina to the Confederacy, be quick." The governor declared, "[T]he country is in a dangerous excitement." He had spent more than two days without rest, "trying to defend the laws and peace of the State against our own bayonets." He drew the line. Davis would stop "these outrages," or else, Vance wrote, "I shall feel it a duty which I owe to the dignity and self-respect of the first State of the Confederacy . . . to issue my proclamation recalling her troops from the field to the defense of their own homes." Davis assured the governor that new orders would protect Raleigh, and calm finally came to the city. The crisis averted, Vance advised, "The troops are passing quietly, and no further disturbance apprehended. Quiet is restored."[57]

Blame rolls downhill. Confederate Inspector General Samuel Cooper ordered General Benning to report on the role his troops played in the Raleigh *Standard* incident, "if not with your consent, at least with your knowledge what was to occur."[58]

A natural warrior and self-taught brigade commander, "Rock" Benning's artful explanation testifies to his reputation as one of the most successful lawyers in Georgia. Replying after Chickamauga, he flatly rejected any accusation of his personal involvement or any "suspicion that any such outbreak was contemplated." In fact, he righteously

56. Vance to Davis, ibid., 765.
57. "Diary of Turner Vaughan, Co. 'C,' 4th Alabama Regiment, CSA," *Alabama Historical Quarterly* 18 (1956): 595; Vance to Davis, September 10, 1863, *OR,* Ser. 1, 51, pt. 2:763–64; Vance to Davis, September 11, 1863, Ser. 1, 51, pt. 2:764–65; Davis to Vance, Vance to Davis, September 15, 1863, ibid., 767–68.
58. Cooper to Benning, September 18, 1863, ibid., 768.

stated, "If I had suspected such a thing I should have taken the most rigorous measures to suppress it." As it happened, when his brigade reached Raleigh, he made forwarding arrangements and then, he claimed, "lay down with my head on a cross-tie, and slept." Benning protested that he did not learn about the *Standard* affair until after his troops boarded the trains, "too late for me to do anything, preventive or remedial." He denied that one of his officers had taken part in the outrage by saying, "the imputation of complicity is in an especial manner unfounded and unjust." Rather, "He was conspicuous in the suppression of the outbreak . . . he told me himself," Benning said, "and he is a man of character and perfect veracity." Benning patriotically added that the hero in question received two wounds "in the last of the two battles on the Chickamauga." Benning then offered a "full explanation." An unidentified group of North Carolinians had ridden with Benning's troops to Raleigh "for the sake of dispatch." His men told him that the Carolinians "freely avowed themselves the authors of the deed, and claimed credit for it." He acknowledged that they "led some of my men into it . . . but I think not many, and these merely unorganized individuals, each acting for and by himself." Benning, unfortunately, did not learn about the guilty parties until they had already left the train, "so that I had no opportunity to question them myself. Thus, sir," he concluded, "you have such an account of this affair as it is in my power to give you." Benning's protests notwithstanding, Lt. Col. E. M. Seago of the 20th Georgia had sent publisher Holden a threatening note that a prosecutor would call a smoking gun. Nevertheless, no one gave the incident any further thought.[59]

The 2nd South Carolina's train broke down one night, causing a "long stop." At daylight, they discovered themselves next to a turpentine distillery where "[h]undreds of barrells of resin were stacked up, and turpentine covered the ground in many places." Some men lit resin barrels to warm themselves. Fires soon burned out of control, including the turpentine-saturated ground. John Coxe saw flames reach the buildings as the train pulled out; he guessed that the fire consumed

---

59. Benning to Cooper, September 28, 1863, ibid., 770–71; Yearns and Barrett, *North Carolina Civil War Documentary*, 298.

the entire facility. General Kershaw "enjoined the men in [the] future to be more careful of the preservation of private property." The train rolled away.[60]

The two routes converged at Atlanta. The Western & Atlantic Railroad carried the troops on the final leg. Construction of the state-owned railroad, started in 1839, had taken more than ten years to complete. Lt. Col. Stephen Long, a West Pointer active in early railroad construction, surveyed the original route. He achieved a minor engineering miracle in the rugged terrain, laying out a route with a governing grade (maximum elevation change) of less than 1 percent, accomplishing it with curves equivalent to 28 complete circles in the 138-mile route. Railroad men named the community that sprang up at the southern end of the line Terminus; citizens later changed it to Marthaville, and then Atlanta.[61]

Heavy traffic jammed the Western & Atlantic. Meddling army officers aggravated the strain. The quartermaster in Atlanta complained, "Troops are being forwarded as rapidly as we can get cars. Two trains of empty cars were seized at Resaca yesterday and not allowed to come down, and it interferes greatly with movement of troops. Please have cars promptly returned." Traffic northbound from Atlanta created a massive "railroad congestion. . . . [O]ur transit was greatly impeded." The 15th Alabama waited a full day in Atlanta "on account of the crowded condition of railroads and insufficiency of rolling stock."[62]

The 2nd South Carolina boarded a W&A train and then waited hours before leaving the station. The undersized locomotive, "too light for the weight of our train . . . had much difficulty climbing grades." The little engine Kentucky made three attempts before successfully "'puff[ing] up' the grade of Allatoona Mountain." The 2nd "found a complete tie up" in Dalton. The railroad's clogged yard facilities could not manage rapid turnarounds. "There were many trains

60. John Coxe, "Chickamauga," 291.

61. Bogle, "Western & Atlantic Railroad," in Savas and Woodbury, *Campaign for Atlanta,* 313–14.

62. Col. M. H. Wright to Col. J. P. Jones, Atlanta, September 19, 1863, *OR,* Ser. 1, 30, pt. 4:672; Coxe, "Chickamauga," 292; Dickert, *Kershaw's Brigade,* 263; Oates, *War Between the Union and the Confederacy,* 253.

there, and every piece of siding was jammed with them," said John Coxe. It could have been worse. The 46th Georgia's train stood idle on a siding at Kingston as the war passed them by. On investigation, the 46th's commander, Colonel P. H. Colquitt, found the locomotive's boiler unlit and the engineer missing.[63]

The 2nd's locomotive needed to take on water, but the water tank at Dalton stood empty because of a broken pump. This caused "great confusion," with "engineers, conductors, firemen, and many army officers and soldiers making all sorts of suggestions for relieving the situation, but no relief came." General Joseph B. Kershaw, a capable citizen-soldier and lawyer who would lead McLaws' division in his absence at Chickamauga, took matters into his own hands. He found twenty buckets, "ordered [the] train forward to a creek about two miles distant," and formed a bucket brigade "in the nature of an endless chain." An hour later, off they went, stopping twelve miles north of Dalton, where Yankee cavalry had torn up the track and wrecked the bridges.[64]

Accidents and breakdowns occurred so frequently that the soldiers found them almost unworthy of comment. A tragic exception occurred when two "off time," or unscheduled, Western & Atlantic trains "met on a curve going at full speed" north of Cartersville, Georgia, on September 16. They crashed in a spectacular head-on accident, and "great was the momentum and sudden the concussion." A few sick and wounded soldiers rode the southbound train. The 1st Tennessee Battalion and the 50th Tennessee Regiment, en route from Mississippi, headed to battle on the northbound. The impact trapped one poor soul "caught between the tender and the engine by the thigh. No efforts could extricate him." The newspapers spared none of the graphic details. The man "burned and screamed and begged to be cut loose for some three hours before [his] life was extinguished." Reports ranged from fourteen to eighteen dead, and forty to sixty-eight injured. The Columbia *Tri-Weekly Carolinian* of September 20 reported that "Everyone standing on the platforms [flatcars] was killed." One survivor, W. J. Brigham, wrote to his aunt, "[S]ome of them had their

63. Coxe, "Chickamauga," 292; Glenn Tucker, *Chickamauga: Bloody Battle in the West* (New York: Bobbs-Merrill, 1961), 99–100.
64. Coxe, "Chickamauga," 292.

arms or a leg amputated on account of being smashed up so badly. I like to been killed . . . myself. . . . I got loose by some meanes and run up a steep bank before I knew I was hert . . . [I]t was an awful sight to see so many laying smashed up and here them groaning and calling for help."[65]

An extended discussion of whether, how, and when to include artillery in the Longstreet movement provides another example of indecisiveness by the Confederate leadership. President Davis, leaving no hair unsplit, got involved. The original plan did not contemplate sending any artillery. On Monday, September 14, however, Porter Alexander's and Henry Dearing's batteries and Benjamin F. Eshleman's Washington Artillery received orders to catch up with Longstreet. They would take their guns, harness, and fully-stocked ammunition limbers but were told to leave their horses at Petersburg. Exercising iron discipline, officers would ride with each detachment to oversee the many transfers and ensure that the men "be kept upon the cars, and . . . prohibited from straggling or leaving the places designated by the commanding officer."[66]

Lawton ordered a major in Columbus, Georgia, to requisition, but "*not* purchase," replacement artillery horses. Ordnance Chief Gorgas had cannons in Atlanta ready for shipment to Wilmington. President Davis suggested swapping them for Alexander's, a good, if belated, off-the-cuff suggestion that central planning might have anticipated, but Alexander's batteries probably had already left Richmond. Regardless, Porter Alexander received orders on September 17 to take his twenty-six cannons *and* the battalion's horses to Georgia. The chief of artillery rescinded the order to take the horses the next day, but Alexander had already left with at least some of them.[67]

65. *Daily Southern Guardian*, Columbia, S.C., September 19, 1863, probably copied from an Atlanta newspaper; W. J. Brigham to Miss Nannie Ellis, November 28, 1863, Brigham Family Papers, Small Collection, Tennessee State Library and Archives, Nashville.

66. Orders of Col. J. B. Walton, chief of artillery, September 14, 1863, *OR*, Ser. 1, 51, pt. 2:766–67.

67. Lawton, Quartermaster Receipt Book, September 14, 1863; Davis to Lee, September 16, 1863, *OR*, Ser. 1, 29, pt. 2:725–27. S. Cooper, the adjutant and inspector general, wrote to Col. Withers that "The horses of Alexander's battalion will be retained here [in Richmond]" (September 18, 1863, *OR*, Ser. 1, 51, pt.

General Lee wanted positive assurance that Alexander had horses waiting for him in Georgia before sending the artillery from Virginia. If not, wrote Lee, "it would be worse than useless to carry them, as they would not only undergo the wear and tear and damage of transportation, but we might possibly lose them." He had good reason for concern, and Alexander's travel experience confirmed Lee's worst fears. Alexander would not reach Longstreet until September 25, five days after the battle ended, his men having spent interminable hours on railroad sidings.⁶⁸

The need to send the artillery at all had been the subject of controversy. Davis had asked Braxton Bragg on September 16 whether his cannons could support Longstreet without the delay, or necessity, of sending Alexander's battery. Bragg, a first-rate artillerist, responded, "We can do with what we have as the country is unfavorable to the use of artillery." Rosecrans had written to Lincoln on September 19, "The battle ground was densely wooded and its surface irregular and wooded. We could make but little use of our artillery." But General Benning at times found himself in open fields where the Yankees employed their artillery to great effect, and his After Action Report indicates that his brigade "felt much in this engagement the want of artillery to oppose not only to the enemy's artillery but to his infantry; but none came to our aid. None had been attached either to my brigade or to Brigadier-General Robertson's." Robertson agreed with Benning's assessment.⁶⁹

2:768). Col. J. B. Walton, chief of artillery, confirmed the order to Maj. S. P. Mitchell (*OR*, Ser. 1, 51, pt. 2:769).

68. Lee to Davis, September 14, 1863, *OR*, Ser. 1, 29, pt. 2:719–20; Gary W. Gallagher, ed., *Fighting for the Confederacy: The Personal Recollections of General Edward Porter Alexander* (Chapel Hill: University of North Carolina Press, 1989), 449.

69. Dunbar Rowland, ed., *Jefferson Davis, Constitutionalist: His Letters, Papers, and Speeches* (Jackson, Miss.: J. J. Little & Ives, 1923), 6:35, citing the president's letter book; Bragg, telegram to Davis, September 17, 1863, William R. Perkins Library, Duke University, Durham; Basler, *Collected Works of Abraham Lincoln*, 5:473; Benning After Action Report, October 8, 1863, *OR*, Ser. 1, 30, pt. 2:517–19; Robertson After Action Report, October 4, 1863, ibid., 510–12.

Alexander's artillerymen waited out long delays at each terminus. Every change of trains meant that they had to dismount and remount the cannon tubes when offloading and reloading the carriages and caissons. Leaving Petersburg at four o'clock on Thursday afternoon, September 17, they reached Wilmington after midnight on Sunday, September 20, having averaged four miles per hour in negotiating the 240 miles. Following a twelve-hour layover, they ferried the Cape Fear River at two o'clock in the afternoon and boarded the Wilmington & Manchester. They arrived at Kingsville, South Carolina, at six o'clock the next evening, taking 26 hours to travel 192 miles. There Alexander learned some details about the battle already engaged at Chickamauga, that "A part of the infantry of [the Longstreet] corps, but only a part, had been engaged in the battle." General Hood had lost a leg.[70]

Another train change followed a six-hour layover, and there was yet another delay for several unexplained hours in Branchville. Alexander, his men, and their guns finally arrived in Augusta at two o'clock in the afternoon of Tuesday, September 22. They completed the 140-mile trip in good time, 12 hours, in spite of stopping to round up horses that had fallen out or jumped through an open car door. They changed trains again, and left at seven o'clock for Belair(?), where they idled on a sidetrack until daylight. They finally reached Atlanta, 172 miles distant, at 2:00 P.M. on September 23. They left before dawn on September 24 on the Western & Atlantic, "its crowded condition is told in our being 22 hours in making the 115 miles to Ringgold, Geo., the terminus of train service. Our entire journey by rail had been about 843 miles in about 178 hours." They spent a day refitting with wagons and supplies "to get us in the best shape." One of Alexander's soldiers wrote to his father of the "tedious journey of 7 days in which we have met with a great many accidents and delays but strange to say have had but one man killed and one wounded. The horses are very much used up but not permanently damaged and I hope will soon be in good condition."[71]

70. Gallagher, *Alexander*, 285–87.
71. Ibid.; Joseph C. Haskell(?), September 25, 1863, Rachel Susan Bee Cheves Papers, Special Collections Library, Duke University.

Leaky security and good Union intelligence betrayed Confederate hopes to conduct their rail movements in secrecy. Even as Longstreet's divisions boarded trains in Virginia, Major General Stephen A. Hurlbut, commander of the Union's 16th Corps in Memphis, reported that "a gentleman just in from Mobile" claimed that "nearly all" of Joseph Johnston's army had left Mississippi to reinforce Bragg "at and near Chattanooga." Hurlbut believed the report because he considered the source reliable and because of "the fact that the country south of Corinth is full of irregular cavalry, masking some movement." On September 11, Meade's scouts reported activity in the Confederate lines, but they could not positively call it a withdrawal. On the twelfth, Union officers in New Bern, North Carolina, passed on a report from a Pennsylvanian detained in the Confederacy since the start of the war. A railroad man, he estimated that thirteen thousand soldiers were rolling south.[72]

Intelligence assessment remains among the more murky challenges in war. The Confederates, knowing the propensity of Yankee commanders to take counsel of their fears, routinely sent "deserters" through the lines to spread false information. On September 14, prisoner interrogations led Meade to report (correctly) that McLaws' division had passed through Richmond. He later reported (incorrectly) that Lee commanded the movement, leaving Longstreet in command of "the rebel army of the Potomac." Still later, Meade reported (partly correctly) that Longstreet's corps had gone, "and perhaps . . . some regiments of Ewell and Hill." Meade (incorrectly) believed that Lee "no doubt . . . deemed [his remaining force] sufficient" but he still put the Army of the Potomac on alert "in readiness for an advance." A Confederate deserter reported that Hill's corps headed toward Tennessee via Lynchburg, but Meade (correctly) rejected the story. By the end of the day he had hard information that Longstreet had passed

72. Hurlbut to Halleck, September 9, 1863, *OR*, Ser. 1, 30, pt. 3:477; Meade to Halleck, *OR*, Ser. 1, 29, pt. 2:167; Maj. Gen. John J. Peck, District of North Carolina, to Maj. Gen. Foster, Dept. of Virginia and North Carolina, September 12, 1863, ibid., 173–74.

through Richmond and that Generals Ewell and Hill remained with Lee.[73]

Many Union generals shared another characteristic: grossly overestimating the enemy's strength. A deserter convinced General John J. Peck that the Confederates had dispatched a thirty-thousand-man movement. Peck wrote, "I am very certain that General Hood's division is to remain in North Carolina for the purpose of collecting deserters from Lee's army, of keeping down the Union feeling, and of sustaining the Confederacy." Stanley Horn reports that General Rosecrans overestimated the combined Confederate armies facing him at Chickamauga "until he thought himself confronted by no less than 120,000."[74]

Regardless of misinformation, misinterpretation, incomplete or wildly inaccurate reports that a commander has to sift through to make decisions, General in Chief Henry W. Halleck knew enough: the Confederates were up to something, and he could guess what. He warned both Burnside and Rosecrans to prepare for an attack. Union forces also tried to break southern coastal railroads, such as the Wilmington & Weldon, to slow down Longstreet. An officer bringing up the rear of Longstreet's corps described the "hard time" that "the late Yankee raid" exacted in his reaching Wilmington: "All the water-tanks had been burned or destroyed and the engine had to be filled by a line of men with buckets, and as we only had such buckets as we could borrow in the neighborhood it was a slow process."[75]

73. Meade to Halleck, September 14, 1863, *OR,* Ser. 1, 29, pt. 2:177–80; Asst. Adj. Gen. S. Williams, headquarters, Army of the Potomac, to corps commanders, September 14, 1863, ibid., 179; Gen. J. G. Foster at Fort Monroe to Halleck, September 14, 1863, ibid., 184, 187–88.

74. Peck to Foster, September 16, 1863, *OR,* Ser. 1, 29, pt. 2:199; Stanley F. Horn, *The Army of Tennessee: A Military History* (New York: Bobbs-Merrill, 1941), 261.

75. Halleck to Burnside and Rosecrans, September 15, 1863, *OR,* Ser. 1, 29, pt. 2:193. The Union War Department also knew that Confederate troops had destroyed the Raleigh *Standard* and the "secession papers" by September 16. Maj. Gen. J. G. Foster to Halleck, Norfolk, September 16, 1863, ibid., 199; Brig. Gen.

Halleck's telegram did not take Rosecrans by surprise. Major General Alexander M. McCook, commanding the 20th Corps, advised him on September 13 that a captured Kentucky officer was "morally certain" that reinforcements from Virginia approached Bragg by way of Atlanta. General Robert H. G. Minty's cavalrymen reported the presence of part of Longstreet's corps, possibly Benning's brigade, on September 15; they confirmed it on the seventeenth.

On September 16, General James A. Garfield, Rosecrans' chief of staff, told General Gordon Granger, who commanded Rosecrans' Reserve Corps, that Halleck's telegram "confirms our reports that Longstreet has joined Bragg or is on the way to do so with 3 Divisions." Slipping out of the noose, Rosecrans ordered his scattered columns to concentrate southeast of Chattanooga.[76] Any hope that Bragg, Davis, or Longstreet might have entertained about achieving tactical surprise against Rosecrans had vanished.

A disappointed Jefferson Davis passed the bad news on to General Lee: "The enemy [Rosecrans] has retired before us at all points. . . . The demonstrations of the enemy in your front have very probably resulted from the knowledge that Longstreet's corps had been detached." The frustrated president added, "I cannot imagine how the information was acquired at so early a date as that which you mention. I have despaired in the present condition of Richmond of being able to keep secret any movement which is to be made from or through this place."General Lee replied, "The enemy is aware of Longstreet's departure. They report in their papers the day he passed through Augusta."[77]

When Longstreet and his staff reached Catoosa Station, they found no one from General Bragg's headquarters there to meet them. Mox-

---

Naglee to Gen. Foster, Norfolk, September 16, 1963, ibid., 198; Charles Minor Blackford to his wife, September 23, 1863, Blackford, *Memoirs,* 1:138.

76. McCook to Garfield, September 13, 1863, *OR,* Ser. 1, 30, pt. 3:603–4; Joseph G. Vale, *Minty and the Cavalry: A History of the Western Armies* (Harrisburg: Edwin K. Meyers, 1886), 216–17, 220; James A. Garfield Papers, Library of Congress, Washington, D.C.; *OR,* Ser. 1, 30, pt. 1:921–24.

77. Davis to Lee, September 16, 1863, *OR,* Ser. 1, 29, pt. 2:726–27; Lee to Davis, September 23, 1863, ibid., 742.

ley Sorrel would recall, "A sharp action had taken place during the day and it would appear that if Bragg wanted to see anybody, Longstreet was the man. But we were left to shift for ourselves." They set off to find Bragg, got lost in the dark, and almost stumbled into a Union picket line, making "a sharp right-about gallop" to escape. They continued their search for Bragg, "about whom by this time some hard words were passing." Sorrel breezily summarized, "But all things have an end, even a friendly hunt for an army commander." When they finally found Bragg's headquarters, the general was fast asleep for the night. Through an astonishing communications lapse, Bragg had only a vague idea about how many soldiers Longstreet had with him, or when they would arrive.[78] It joined the list of many confusions. Longstreet would have a much easier time finding his former West Point roommate, William Starke Rosecrans.

Confederate commanders made the most of the poorly coordinated arrivals: "The corps arrived in detachments but, as fast as they came, were sent off to Bragg. The commands were very much split up and parts of brigades and regiments left as they came up in detached trains for the front." Five small brigades would reach north Georgia in time to fight at Chickamauga, three on the nineteenth, two more on the twentieth. As their comrades fought and died, Porter Alexander's artillerymen sat on a siding, five days' ride away.[79]

Though the Army of Tennessee welcomed Longstreet's help, some felt bitter about the timing of the reinforcements' arrival. On "a bright good morning," the Army of Tennessee greeted the first brigades, but as George William Brent wrote, with Chattanooga and Knoxville fallen, "they come after the damage has been done, a lock and key on the stable after the horse has been stolen. Such has been the action of Jeff Davis in the Western Campaign, always too late."[80]

This seems harsh, considering the price the Army of Tennessee's re-

78. Sorrel, *Recollections,* 192–93; Connelly, *Autumn of Glory,* 191.
79. Benjamin Abbott to Green Haygood, Chickamauga, September 26, 1863, *"Dear Mother,"* ed. Mills Lane, 272.
80. Asst. Adj. Gen. George William Brent, Army of Tennessee, diary, September 16, 1863, Braxton Bragg Papers, MS 2000, Western Reserve Historical Society, Cleveland, Ohio.

inforcements paid at Chickamauga. The 30th Tennessee came from Mississippi, via Mobile and Atlanta. They reached "the burnt bridge across the Chickamauga about sun down" on September 15, in plenty of time for the "great Slaughter." The 30th's quartermaster, Samuel Robert Simpson, wrote that "it was awfull to look at, dead men laying thick on the ground, horses, guns, broken cannon & all the implements of war scattered all over the face of the earth." Simpson helped evacuate wounded from the battlefield until October 1 and reported that the 30th had "but 41 men left."[81]

Longstreet's tough, confident veterans and, more important, their general's battlefield leadership, made a decisive contribution to victory at Chickamauga. One of Bragg's soldiers wrote to his mother, "The eastern Rebbs that came over to help Bragg said that if the Western Yankees fought as good [poorly] as the Eastern ones did that we would whip them every time. The Eastern Rebbs fight much better than the Western Rebbs do. The Rebbs crack Division was Longstreets of Virginia & I tell you they fight well. They are the best looking Rifles I ever saw."[82]

Archer Jones hails the Longstreet movement as a "Napoleonic concentration over a vast space" to win a strategic victory at Chickamauga. Jones and Herman Hattaway exaggerate by describing Longstreet's brigades "rushing to [Bragg] by rail." Thomas Lawrence Connelly, however, derides it as "more myth than genuine fact," calling "the much-heralded stream of reinforcements . . . a mere trickle." He attributes "the haphazard nature of this reinforcement" to a "lack of central control," compounded by poor communication between Bragg and Davis. He dismisses Davis' attempt at grand strategy as meddling. Longstreet biographer Donald Sanger also belittles the movement, asserting that "Nine days had been consumed by a journey that ought to have been accomplished in two or three." According to Porter Alexander, however, "It scarcely could be considered rapid transit, yet

81. Samuel Robert Simpson Papers.

82. "Son" to "Dear Mother," October 3, 1863, National Archives Civil War Collection: Confederate and Federal 1861–1865, Federal Collection, Box F 25, Folder 11, Letters—Pierce, Nat. G—1863.

under the circumstances it was really a very creditable feat for our railroad service under the attendant circumstances."[83]

Jones presses the fringe of historical romance. He and Alexander come closer, however, to understanding the genuine accomplishment of the Longstreet movement than either Connelly or Sanger. If hardly a rush, the movement certainly qualified as more than a trickle. Chickamauga stands as a great Confederate victory, even though only half of Longstreet's soldiers got there in time to fight. The battle achieved the urgent and imperative Confederate objective of stopping Rosecrans cold. It saved Atlanta—and the rebellion—for a year.

Few believed that Bragg could have defeated Rosecrans at Chickamauga without help; he certainly failed to exploit the victory. Longstreet's leadership and his veteran infantry's confidence and courage provided necessary stiffening to the Army of Tennessee. Rosecrans' equally stubborn westerners proved themselves tough, hard-nosed fighters. According to one of Hood's Texans, "Brave fellows they were. These troops are better fighters than the Virginia army, they coming from the northwestern states, kinder frontiersmen."[84] From a military standpoint, then, the Longstreet movement proved very successful.

Sanger also underestimated the enormous difficulty involved in conducting the Longstreet movement. Daniel McCallum, John Garrett, Tom Scott, Prescott Smith and their associates, who would so skillfully engineer the 11th and 12th Corps movement, could not have completed a movement of Longstreet's magnitude in "two or three" days, even with the Union's great resources. At the other extreme, Alexander describes the difficulty with "the use of one long roundabout line of single-track road of light construction," inadequate equipment, and different track gauges. He concludes, "The task would have taxed a

83. A. Jones, *Command and Strategy*, 176; Hattaway and Jones, *How the North Won*, 450; Connelly, *Autumn of Glory*, 152–153, 191; Donald Bridgman Sanger and Thomas Robson Hay, *James Longstreet* (Baton Rouge: Louisiana State University Press, 1953), 199; Alexander, *Military Memoirs of a Confederate* (New York: Charles Scribner's Sons, 1912), 449.
84. Hanks, "B. F. Beton's Company," 25–26.

double-tracked road with modern equipment,"[85] an exaggeration that Alexander, a first-rate engineer and gunnery expert who would become a railroad president after the war, could hardly have believed.

Lawton, Sims, and their associates did their best with what they had. They could have done better only if the Confederacy had organized its railroads when it still had the time. This speaks to the question of whether the Confederacy in 1863 still—or ever—held the advantage of interior lines. The fact remains that only five brigades of Long-street's troops reached northwest Georgia in time to fight, but they helped the Confederates at Chickamauga to outnumber Rosecrans' Cumberlanders by between 12 and 14 percent.[86]

Longstreet's absent three brigades would have added another 10 percent to Bragg's firepower and, perhaps, changed the outcome of the war. An interesting historical "what if" asks what might have happened if the Confederates had driven Rosecrans from Chattanooga, and across the Tennessee River toward Nashville. If Sherman had to force the Tennessee River and recapture Chattanooga, the delay would have affected the timing and, perhaps, the outcome of the Atlanta campaign. That in turn might have affected the outcome of the presidential election in 1864. But the three brigades got there too late.

Porter Alexander believed that the Confederacy "still held unimpaired" the advantage of interior lines in September 1863, which gave it "the sole opportunity ever presented the South for a great strategic victory." The Yankees took Knoxville only because of "the dilatory consideration and slow acceptance of the proposed strategy" to rein-

85. Alexander, *Memoirs,* 449.

86. William Mathias Lamers, *The Edge of Glory: A Biography of General William S. Rosecrans, U.S.A.* (New York: Harcourt, Brace and World, 1961), 362. Accounts of actual manpower present vary, according to Lamers. Rosecrans had between 58,333 and 59,935 men, Bragg between 66,326 and 71,551. Chickamauga produced some of the heaviest casualties of the war. The Union lost 1,657 killed, 9,765 wounded, and 4,757 missing. Bragg lost 2,316 killed, 13,202 wounded, and 1,468 missing. Glenn Tucker notes that Rosecrans fought all his battles against numerically superior forces, the only Union general to do so. He won at Corinth and Stones River but his luck ran out at Chickamauga. *Chickamauga,* 365.

force the West. Alexander faults Davis' and Lee's complete lack of any sense of urgency, which led to "incomplete success" at Chickamauga. He would have sent troops to Bragg as soon as Lee withdrew from Gettysburg, "and [at] every subsequent movement planned to facilitate it." He says that the partial success facilitated by the troops that did reach north Georgia in time "shows the soundness of our strategy" in spite of other flaws that attended the battle and its aftermath.[87]

Moxley Sorrel also believed that the Confederacy still held the great advantage of interior lines. He thought that Longstreet's troops would help Bragg "strike a swift, crushing blow" against Rosecrans and "enable masterly reinforcements to return rapidly to Virginia without endangering the safety of the Confederate capital or that of Lee's army." Sorrel admits to two factors that threatened the advantage. First, "to anyone familiar with the railroad service of the South in the last part of 1863 little need be said of the difficulties facing the Quartermaster-General." Second, the Confederacy took the calculated risk that the Army of the Potomac would not disrupt the plan. Fortunately for the Confederates, "This expectation proved correct. Meade was silent and inactive. . . . [H]is well-known prudence and lack of initiative might be trusted to keep him quiet during our great strategic coup."[88]

The Confederacy encountered such great difficulty in getting Longstreet's troops to Atlanta that only half made it in time to fight at Chickamauga. How efficiently the railroad men could have organized their return to Virginia would have provided an acid test of the interior lines advantage. Considering the wear and tear on already distressed rolling stock in carrying Longstreet's troops to Georgia, one doubts that they could have returned the soldiers to Virginia as easily as Sorrel suggests. The Longstreet movement rudely exposed the distressed condition of the southern railroads in the late summer of 1863. The delays and ragged nature of the movement reflected a failing transportation infrastructure. Thomas Ziek argues in his excellent and well-researched thesis that deteriorated railroads had cost the Confederacy the advantage of interior lines by September 1863. The movement's

87. Alexander, *Memoirs,* 447–50.
88. Sorrel, *Recollections,* 188–90.

success was also hampered by President Davis' two-week delay in ordering Longstreet to Georgia.

The interior lines advantage, moreover, did not face a rigorous test. As Sorrel observes, General Meade gave the Confederacy crucial relief. Had he maintained Anaconda-type pressure on the Army of Northern Virginia, the Davis government could not have risked releasing Longstreet's divisions to reinforce Bragg. Had Meade advanced, catching Longstreet on the move, en route to or even after Chickamauga, the Confederacy would have faced a serious crisis. Generals Grant and Sherman would demonstrate how well the Union learned that lesson the next spring.

The Longstreet movement does not advance the argument that the Confederacy possessed an advantage based on interior lines. It may never have had it. It certainly never took the most rudimentary steps to improve the condition of its rails to best exploit its interior lines. Indeed, it permitted its railroads to decline. Joining unconnected same-gauge tracks almost certainly would have allowed all of Longstreet's troops to reach Chickamauga in time, even with Davis's inexcusable delay in deciding to send them. The possible difference to American history is incalculable. But it did not happen. The Longstreet movement deserves its place in the history of logistics as well as the drama of the Civil War. It cannot, however, support a claim that the Confederacy enjoyed an advantage based on interior lines, at least not as of September 1863.

Thomas A. Scott, vice president of Pennsylvania Central
Railroad and assistant secretary of war.

Courtesy Massachusetts Commandery of the Military Order of the
Loyal Legion of the United States (MOLLUS) and United States
Army Military History Institute (USAMHI)

Colonel Daniel C. McCallum, chief of U.S. Military Railroad.

Courtesy Massachusetts Commandery of MOLLUS and USAMHI

John W. Garrett, president of Baltimore & Ohio Railroad.

Courtesy B&O Railroad Museum

William Prescott Smith, master of transportation for B&O Railroad.

Courtesy Library of Congress

General Josiah Gorgas, Confederate chief of ordnance.
Courtesy Massachusetts Commandery of MOLLUS and USAMHI

Confederate Quartermaster General Alexander R. Lawton.
Courtesy USAMHI

Destruction of B&O Railroad bridge at Harpers Ferry, 1862.

Destruction of railroad at Manassas Junction on General Pope's retreat, August 1862.

Courtesy Massachusetts Commandery of MOLLUS and USAMHI

Destruction of Orange & Alexandria Railroad by retreating Confederates, 1862.

Courtesy Library of Congress

USMRR locomotive and tender built by William Mason of Taunton, Massachusetts, and named for USMRR field engineer Herman Haupt.

Courtesy Massachusetts Commandery of MOLLUS and USAMHI

Railroad bridge over Potomac Creek built by Haupt's USMRR Construction Corps in forty-four hours in 1862. Haupt rode the first locomotive across the bridge to demonstrate its soundness.

Courtesy Massachusetts Commandery of MOLLUS and USAMHI

Howe bridge built by General Hooker's engineers over Tennessee River at Bridgeport, Alabama, fall 1863.

Courtesy Massachusetts Commandery of MOLLUS and USAMHI

Wagon bridge over Tennessee River at Chattanooga built during siege, 1863.

Courtesy Massachusetts Commandery of MOLLUS and USAMHI

Rail supplies at City Point, Virginia, during General Grant's siege of Petersburg, 1864. The Union armies could call on resources that Confederate supply officers could only envy.

Courtesy Massachusetts Commandery of MOLLUS and USAMHI

USMRR at Chattanooga, ca. 1864, with Lookout Mountain in background. The city served as General Sherman's supply base during the Atlanta campaign.

Courtesy Library of Congress

Railroad station in Atlanta after General Hood destroyed his ammunition train, 1864.

Courtesy Massachusetts Commandery of MOLLUS and USAMHI

4

"A Serious Disaster"

The Federal Government Responds to Defeat at Chickamauga

> If we hold this point we shall save the campaign, which will be great gain even if we lose this army.
> —Major General James A. Garfield

September 20, 1863: Army of the Cumberland telegraphers began tapping out grim news. General Braxton Bragg's Army of Tennessee, reinforced by part of James Longstreet's command, crashed into General William S. Rosecrans' Cumberlanders at Chickamauga Creek, southeast of Chattanooga, Tennessee, on September 19. On the second day of hard but inconclusive fighting, Longstreet exploited a chance opening in the Union line, punched fifteen thousand men through it, rolled up Rosecrans' right flank, and came close to shattering his army. The tough, veteran Cumberlanders, victors at Stones River nine months earlier, crumbled. Many fled the battlefield in disorder.

Rosecrans, mistakenly believing that the Confederates had broken his army, rode back to prepare a defensive line in Chattanooga. Although possessed of unquestioned personal bravery, he unwittingly abandoned his army as it fought for its life. His senior corps commander, General George H. Thomas, a Virginian loyal to the Union, rallied his men on a grassy knob called Snodgrass Hill. An inspired tactician and defensive genius, Thomas had learned artillery tactics from his former comrade Braxton Bragg at Buena Vista in the Mexican War. The most underrated Union officer in the Civil War, Thomas held the Union right flank with a stubborn horseshoe defense that earned him the enduring nickname "The Rock of Chickamauga."[1]

A bright, if temperamental, officer, Rosecrans had demonstrated his fighting generalship at Corinth, Iuka, and Stones River. His campaign for Chattanooga, once he started, showed boldness and resolve. His always restless intellect, however, combined with a relentless energy that on occasion drove him past the point of extreme exhaustion. He may have spent his emotional stamina before the fighting began at Chickamauga. His first reports warned of "a serious disaster; extent not yet ascertained." A panicked Assistant Secretary of War Charles A. Dana, the eyes and ears of Secretary of War Edwin M. Stanton, and, some said, his spy, horrified Washington with the overwrought message, "Chickamauga is as fatal a name in our history as Bull Run. . . . [O]ur soldiers turned and fled. It was a wholesale panic. . . . Our wounded are all left behind." The next day Rosecrans advised General in Chief Henry W. Halleck in Washington that, based on prisoner reports, soldiers had come from all parts of the Confederacy to fight at Chickamauga. "It seems that every available man was thrown against us." That same day, however, Major General Lovell H. Rousseau,

1. The Union leadership never completely trusted Thomas, who lost his congressional sponsors when Virginia seceded, and lacked any gift for self-promotion. Grant thought him "slow." The Union army, however, only broke Confederate forces defending prepared positions twice during the Civil War, at Missionary Ridge and Nashville. Thomas commanded the Union forces in both actions. Thomas' family disavowed him, and many southerners considered him a traitor. Francis F. McKinney, *Education in Violence: The Life of George H. Thomas and the History of the Army of the Cumberland* (Detroit: Wayne State University Press, 1961), 90, 93, 274, 281. Moxley Sorrel, Longstreet's chief of staff, however, considered Thomas "one of the ablest of [the Union's] soldiers, perhaps none equalled him, and I heartily wish he had been anywhere but at Chickamauga" (Sorrel, *Recollections,* 196).

rounding up stragglers separated from their regiments, reported to Rosecrans, "I find the troops in fine spirits and ready to re-enter the fight, though they have suffered severe loss. What is left is all right." Rosecrans recovered his composure and reported the army intact with high morale: "The enemy confront us, but we have taken the starch out of him." A defeated man does not use these words, but Union leaders lost confidence in Rosecrans because of his erratic behavior in the ensuing weeks.[2]

The Confederates, whose generals seemed more interested in fighting each other than the Yankees, failed to exploit their victory. Rapid and vigorous pursuit would have sorely tried the Army of the Cumberland. Whether Bragg could have destroyed Rosecrans' army seems debatable, but Rosecrans helped his chances. Declaring it not "practical or expedient" to defend Lookout Mountain south of Chattanooga, he gave Bragg the opportunity—quickly taken—to break the Nashville & Chattanooga Railroad and interdict Rosecrans' line of communication. This mistake reduced his army's only supply line from a twenty-eight-mile rail line to a sixty-mile mule-killing trail. The situation convinced Bragg that he need not attack Rosecrans. He would starve him out. As an Illinois soldier wrote, "time, rain and mud would accomplish [Bragg's] purpose." Bragg's inability to judge when to stick in and twist the tactical knife undermined his sound strategic sense. He also possessed a phenomenal talent, and propensity, for alienating people. With Rosecrans in trouble, Bragg could turn his attention to the more appealing enterprise of purging suspected disloyal officers from his command.[3]

2. Rosecrans to Halleck, September 20, 1863, *OR,* Ser. 1, 30, pt. 1:142–43; Dana to Stanton, September 20, 1863, ibid., 448; Rosecrans to Halleck, September 21, 1863; Stanton Papers, Library of Congress; Maj. Gen. Lovell H. Rousseau to Rosecrans, September 21, 1863, *OR,* Ser. 1, 30, pt. 3:762; Rosecrans to Hooker, September 27, 1863, *OR,* Ser. 1, 29, pt. 2:64. Bruce Catton says that Rosecrans "had everything except that final ten percent that lifts a man into greatness." *Grant Takes Command* (Boston: Little, Brown, 1968), 30. Excellent accounts of Chickamauga are found in Cozzens, *This Terrible Sound,* and Tucker, *Chickamauga.*

3. John J. Nicolay and John Hay, *Abraham Lincoln: A History* (New York: Century, 1890), 8:112; Capt. B. F. Campbell to Col. Silas Miller, in *The History*

Rosecrans had faults as well. He constantly demanded more troops and supplies. When he did not get them, he accused Washington of refusing to support him. Such complaints fell on increasingly deaf ears in a hardening war. His army stood idle while Grant engaged the Confederates at Vicksburg; his failure to advance against Bragg at that time drew criticism from President Lincoln, who noted that Rosecrans had an excellent opportunity to attack when Joseph Johnston's troops went to relieve Vicksburg. Never one to underestimate his problems, Rosecrans compiled an exhausting list of the obstacles he faced. To a reporter, he likened his problems in middle Tennessee to Napoleon's crossing the Alps; the journalist thoughtfully published Rosecrans' campaign strategy in the New York *Herald*. A sharp tongue and abrasive nature gave Rosecrans a tendency to lash out at the wrong times and at the wrong people. Two men with great power and long memories had felt Rosecrans' wrath. He had taken Secretary of War Stanton to task for an innocent mistake early in the war, turning him into an "implacable enemy." He had also alienated Ulysses S. Grant by accusing him, perhaps with some reason, of moving too slowly at Iuka.[4] Although Rosecrans faced his share of challenges, he never understood that the leaders in Washington had their own problems; they wanted results, not a laundry list of his problems. In the eyes of Lincoln, the fact that Grant did not complain or blame his problems on others was not the least of his considerable assets as a commander.

The vultures began circling over Rosecrans' career. Charles Dana, in daily poison pen letters to the secretary of war, played on Stanton's

---

of the Thirty-sixth Regiment Illinois Volunteers, ed. L. G. Bennett and William M. Haigh (Aurora, Ill.: Knickerbocker & Hodder, 1876), 502–3; James Lee McDonough, *Chattanooga: A Death Grip on the Confederacy* (Knoxville: University of Tennessee Press, 1984), 20–40; Judith Lee Hallock, *Braxton Bragg and Confederate Defeat* (Tuscaloosa: University of Alabama Press, 1991), 2:89–97.

4. Basler, *Collected Works of Abraham Lincoln*, 6:377; Rosecrans to Halleck, August 1, 1863, *OR*, Ser. 1, 23, pt. 2:585–86; J. Cutler Andrews, *The North Reports the Civil War* (Pittsburgh: University of Pittsburgh Press, 1955), 444; Lamers, *Edge of Glory*, 252, 124; William Wirt Calkins, *The History of the 104th Regiment of Illinois Volunteer Infantry* (Chicago: Donohue and Henneberry, 1895), 159.

antipathy toward Rosecrans by characterizing the general as unstable and ready to abandon Chattanooga. The outpourings of Rosecrans' fertile imagination did little to help his case. He made a bizarre recommendation that the Union should consider offering amnesty; it remains unclear why he believed that undefeated, unrepentant Confederates would consider accepting it. The proposal struck President Lincoln as coming from a man "confused and stunned like a duck hit on the head." Lincoln stayed informed, but otherwise uninvolved, in western theater activities during this period. He spent his time trying to knit together the seemingly unraveling General Rosecrans. Abetted by the disloyalty of his chief of staff, General James A. Garfield, the vultures began descending. Garfield had criticized Rosecrans's generalship in a July 27, 1863, letter to Secretary of the Treasury Salmon P. Chase. Garfield told Stanton a month after Chickamauga that he no longer considered Rosecrans up to the job. Lincoln promoted Grant to command of the western armies on October 16, 1863. Grant promptly fired Rosecrans and replaced him with George Thomas, whom he ordered to hold Chattanooga "at all hazards." Thomas, proving that Grant chose well, replied, "I will hold the town till we starve."[5]

The Confederacy paid dearly for its victory at Chickamauga. Senior officers killed included General Benjamin Hardin Helm, related by marriage to Mary Todd Lincoln. General Hood lost a leg; his aides thereafter would have to strap him onto his horse to enable him to

5. Tyler Dennett, ed., *Lincoln and the Civil War in the Diaries and Letters of John Hay* (New York: Dodd, Mead, 1939), 106; Lamers, *Edge of Glory*, 389. Garfield's apologists believe he was simply a soldier doing his duty, but critics describe him as a ruthless opportunist. As chief of staff, Garfield owed his loyalty to Rosecrans. He might have insisted that his boss get more rest. He could definitely have made his concerns known more constructively. Garfield's apologists include Robert Granville Caldwell, *James A. Garfield: Party Chieftain* (New York: Dodd, Mead, 1931), 125; Allan Peskin, *Garfield* (Kent, Ohio: Kent State University Press, 1978), 217; Theodore Clarke Smith, *The Life and Letters of James Abram Garfield* (New Haven: Yale University Press, 1925) 1:309–11. For a critic, see John M. Taylor, *Garfield of Ohio: The Available Man* (New York: W. W. Norton, 1970), 81–91.

ride. On September 23, Secretary Stanton read reports of the battle in the Richmond *Enquirer*. He recognized that unless Bragg recaptured Chattanooga, and its important rail center, the Confederate victory accomplished nothing from a strategic standpoint. That same day, Charles Dana and James Garfield each sent telegrams to Washington urging the government to send twenty to twenty-five thousand "competent troops" to reinforce the Cumberlanders. Garfield added, "If we hold this point we shall save the campaign, which will be great gain even if we lose this army."[6]

The Cumberlanders were beaten at Chickamauga but not whipped. Their morale intact, they dug in, ready to fight. The Confederates could only take Chattanooga by siege. Quartermaster General Montgomery Meigs reported that would "take time." He believed that the Confederate concentration in the West had failed to gain the expected great strategic victory. If the Cumberlanders could hold Chattanooga and pro-Unionist east Tennessee, they would deny the Confederates their only source of copper, as well as invaluable coal fields and nitre deposits. They would sever the northernmost railroad link between the eastern and western Confederacy and continue to point a dagger at Atlanta. Dana's and Garfield's telegrams sealed the decision. The secretary of war determined that the Union must hold Chattanooga.[7]

Stanton called a special meeting at the War Department in the early hours of Thursday, September 24. President Lincoln came in from his summer quarters at the Soldiers' Home outside Washington. Secretary of the Treasury Salmon P. Chase and Secretary of State William H. Seward both attended at Stanton's invitation. Soldiers present included General in Chief Henry Halleck; Colonel Daniel C. McCallum, chief

6. Newspaper text telegraphed to Stanton by Gen. Solomon A. Meredith at Fort Monroe, Va., September 23, 1863, *OR,* Ser. 1, 30, pt. 3:789–91; Dana to Stanton, September 23, 1863, *OR,* Ser. 1, 30, pt. 1:98; Garfield to Chase, *OR,* Ser. 1, 30, pt. 3:792.

7. Rosecrans to Hooker, September 27, 1863, *OR,* Ser. 1, 29, pt. 1:164; Meigs to Stanton, September 27, 1863, *OR,* Ser. 1, 30, pt. 3:890–91; for Chattanooga's importance for Confederate resources, see Connelly, *Army of the Heartland,* and Goff, *Confederate Supply.*

of the U.S. Military Railroads (present only "for awhile"); and Major Thomas T. Eckert of the U.S. Military Telegraph.[8]

Accounts of the meeting differ as to details but confirm the substance. Stanton presented Dana's and Garfield's telegrams recommending reinforcements. According to Salmon Chase, Stanton asked how long it would take General Burnside's twenty thousand men in Knoxville to reach Chattanooga. Halleck replied that the 110-mile march across hostile territory would take ten days if "not interrupted," an unlikely prospect. Halleck added that General William Sherman's divisions, three hundred miles away but already marching toward Chattanooga along the Memphis & Charleston Railroad, could not possibly reach Rosecrans in time to help him. As it happened, Sherman did not arrive in Chattanooga until November 23. Stanton then asked Halleck how quickly troops from the Army of the Potomac in Virginia could reach Chattanooga. The general guessed sixty days, "perhaps forty." Eckert, a Pennsylvania Railroad telegrapher, and future president of Western Union, also suggested forty days, perhaps less. Stanton responded that if traders could ship twenty thousand bales of cotton to Chattanooga in five days, then certainly the Union could ship twenty thousand soldiers. An astonished President Lincoln expressed doubt that the army could march the troops from the field in five days. Stanton stood his ground, saying that he had "carefully investigated" the proposal with "the ablest railroad men of the country." Supported by Chase and Seward, he finally convinced the others to reinforce the Army of the Cumberland with soldiers from the Army of the Potomac. In fact, troops would begin marching toward the railheads within twelve hours. They started to board trains the following morning, September 25.[9]

8. Dennett, *Diaries and Letters of John Hay,* 93.

9. Salmon P. Chase papers, National Archives, Washington, D.C., microfiche; *The Salmon P. Chase Papers,* ed. John Niven, James P. McClure, and Patrick Delana (Frederick, Md.: University Publications of America, 1987), microfiche, 1:450–54; *Inside Lincoln's Cabinet: The Civil War Diaries of Salmon P. Chase,* ed. Donald David (New York: Longmans, Green, 1954), 201–3; David Homer Bates, *Lincoln in the Telegraph Office: Recollections of the United States Military Telegraph during the Civil War* (New York: Century, 1907), 174; Benjamin P. Thomas and

The dynamics of the meeting reveal the distinctly different cultures of the civilians and soldiers present. Stephen E. Ambrose observes that, in spite of the clear superiority of northern railroads, the Confederacy had successfully completed two major strategic rail movements at this stage of the war, while the Union had never attempted one. Contrasting forward-looking civilians with a military mind-set wedded to the past, Ambrose notes that the civilians supported Stanton's bold proposal while the military leadership, absent precedent, thought it impossible.[10]

It seems curious that a genuine railroad expert at the meeting, who could have objectively judged the merits of Stanton's plan, apparently either did not offer, or was not asked, his opinion. U.S. Military Railroad chief Daniel McCallum certainly qualified as one of the "ablest railroad men" in America. The former superintendent of the Erie Railroad now commanded the largest railroad system in the world in the USMRR. McCallum, however, said nothing that either Chase, Hay, or Eckert recalled. One Stanton biographer claims that Stanton sent for McCallum during the meeting and states that McCallum said he could complete the troop movement in seven days. He adds that Eckert alerted McCallum to the agenda and prepared his analysis. One must believe that Stanton would have included McCallum, a critical resource, in the meeting from the start. Besides, if McCallum actually made such a dramatic statement, someone would have remembered it.[11]

Harold M. Hyman, *Stanton: The Life and Times of Lincoln's Secretary of War* (New York: Alfred A. Knopf, 1962), 286–87.

10. Stephen E. Ambrose, *Halleck: Lincoln's Chief of Staff* (Baton Rouge: Louisiana State University Press, 1962), 153–54. Ambrose acknowledges Halleck's reputation as a poor fighting general but praises the man's exceptional administrative ability, perceptively observing that Halleck, when put in the right job, made significant contributions to Union victory off the battlefield. Halleck thus represents an example of the changing nature of war and the essential noncombat management skills necessary to win the Civil War.

11. Frank Abiel Flower, *Edwin McMasters Stanton: The Autocrat of Rebellion, Emancipation, and Reconstruction* (New York: W. W. Wilson, 1905), 204. Flower's reliability is questionable; he cites a subordinate in the Military Railroad who claimed to have heard the story from Eckert, who repeated what McCallum told

Stanton had almost certainly made up his mind to send troops to Chattanooga before he called the meeting. Late in the evening of September 23, he had telegraphed Brigadier General Jeremiah T. Boyle, commanding the Military District of Western Kentucky, in Louisville. He asked pointed questions about the capacity and condition of the railroads between Louisville and Chattanooga via Nashville. Boyle replied by 4:00 A.M. on the twenty-fourth that the roads could carry three thousand, possibly four thousand, men per day. Troop trains took 16 hours to travel the 185 miles from Louisville to Nashville; Chattanooga lay 150 miles beyond.[12]

The decision made, Stanton acted quickly. He put McCallum in charge and summoned three more "ablest railroad men" to Washington. Stanton knew them well and had almost certainly consulted with at least one of them before proposing to reinforce Chattanooga by rail. Civilians would organize and conduct the largest military transportation effort of the war. John W. Garrett, the bright, analytical president of the Baltimore & Ohio Railroad, brought William Prescott Smith, the B&O's master of transportation. The secretary of war had known, liked, and trusted Garrett since before the war, when the B&O-controlled Central Ohio Railroad retained Stanton as general counsel. Prescott Smith also knew his business: the master of transportation managed the movement of the B&O's freight and passengers, a position comparable to today's operations vice president. Thomas A. Scott arrived last. He had organized and managed the U.S. Military Telegraph with his assistant, the young Andrew Carnegie. He then served as Stanton's first assistant secretary of war. A Herman Haupt protege, the affable and politically astute Scott had made a meteoric rise to vice president of the Pennsylvania Central Railroad at age thirty-seven (Garrett was only forty-one). He would become one of the outstanding business leaders of the nineteenth century. During his presidency, Scott's Pennsy operated more track than Britain and France combined.

---

him. Flower also contradicts Eckert, according to George C. Gorham, *Life and Public Services of Edwin M. Stanton* (Boston: Houghton Mifflin, 1899), 2:123–25.

12. Stanton to Boyle, September 23, 1863, *OR,* Ser. 1, 29, pt. 1:147; Boyle to Stanton, September 24, 1863, ibid., 149.

Scott had already prepared his road to assist a major military rail movement, strongly suggesting that Stanton had researched the possibility.
"Have ordered all our troop extra pass[enger] & baggage cars to be
ready," Scott reported to McCallum on September 24.[13]

Garrett, Scott, and Smith met with McCallum at the War Department. Major Eckert had spent the night poring over railroad timeta-
bles. Freight trains could reach Chattanooga from Washington in seven
days, passenger trains even faster. Eckert now believed, to Stanton's
delighted relief, that they could complete the movement in fifteen days
or less. Tom Scott stated that they could do it faster than that. He knew
whereof he spoke: he had inspected the Kentucky and Tennessee railroads during a fact-finding mission to the western armies in February
1862. He had studied the mechanics of large troop movements at that
time, in part for his own education, but also in response to Army of
the Potomac commander General George B. McClellan's soon-aban-
doned proposal for a major Union offensive through Kentucky. He
had advised Stanton in 1862 that, with an all-out effort, the federal
government could send sixty thousand troops from Washington to
Pittsburgh in six days.[14]

The four men divided the tasks; each assumed responsibility for part
of the route. McCallum's Military Railroad would ship the soldiers
from the Army of the Potomac in Virginia to Washington. The troops
would change to B&O cars in Washington for the trip to the Ohio
River. Garrett, Smith, and other B&O officers would oversee their passage from Washington to Louisville, Kentucky. They would cross the
Ohio River at Benwood, West Virginia, on a hastily constructed pon-
toon bridge and then change trains again. The Central Ohio, two

13. Scott to McCallum, September 24, 1863, National Archives, Quartermaster Department records.

14. Bates, *Lincoln in the Telegraph Office*, 174–76. Bates managed the War Department Telegraph Office, where President Lincoln spent hours reading dis-
patches during battles, and Eckert became a good friend of Lincoln at that time.
Kamm, *Scott*, 88, citing Stanton Papers, February 1, 1862; Stephen W. Sears,
George B. McClellan: The Young Napoleon (New York: Ticknor & Fields, 1988),
148. Stanton does not appear to have acknowledged Scott's report in shaping his
decision to reinforce Chattanooga.

other Ohio roads and then the Indiana Central Railroad, all with connected 4-foot 10-inch "Ohio" gauge tracks, would carry them to Indianapolis. There a gauge barrier with the standard-gauge Jeffersonville, Madison & Indianapolis Railroad required a fourth set of trains. The JM&I would take them to Jeffersonville, Indiana, where they would recross the Ohio River on ferries and a bridge of coal barges to Louisville, Kentucky, for their fifth, and final, change of trains.[15]

McCallum assigned Tom Scott to manage the route from Louisville to Chattanooga. The soldiers would take the Louisville & Nashville Railroad to Nashville, then the Nashville & Chattanooga Railroad to Bridgeport, Alabama, twenty-eight miles southwest of Chattanooga. The troops could ride the entire distance in L&N cars because the USMRR had previously connected the compatible five-foot-gauge tracks of the two railroads. The Confederates had burned the railroad bridge at Bridgeport and controlled the south bank of the Tennessee River to Chattanooga. The total distance exceeded 1,233 miles over nine railroad companies' tracks.[16] Train changes meant organizing five sets of thirty trains, each with twenty cars, which far exceeded the capacity of any one participating railroad.

The railroad men considered alternate routes. By crossing the Ohio River at the B&O terminus at Parkersburg, West Virginia, they could have sent the soldiers over the Cincinnati, Wilmington & Zanesville Railroad directly to Cincinnati, Ohio, then by river steamers to Louisville. Conflicting evidence suggests that the dry summer, however, may have left the meandering Ohio River too low to float the shallow-draft vessels. A second option involved crossing the Ohio River again at Cincinnati and taking the Covington & Lexington Railroad to Lexington, Kentucky and the Louisville & Lexington Railroad to Louisville. R. B. Bowler, president of the Covington & Lexington, advised Stanton that, given two days' notice, he could carry 8,000 troops a day from Covington to Louisville, 156 miles, in 12 hours. The L&L, however,

---

15. Turner, *Victory Rode the Rails*, 289; Weber, *Northern Railroads*, 182; Kamm, *Scott*, 166–67.

16. Turner, *Victory Rode the Rails*, 289; Weber, *Northern Railroads*, 182; Kamm, *Scott*, 166–67.

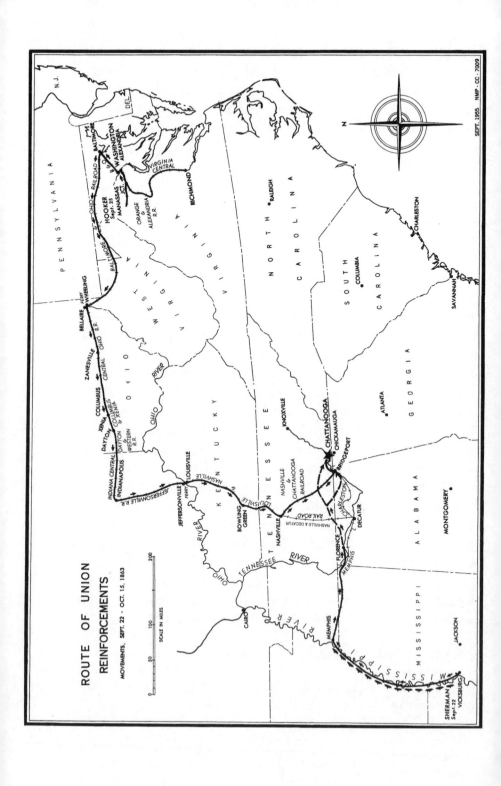

ROUTE OF UNION
REINFORCEMENTS

MOVEMENTS, SEPT. 22 - OCT. 15, 1863

SCALE IN MILES

0   50   100   200

SEPT. 1955   NMP - CC - 7009

used 4-foot 4^1/$_2$-inch-gauge track. This meant changing trains at both Lexington and Louisville.[17] Bowler's route would have cut more than one hundred miles off the Columbus-Indianapolis route. No record of the reasoning behind the decision remains, but the railroad men may have questioned Bowler's estimated eight-thousand-man capacity, the implications of the additional train change for transfer delays, and possibly concerns about questionable maintenance. They may also have worried about Confederate cavalry or guerrilla raids. Self-interest probably also factored into the decision. Overriding Prescott Smith's advocacy of the Cincinnati-Louisville river route, they chose the longer route. Scott left immediately for Louisville.

John Garrett's business interests almost certainly influenced his promoting the Bellaire-Jeffersonville route for the 11th and 12th Corps movement. The Baltimore & Ohio owned a two-thirds interest in the Central Ohio Railroad. Garrett, accordingly, would naturally have tried to direct the business to his company. The planners chose it over the hundred-mile shorter route through Parkersburg, Cincinnati, Covington, and Lexington. Garrett also squashed a later suggestion to reconsider using Ohio River steamboats for the 11th and 12th Corps movement, possibly for business reasons.[18]

The Kentucky route might have saved half a day or more, even with the extra change of trains. North central Kentucky did not suffer any cavalry or guerrilla activity during the movement. Tom Scott would recommend changing the Louisville & Lexington track gauge to five feet, suggesting a road in reasonable condition. Even if the change of trains at Lexington entered into the decision to choose the northern route, the Kentucky roads could have carried the highest priority cargo, infantrymen. They could have walked from one train to the next, the army shipping their equipment by the longer route. His contemporaries

17. Bowler to Stanton, September 24, 1863, *OR,* Ser. 1, 29, pt. 1:153; Kamm, *Scott,* 166. The actual condition of the Ohio River at the time is uncertain. W. F. Hecker, the B&O's agent in Cincinnati, telegraphed the War Department on September 24, "Mail boats are running regularly[.] State of water between Cincin and Louisville thirty three (33) inches draft of boat twenty (20) inches light. Plenty light draught boats here." National Archives, Quartermaster Department files.

18. Garrett to Stanton, October 6, 1863, *OR,* Ser. 1, 29, pt. 1:192.

considered Garrett's behavior neither unethical nor remarkable. Former Secretary of War Simon Cameron routinely routed government traffic from the Philadelphia, Wilmington & Baltimore Railroad to his longer and higher-priced Northern Central in order, he said, to keep up with heavy wartime volume. PW&B president Felton claimed that shipping troops over Cameron's road cost the government fifteen hundred dollars more per regiment. Tom Scott's critics unfairly accused him of the same practice.[19] Garrett, however, certainly had sound reasons for questioning a shift to the water route in the middle of the 11th and 12th Corps movement, if not earlier. The original route had worked out well, and everyone involved knew his job. It made less sense at that time to change for unproven gains.

A sense of great urgency pervades the official correspondence. Learning that the Army of the Potomac had no immediate plans for an offensive, Halleck, using the direct authority of President Lincoln, sent an order to General Meade that "the Eleventh and Twelfth Corps are positively to be sent [to Washington] with the least possible delay. Every effort must be made to have them ready [to board trains] tomorrow morning." The time was 9:45 A.M. on Thursday, September 24. Halleck then telegraphed General Rosecrans that help was on the way. Stanton advised Charles Dana.[20]

Within the hour, Meade telegraphed General Oliver Otis Howard, whose 11th Corps bivouacked west of the Orange and Alexandria Railroad line. He ordered Howard to break camp and move out at once with "five days cooked rations" and "not wait to be relieved by other troops." Meade also ordered General Henry Warner Slocum, whose 12th Corps stood picket duty along the Rappahannock River, to march toward the railheads as soon as the 1st Corps relieved the 12th. Meade added, "The utmost promptitude and dispatch must be shown in exe-

19. Kamm, *Scott,* 59–61. Kamm notes that the PW&B still carried 80 percent of the traffic. He acknowledges that Scott certainly stayed mindful of the Pennsy's interests but gained nothing personally in his role as assistant secretary of war.

20. Halleck to Meade, September 24, 1863, *OR,* Ser. 1, 29, pt. 1:148; Stanton to Dana, September 24, 1863, ibid., 150–51.

cuting this order, and the troops be kept on the march if necessary all night."[21]

Halleck chose General Joseph Hooker to command the movement. The handsome, ambitious "Fighting Joe" boosted himself by running down his rivals. "He speaks badly," said President Lincoln. He had once offered to fill the nation's need for a dictator, a risk that the president said he would take if Hooker could win battles. That prospect dimmed after Hooker led the Army of the Potomac to humiliation at Chancellorsville. The biographer of "the profane, hard drinking" Fighting Joe Hooker traces a history of debts unpaid, including money borrowed from both Henry Halleck and William Sherman, and more references to alcohol abuse than one can ignore. His disgrace at Chancellorsville stemmed from an admitted failure of nerve, possibly complicated by alcohol withdrawal. Despite Hooker's reputation, Dr. Robert Hubbard, medical director of the 11th Corps, recorded that the general "does not look in the least like an intemperate man and if he has ever been dissipated his health & vigor do not seem to have been impaired thereby."[22] Good with troops, Hooker ably commanded a corps at Antietam until a Confederate bullet almost took his foot and his life. President Lincoln apparently respected his fighting ability. As an unemployed officer in Washington, Hooker was a visible reminder of the Army of the Potomac's failures. Sending him west was one way to blot out the memory.

21. Asst. Adj. Gen. S. Williams (for Meade) to "Commanding Officer Eleventh Corps," September 24, 1863, *OR,* Ser. 1, 29, pt. 1:148; Meade to "Commanding Officer Twelfth Corps," ibid.

22. T. Harry Williams, *Lincoln and His Generals* (New York: Alfred A. Knopf, 1952), 212; Walter H. Hebert, *Fighting Joe Hooker* (New York: Bobbs-Merrill, 1944). Hebert gives credibility to the alcohol withdrawal argument, citing Darius N. Couch in *Battles and Leaders of the Civil War* (New York: Century, 1884, 1888), 3:170, and *The Reminiscences of Carl Schurz* (New York: McClure, 1908), 2:431. See also Charles E. Slocum, *The Life and Services of Major General Henry W. Slocum* (Toledo: Slocum, 1913), 87; Dr. Robert Hubbard, Medical Director of the 11th Corps, to "Darling Nellie," October 5, 1863, Letters of Dr. Robert Hubbard, U.S. Army Military History Institute, U.S. Army War College, Carlisle Barracks, Penn. [hereinafter cited as MHICB].

Stanton, armed with Lincoln's authorization, invoked the 1862 federal law that authorized the president to take military control of the railroads in time of emergency and ordered "That Major-General Hooker be, and he is hereby, authorized to take military possession of all railroads, with their cars, locomotives, plants, and equipments, that may be necessary for the execution of the military operation committed to his charge; and all officers, agents, and employes of said roads are directed to render their aid and assistance therein, and to respect and obey his commands."[23] The full authority of the federal government backed the movement. Those in charge exercised it.

One must guess why Halleck, presumably with Meade's consent, chose the 11th and 12th Corps. Hooker's biographer reasons that they had the shortest service with the Army of the Potomac, brought into it from the Army of Virginia after Second Manassas. Perhaps so, considering how often its many commanders reorganized the eastern army, but troops had fought under Oliver Howard and Henry Slocum since First Manassas. Slocum had taken command of the 12th Corps on October 15, 1862, and Howard had commanded the 11th since April 2, 1863.[24] The decision was probably influenced more by personalities.

The 11th Corps was a hard-luck outfit. The army blamed it for letting Stonewall Jackson smash the Union right at Chancellorsville, roll up half the army, and hand Robert E. Lee one of the greatest victories in the history of American arms. Major General Oliver Otis Howard was a devout Christian, abolitionist, and abstainer. No one questioned his bravery. He lost his right arm at Seven Pines during the Peninsula campaign yet returned to command his brigade in less than three months. Even though his brigade bolted at First Manassas, the army promoted him to brigadier general. In spite of the harsh lesson learned at Chancellorsville, one of his officers failed to protect his flank one

23. Stanton's General Order, September 24, 1863, *OR*, Ser. 1, 29, pt. 1:151.

24. Hebert, *Hooker*, 251; Slocum, *Life and Services*, 13–37, 54; Edmund R. Brown, *The Twenty-seventh Indiana Volunteer Infantry in the War of the Rebellion* (Washington, D.C.: n.p., 1899), 435; Lee considered the 11th and 12th "two of the smallest and most indifferent corps" of the Army of the Potomac (*OR*, Ser. 1, 29, pt. 2:769).

month later on the first day at Gettysburg. Once again the obliging Confederates crushed Howard's exposed flank, destabilized the Union line, and inflicted more than five thousand casualties on the 1st and 11th Corps.[25]

George Thomas' biographer dismisses Howard as a "diligent mediocrity." An admiring Dr. Hubbard, however, rode in Howard's railroad car to Tennessee. He wrote to his Darling Nellie, "He is a noble man as no one can associate with him intimately without loving him. He has the truthfulness and artlessness of an ingenuous child but great decision and firmness with the courage of a lion. His conscience decides his course always."[26] His critics notwithstanding, Howard served commendably at Chattanooga and during the Atlanta campaign. General Sherman promoted him over Hooker to command the Army of the Tennessee following the death of General James B. McPherson outside Atlanta in 1864.

General Henry Slocum commanded the 12th Corps. A Quaker's son, Slocum roomed with Philip H. Sheridan before graduating seventh in West Point's class of 1852. He rose rapidly in rank and responsibility to major general and corps command at age thirty-six. The fighting 12th led the Army of the Potomac into Chancellorsville and then covered the retreat. Slocum's understrength regiments held Culp's Hill at Gettysburg on July 2 and then took part in the hard fight to clear the hill the next day. They showed their toughness during the muddy, frustrating pursuit of General Lee after Gettysburg. Slocum's criticism of Hooker at Chancellorsville and of Meade's timid pursuit of Lee after Gettysburg probably convinced Meade to transfer him. Slocum despised Hooker and offered to resign rather than serve under him, citing his "well known" opinion of Hooker "as an officer and a

25. In his memoirs, Howard describes his prudent and thorough preparations for defending the Union right flank at Chancellorsville in such great detail that the reader is almost as astonished as the general by the Confederates pouring through his lines (*Autobiography,* 1:366–71). For an unfavorable assessment of Howard, see Frederick Stephen Wallace, *The 61st Ohio Volunteers, 1861–1865* (Marysville, Ohio: published privately by Theodore Mullen, 1902), 13–14.

26. McKinney, *Education in Violence,* 268; Hubbard to "Darling Nellie," Hubbard Letters, September 27, 1863, MHICB.

gentleman" and having "so little confidence in his ability." Halleck hoped to keep Slocum and Hooker apart, but Grant found it easier to exile Slocum to Missouri. Hooker's petulant resignation after Sherman passed him over in favor of Howard for McPherson's command resurrected Slocum's career. He commanded the combined 11th and 12th Corps, renamed the 20th Corps, and later the Army of Georgia, during the March to the Sea and the Carolinas campaigns.[27]

The two corps would travel light. Hooker told Slocum that the troops would get food and hot coffee twice a day en route. The corps would take the absolute minimum of camp equipment and "only such medicines as will be required on the march." Officers limited their personal mounts. The troops would, however, carry full ammunition loads. Infantry would go first, with artillery following "at leisure," followed by equipment and transportation. The army planned to reassign the 11th and 12th Corps' draft animals because Halleck mistakenly believed that Rosecrans could replace them in Tennessee. The Army of the Cumberland's animals, however, were at the moment dying of starvation in Chattanooga.[28]

Stanton had wasted no time. Confederate leaders took two weeks before Longstreet left for Georgia. The federal government, in contrast, decided to reinforce Rosecrans within twelve hours after Dana and Garfield proposed the idea. Stanton knew the railroad men who could successfully manage an operation of the magnitude proposed,

27. See A. Wilson Greene, "'A Step All-Important and Essential to Victory': Henry W. Slocum and the Twelfth Corps on July 1–2, 1863," in *The Second Day at Gettysburg: Essays on Confederate and Union Leadership,* ed. Gary W. Gallagher (Kent, Ohio: Kent State University Press, 1993), 87–135; Slocum, *Life and Services,* 155, 178, 200; Slocum to Lincoln, September 25, 1863, *OR,* Ser. 1, 29, pt. 1:156; Grant to Halleck, October 26, 1863, *OR,* Ser. 1, 31, pt. 1:739–40. For descriptions of the 12th Corps's pursuit of Lee, see Capt. Richard Titus, 150th New York, to his father, July 6, 1863, Dutchess County Historical Society Collection, MHICB, and A. Wilson Green, "From Gettysburg to Falling Waters: Meade's Pursuit of Lee," in *The Third Day at Gettysburg and Beyond,* ed. Gary W. Gallagher et al. (Chapel Hill: University of North Carolina Press, 1994), 161–201.

28. Hooker to Slocum, September 24, 1863, *OR,* Ser. 1, 29, pt. 1:152; Halleck to Rosecrans, Rosecrans to Halleck, September 24, 1863, ibid., 151.

and he had no hesitation in enlisting their expert help. President Lincoln had expressed doubt that the army could withdraw the soldiers from the field in less than five days. But within that time, twenty-three thousand Union soldiers, their artillery, horses, wagons, and equipment rolled toward Chattanooga.

5

The 11th and 12th Corps Movement

The Success of Northern Management

> We are continuing to strain every energy to accomplish prompt movement.
>
> —John Garrett to Edwin Stanton

Although thrown together as a pick-up team, the railroad men demonstrated a thorough knowledge of their business, a creative flexibility with a gift for innovation, confidence, decisiveness, and phenomenal energy levels. The extreme urgency of their assignment fostered a strong spirit of cooperation. Garrett and Scott disliked each other, both personally and as business competitors, but they had a job to do, so they set aside their differences and went to work.

Daniel McCallum's Military Railroad personnel supervised the first stage, shipping twenty-three thousand soldiers, their artillery, equipment, animals, and wagons from the Army of the Potomac in northern Virginia to Washington. The task pressed the capacity of the single-track Orange & Alexandria Railroad, which continued to perform its mission of sustaining the seventy-seven thousand soldiers remaining with the Army of the Potomac.

The suddenness of the movement, the absence of prior notice, and the obvious urgency of their orders took the soldiers by surprise. The 111th Pennsylvanians, standing picket duty at Raccoon Ford, had just finished negotiating a business deal:

"Hello, Yank! Are you all over there?"

"You bet we're here, Johnnie. Do you want to surrender and come back into the Union?"

"I'll surrender you if I get ahold of you," would be drawled back. "But, say, Yank have you'uns got any coffee?"

"Dead loads of it, Johnnie Reb. We make it in French pots, and serve it with sugar and cream."

"Will ye trade some of it for tobacco?"

"Well, I don't care. But if you try to play Indian on me I'll put you where we put the rest of you at Gettysburg."

The negotiators waded to the middle of the stream to close the deal.[1]

Both wild and thoughtful speculation whirled along the camp grapevines. The soldiers knew about Chickamauga from "the cheering and jollification in the Confederate camp [which meant] that they had received some good news from somewhere." Still, they had recently moved into the area and did not expect to go anywhere so soon.[2]

Chaplain Lyman Ames of the 29th Ohio noted, "This move seems sudden and unexpected to Div. commander [General John W. Geary]." Isaac W. Gardner wrote his parents that his 1st Ohio Light Artillery had built new stables and had started digging defensive positions "until about 2 o'clock when we received orders to cease work as we had got to march." Lt. Colonel Ario Pardee, commanding the 147th Pennsylvania, dryly summed it up later in a letter to his father:

1. John Richards Boyle, *Soldiers True: The Story of the 111th Pennsylvania Veteran Volunteer Infantry, 1861–1865* (New York: Eaton & Mains, 1903), 145.

2. Sgt. Michael S. Schroyer, 147th Pennsylvania, *Snyder County Historical Society Bulletin* 1 (1939): 370–71, Susan Boardman Collection, MHICB. Schroyer had enlisted in 1862 with his brothers, William and Lewis, now both dead of typhoid fever, in whose memory he wrote in his diary, "Sleep, Sleep a Soldiers Sleep thy weary march is over."

"You were undoubtedly surprised to hear of our transfer to the Army of the Cumberland but I can assure you not as much as we were."[3]

A Pennsylvania artillery sergeant wrote a quick letter to his father:

> [M]arching orders came . . . but when we saw the head of our column going towards the rear we were entirely taken by surprise and could not imagine where we were going. Everyone had an opinion . . . it leaked out we were going to Alexandria to be shipped off but where we could not tell. . . . All the troops around here say we are going to Chattanooga to reinforce Genl Rosecrans. [A]t least the 11th Corps were shipped there & we are to follow as fast as cars are furnished so you need not expect to hear from me in Va again . . . trains are leaving hourly.[4]

Few regretted leaving Virginia. Henry Henney of the 55th Ohio recalled, "The boys feel jubilant." Sergeant David Nichol, the Pittsburgh artilleryman, reported, "This news was hailed with delight by all. [A]ny place but Virginia. . . . [T]his change will put new life in the men & I think in this new field of operation every thing will go on better." Chaplain Lyman Ames of the 29th Ohio wrote in his diary, "Men are becoming tired of the monotony of marching over and over again the state of Va. Something new is their motto."[5]

The land they had purchased so dearly, however, had become part of them. The 73rd Ohio "bid farewell to the noble old Army of the Potomac . . . to the desolate fields of Old Virginia . . . to her bloody battle-grounds, and the dust of our sleeping comrades!" The 2nd Massachusetts "left Virginia . . . whose roads had been pressed by many

3. Chaplain Lyman Daniel Ames diary, September 24, 1863, *Civil War Times Illustrated* Collection (CWTI), MHICB; Isaac W. Gardner, 1st Ohio Light Artillery, to his parents, October 2, 1863, Harrisburg Civil War Round Table Collection (HCWRT), MHICB; Ario Pardee to "Dear Pa," October 11, 1863, MHICB.

4. Sgt. David Nichol, Knap's Battery, 1st Pennsylvania Light Artillery, to his father, September 27, 1863, HCWRT, MHICB.

5. Henry Henney diary, September 25, 1863, CWTI, MHICB; Nichol to his father, September 27, 1863; Ames diary, September 27, 1863.

weary feet, left the graves of [their] dead heroes, left the noble army of Virginia [the Army of the Potomac], not to meet it again until the triumphal days of review in Washington."[6]

General Hooker hoped to conduct the movement in secrecy. His chief of staff, General Daniel Butterfield, told Oliver Howard that they headed for Chattanooga, but added that "you are at liberty to give the impression to your command that you are going toward Mobile." When the 147th Pennsylvania, near the tail of the movement, boarded boxcars on Sunday evening, September 27, Sergeant Schroyer admitted that "of the destination we were ignorant at this time and yet it was wonderful how well so many could guess right concerning the different moves of the army."[7]

Not all guessed correctly. Dr. Hubbard confided to his Darling Nellie on September 25, "It is quite certain I think altho. *it is a secret* that we are going some 20,000 under *Genl. Hooker* to Tennessee and it is my belief that Genl H. is to supersede Genl Burnside"(italics in original). He waffled two days later, saying, "Our destination is still I think unknown to all of us the Genl. [Howard] included. Most think we are to reinforce Rosecrans while others say we are going to the Mississippi River & thence to Mobile." Henry Henney of the 55th Ohio summarized the guesses, writing, "[T]he Western Army, and others suppose we shall go to Charleston [South Carolina, then under Union siege], while others surmise our destination to be Ohio."[8]

The Military Railroad officers maximized boarding capability by spreading the infantry among several stations. This allowed the railroad men to load several trains simultaneously and to move the troops out very rapidly. The precision of the organization greatly impressed General Howard, who wrote: "Instead of having a single long train, Mr. Devereux [John H., Chief of the U.S. Military Railroad in Virginia] furnished us with several short ones. As soon as the first one was loaded

6. Samuel H. Hurst, *Journal History of the Seventy-third Ohio* (Chillicothe, Ohio: n.p., 1866), 81; Quint, *2nd Massachusetts,* 192.

7. Butterfield to Howard, September 26, 1863, *OR,* Ser. 1, 29, pt. 1:160; Schroyer diary, September 27, 1863.

8. Hubbard to Nellie, September 27, 1863; Henney diary, September 25, 1863.

to its full with our material, animals, and men, it moved off, to be followed by the second, filled in like manner. As several stations were used at the same time, it did not take long, with our multitude of helpers, to embark everything which was allowed."[9]

Some artillery batteries traveled far to reach sidetracks with loading platforms. Knap's Battery, Pennsylvania Light Artillery, rode thirty-seven miles from the Rappahannock River to Centreville one day, then twenty-two miles the next so they could board their guns at the Alexandria station. The 1st Ohio Light Artillery set out for Alexandria at 7:00 P.M. on Thursday, September 24, arriving at noon the next day, having marched forty-five miles in seventeen hours. They would not stay in Alexandria long, a good thing in Dr. Hubbard's opinion. He found the town "a wretched 3rd rate place full of contraband sutlers & other hangers on of the Army with a large admixture of all other kinds of sinners male and female."[10]

Hooker demanded tight discipline. He understood perfectly well the enlisted soldier's unique ability and remarkable propensity to disappear when it suited him. He had another good reason to worry. Some of the first men drafted under the Conscription Act had recently joined the 11th and 12th Corps. Some seemed positively lacking in enthusiasm for military service. Hooker held his senior officers "responsible for the preservation of good order and the integrity of their commands. If we suffer from desertion it can only proceed from inattention and neglect." General Butterfield warned General Howard to exercise "the utmost vigilance and energy to prevent any disorganization." Their "vigilance" included stationing guards on each car. General Halleck prudently ordered General Benjamin F. Kelley to guard the Ohio River crossing at Benwood and "to close all drinking saloons at the principal stations." Despite the guards and Hooker's orders that the soldiers generally be confined to the cars, "bounty jumpers managed to drop off in large numbers" from the 111th Pennsylvania's cars.

9. Howard, *Autobiography,* 1:452.
10. David Nichol to his father, September 27, 1863; Isaac W. Gardner to his parents, October 2, 1863, HCWRT, MHICB; Hubbard to Nellie, September 26, 1863.

One hundred "substitute recruits" vanished by the time the 111th reached Louisville. Six "drafted men" deserted from the 147th Pennsylvania as it passed through Indiana, and "None of these were ever brought back to the company."[11] Provost guards did their best to keep the soldiers confined to the trains. When they reached Ohio, a Pennsylvania officer "did not see much of Columbus as guards stationed at the head of the main [terminal?] prevented ingress to soldiers." One soldier of the 73rd Ohio, in one of the first trains, sadly wrote that they rode "right on past our own homes and families, which most of us had not seen for nearly two years. Nor were our friends advised of our coming. The movement was to be kept as secret as possible; and in many places they knew nothing of it until our first trains passed along."[12]

The volunteer soldiers faithfully obeyed General Hooker's order, except when they found it inconvenient. They also stayed alert to opportunities. When the 147th Pennsylvania reached Alexandria, "William Keller came into the car with sixteen loaves of bread, government size and first class, under his arm and distributed it among the boys and no questions were asked as to where he bought it." The soldiers found more than bread. During a layover in Washington, 149th New Yorkers bought food "and a good deal of poor whisky." Army regulations prohibited the sale of alcohol to soldiers, but "Women by scores hovered around the train and supplied the men with whisky which they concealed under their skirts. . . . [E]very man who desired was supplied with what he wanted to drink and a full canteen besides." Limited supervision and the "sudden change from deprivation to plenty" produced a considerable number of very drunk soldiers.[13]

The teetotaling General Howard discovered that in "times of excite-

11. Hooker to Slocum, September 24, 1863, *OR,* Ser. 1, 29, pt. 1:152; Butterfield to Howard, September 26, 1863, ibid., 160; Halleck to Gen. B. F. Kelley, September 24, 1863, ibid., 150; Boyle, *Soldiers True,* 148; Schroyer diary, October 1, 1863.

12. Capt. Alexander Caldwell, 46th Pennsylvania, diary, October 2–5, 1863, CWTI, MHICB; Hurst, *73rd Ohio,* 82.

13. Schroyer diary, October 1, 1863; George K. Collins, *Memoirs of the 149th Regiment, New York Volunteer Infantry* (Syracuse: published by the author, 1891), 180–81.

ment . . . some of our men developed an extraordinary desire for whisky" and found citizens willing "to press a bottle into their pockets." Howard telegraphed towns up the line and ordered them to close the liquor stores until the troop trains passed, but sometimes sterner measures were necessary. As Howard writes in his autobiography, "When we caught an eager vendor, selling bottles secretly in spite of all precautions, we found it a good policy to give him a free ride for some distance, then permit him to walk back."[14]

John Garrett and Prescott Smith sorted out the cars needed for the transfer in Washington. Smith advised McCallum on the evening of September 24 that he would have 140 passenger cars in Washington by noon on the twenty-fifth. He needed more than that to carry the seventy-five hundred men of the 11th Corps, as well as an additional fifty cars for the 11th's regimental and artillery horses. The B&O men actually lined up 194 passenger cars and 44 box cars that afternoon, and promised the army 30 more passenger cars by evening.[15]

McCallum, Garrett, and Smith appealed to nearby railroads for cars. The Philadelphia, Wilmington & Baltimore's superintendent offered McCallum sixty passenger cars and forty "house cars" (boxcars). He sent the passenger cars to Washington and the boxcars to Baltimore, where carpenters at the B&O's Mt. Clare Depot installed seats. McCallum reported to Secretary Stanton that the first seventeen hundred troops would start boarding at 8:00 A.M. on September 25 at Bristoe (now spelled "Bristow") Station, Virginia, thirty-five miles from Washington, less than thirty hours after the War Department had decided to send them to Chattanooga.[16]

Garrett, meanwhile, arranged the rest of the route to Jeffersonville, Indiana. He directed Hugh J. Jewett, president of the Central Ohio, "to concentrate, by 10 P.M. of Saturday the 26th inst.—175 cars—125 for passengers and 50 for baggage, freight, horses, artillery &c." and

14. Howard, *Autobiography,* 1:453.

15. Smith to McCallum, September 24, 1863, *OR,* Ser. 1, 29, pt. 1:154.

16. Stearns to McCallum, September 24, 1863, National Archives, Quartermaster Department files, instructions attached to telegram from W. H. Whiton(?); McCallum to Stanton, *OR,* Ser. 1, 29, pt. 1:154.

"to have the same quantity of cars additionally" for both Sunday and Monday evenings. He told Jewett to expect fifteen thousand troops plus their horses and equipment. He also recommended to General Hooker that the B&O take the soldiers directly from Virginia to the Ohio River in Military Railroad cars. Garrett would swap them with B&O cars on a temporary basis. This saved a change of trains and minimized congestion in Washington.[17]

The 11th and 12th Corps soldiers' arrangements reflected the urgency of the movement. Some rode in passenger cars, but many made do in boxcars with hurriedly installed board seats, "like the old-fashioned school house benches," along the length of each side and in the center. Fifty men packed themselves into poorly ventilated, unlit, and unheated cars; as one soldier would write, "It would be a criminal offense now to huddle livestock in as thickly." The 150th New York's "space in the car allowed nearly room enough for each man to breathe in, provided all did not breathe simultaneously, in which event the sides of the car would have been unable to withstand the pressure." They bore the discomfort stoically, as "comfort is the last thing to be considered in army life, especially in cases like these where great haste is important." Sgt. David Nichol, the Pennsylvania artilleryman, "had rather a rough ride of it at night being very cold and we had no covering still we had to grin & bear it."[18]

The troops nonchalantly tore the cars apart to improve light and air. William D. Harper of the 154th New York told his family, "Our officers thought it was a little too warm in the cars for comfort and that it might be wisdom to make a few air holes and that was enough for the old 154th." The 149th New York's "company axes were at work in a manner to make a railroad official sick. . . . [T]he cars from one end of

17. Summers, *Baltimore and Ohio in the Civil War,* 170, citing the Stanton Papers; Garrett to Hooker, September 25, 1863, *OR,* Ser. 1, 29, pt. 1:158.

18. Edwin E. Bryant, *History of the Third Regiment of the Wisconsin Veteran Volunteer Infantry, 1861–1865* (Madison: Veteran Association of the Regiment, 1891), 216; Cook and Benton, *150th Regiment of New York,* 52; John W. Storrs, *The Twentieth Connecticut: A Regimental History* (Ansonia, Conn.: Press of the Naugatuck Valley Sentinel, 1886), 112; Sgt. David Nichol, letter to "Dear Sister Annie," October 10, 1863, HCWRT, MHICB.

the train to the other were as open as those used in Summer on a street railway." By the time the soldiers reached the Ohio River, only the frames and roofs remained on many cars.[19]

They tried to find comfortable ways to sleep. The 150th New York's historian recalled, "Nature's sweet restorer must have her innings, and we found by actual experiment that the average man required about two and a half to three times more space when sleeping in a recumbent position than he did when awake and sitting up. We also discovered that when we slept in layers more than two deep, the lower strata showed signs of discomfort, and was disposed to kick, and it was no figurative 'kick' either."[20]

They good-naturedly bore the miserable conditions. "When night came," one wrote, "we were huddled together like so many porkers. Our beds were the soft side of the bottom of the car with not even a handful of straw." Some slept sitting all the way to Tennessee, by which time they "had become physically hardened, calloused and toughened to such a degree that [they] could scarcely detect the difference between the hard and soft sides of a board, and could sleep anywhere, everywhere, and at any time." Their resourcefulness took charge. "Something had to be done," one wrote. "To the roof of the car! That's the idea! . . . Some of us who went to the roof to sleep (about half of that car load I think) took the precaution to lash ourselves fast to the plank of which I have spoken, by canteen straps and gun slings." Henry Henney of the 55th Ohio "nearly froze to death in so doing." The next night, however, he wrote, "I passed a comfortable night on top of the train. I had more blankets over me and slept with Bill Warner."[21]

Sleeping on the platforms or roofs to escape crowded and poorly ventilated cars replaced discomfort with danger, as Longstreet's troops

19. William D. Harper Reminiscences, Michael Winey Collection, MHICB; Collins, *149th Regiment, N.Y.,* 183.

20. Cook and Benton, *150th Regiment of New York,* 52.

21. Schroyer diary, September 27, 1863; Sgt. William H. H. Tallman, 66th Ohio, *Recollections of a Private in the War for the Union, 1861–1865* (New York: Century, 1884, 1888), 78; Cook and Benton, *150th Regiment of New York,* 53–55; Henney diary, September 28, 1863.

had found. A Pennsylvania sergeant recorded in his diary, "Henry Lake fell asleep, fell off, run over, and killed." Charles A. Houghton of the 141st New York told his wife, "8 men killed by getting nocked off of the cars." Dr. Hubbard wrote to Nellie, "8 men from our [11th] Corps by carelessness in riding on top of cars have been swept off by bridges and killed." General Howard regretted the casualties but accepted them as inevitable. "Many men mounted, from choice, on the tops of the freight cars," he wrote. "It gave them better air to do so, but it was dangerous at the bridges and in passing through the tunnels. A few men were swept off and hurt." General Hooker also viewed the losses philosophically: "The accidents . . . were caused by the men falling off the tops of cars while under way, a luxury they would indulge in whether their officers were with them or not; at all events no orders to the contrary checked it." A Maine man thought the low casualty rate "highly creditable," considering the amount of whiskey consumed. Those who had imbibed "were generally watched by their sober and more careful comrades."[22]

Some traveled well. Dr. Hubbard enjoyed a pleasant and comfortable journey in General Howard's private car. Rank's privileges included "the most comfortable means of transportation" in "a well fitted sleeping car" with such amenities as a bathing room. Private Luther B. Mesnard of the 55th Ohio enjoyed the trip with "a select party" of only twenty men in his car, their spacious arrangements made possible by "a little sharp practice." They had "a jolly time" with "a violin and banjo good singers, dancers and story tellers in the crowd." Mesnard wrote that he "enjoyed the trip greatly, and crowded more fun and amusement into that week than I ever had known before, this

22. Sgt. Fergus Elliott, 109th Pennsylvania, diary, September 28, 1863, CWTI, MHICB; Charles A. Houghton to "Dear Anna," October 2, 1863, Houghton Papers, MHICB; Hubbard to Nellie, September 29, 1863; Howard, *Autobiography* 1:453; Hooker to Stanton, Oct. 8, 1863, *OR,* Ser. 1, 29, pt. 1:182–83; John M. Gould and Rev. Leonard G. Jordan, *History of the First–Tenth–Twenty-ninth Maine Regiment. . . . By Major John M. Gould. With the History of the Tenth Maine Battalion, by Rev. Leonard G. Jordan.* (Portland: Stephen Berry, 1871), 361–62.

with a lot of boys I had known but a few days and never saw afterwards."[23]

As of 5:00 P.M. on September 25, "two trains of 51 cars of troops and 4 cars with [artillery] battery [had] already left Washington." Forty-two hours had passed since the decision to reinforce Rosecrans. With all the main elements of the movement in place, the B&O would henceforth forward the troop trains "with all practical dispatch." The entire 11th Corps would pass through Washington heading west on Saturday, September 26.[24]

Garrett, Smith, McCallum, and their associates deftly made adjustments as necessary. The Military Railroad routinely ran long trains in the relatively flat terrain south of Washington. The first two trains from Washington, accordingly, pulled twenty-seven and twenty-eight cars. The B&O could easily accommodate forty-car trains to Relay House, Maryland, the junction with its main line, but the grade increased as the railroad snaked west up the Potomac River. A long train, Prescott Smith told McCallum, "works very badly for our engines." He recommended that McCallum send either 20- or 22-car trains or two 30-car trains, which Smith's men would break into three at Relay House. John Devereux explained to Smith that the USMRR ran long trains to Washington to ease the load on Orange & Alexandria tracks crammed with urgent southbound traffic. He added that the last 1,700 men from the 11th Corps would load at 6:00 A.M. on September 26. "The Twelfth Corps we have not got to yet." Operators logged Devereux's telegram into Smith's office at 1:42 A.M. on September 26, forty-eight hours after the decision to send twenty-three thousand soldiers to Tennessee.[25]

The railroad men worked out precise plans in spite of the limited time available to them. Prescott Smith asked McCallum to estimate the number of freight-carrying cars needed, "in addition to the 420 with

23. Hubbard to Nellie, September 27, 1863; Reminiscences of Luther B. Mesnard, 55th Ohio, Civil War Miscellaneous Collection, MHICB.

24. Garrett to Hooker, September 25, 1863, *OR*, Ser. 1, 29, pt. 1:158; McCallum to Smith, ibid., 154–56.

25. Smith to McCallum, September 25, 1863, ibid., 158; Devereux to Prescott Smith, September 26, 1863, ibid., 158–59.

seats." Agents reported the Central Ohio at Bellaire, Ohio, in "the fullest condition of readiness" for the transfer from the B&O. Smith had 260 cars "with seats" on the B&O track on Connecticut Avenue in Washington. He would have another 120 there by evening.[26]

The 11th and 12th Corps movement hit full stride on Saturday, September 26. Eight trains passed Relay House by 8:00 A.M. By 9:45 A.M. three trains with more than two thousand troops in sixty cars reached Martinsburg, West Virginia, 130 miles from Washington, "in good order." The trains stopped there briefly for scheduled hot food and coffee. The 33rd Massachusetts ate "A hasty breakfast among the wrecked locomotives," reminders of Stonewall Jackson's visitation. Sergeant Schroyer of the 147th Pennsylvanians wrote: "All got off the train and in order marched in a line on each side of the tables, loaded with hardtack, pork, and coffee. When all had received their ration, we again boarded the train and continued our journey." Peter Funk and the 150th New York enjoyed "coffee, boiled pork, and soft bread—a luxury for us Yanks." By Saturday noon, seven thousand troops had passed Washington. In an age before military censorship, Dr. Hubbard wrote Nellie that they reached Cumberland twenty-four hours after leaving Washington and, "by following us on any good R.R. map you will see that we have made good progress."[27]

The Appalachian mountains challenged every east-west railroad builder between Massachusetts and Georgia. B&O engineers had constructed models in order to test the design strength of the 113 iron bridges, totaling 7,003 feet, that spanned rivers and gorges between Cumberland and Benwood. They also dug two miles of tunnels before reaching the Ohio River in 1852.[28]

26. Smith to McCallum, September 26, 1863, ibid., 161.

27. Smith to Stanton, September 26, 1863, ibid., 161; Col. Adin Ballou Underwood, *Three Years Service of the 33rd Regiment Massachusetts Volunteers, 1862–1865* (Boston: A. Williams, 1881), 148; Schroyer diary, September 28, 1863; Peter W. Funk, 150th New York, diary, September 25, 1863, Civil War Miscellaneous Collection, MHICB, from the Dutchess County *Red Hook Advertiser;* Hubbard letter, September 27, 1863.

28. Hungerford, *Baltimore & Ohio,* 257–64; James D. Dilts, *The Great Road: The Building of the Baltimore and Ohio, the Nation's First Railroad, 1828–1853* (Stanford: Stanford University Press, 1993), 369–79.

The soldiers traveled over "a most romantically wild mountainous region." A 149th New Yorker marveled at the "wild and picturesque country. . . . As the train made its way around the curves and in and out of the cuts and tunnels many glimpses were had of the grand and beautiful scenery." Another New Yorker added, "Sometime we skirted along the brow of a precipice where one might look down a sheer thousand feet into a sea of foliage of variegated hues, and anon we plunged into the midnight darkness of a tunnel, and then again into the bright sunshine." At one point the trainmen broke the train into two- or three-car sections and lifted them up "the steep ascent" with two additional engines.[29]

The road down the western slope evoked images of bridges "suspended above yawning abysses" and long tunnels. There was great "excitement to prevent [the train] from running away down the steep declivity of the mountain slope . . . and the engineer frequently checked the speed to make sure he could hold his train." Battle-hardened veterans held their breaths until their trains reached the valley. Loyal Unionists waved flags during the day and torches at night. The soldiers traveled among friends.[30]

The railroad men struggled to keep the traffic flowing smoothly. McCallum praised the civilians' "hearty co-operation," which enabled them to forward trains faster than initially expected. He told Stanton, however, that he could have shipped the entire 11th Corps by 5:00 P.M. on September 26, including eleven hundred artillery and officers' horses, but they were "constantly importuning for cars." McCallum's importuning created a problem. Prescott Smith's B&O officers delivered cars "faster than the understanding"; in fact they provided 390 of the 420 cars originally ordered a full day ahead of schedule. McCallum's men, however, violated the planned schedule. Although they

29. Collins, *149th Regiment, N.Y.*, 181–82; Cook and Benton, *150th Regiment of New York*, 52. The B&O had completed its tunnels before it first opened the route in January 1853. A rockfall or cave-in probably blocked the tunnel, forcing the B&O trainmen to use the alternate route over the mountaintop. See Dilts, *The Great Road*, 369–79. For photographs of the rugged terrain, see p. 88ff.

30. Hubbard to Nellie, September 27, 1863; Collins, *149th Regiment, N.Y.*, 181–82.

should have known better, they shipped out the troops as fast as they could board them. This overloaded the Orange & Alexandria and created a massive traffic jam.[31]

The jam notwithstanding, Smith continued to dispatch trains rapidly and tracked their progress over the lengthening route. The first three trains passed Cumberland, Maryland, in the afternoon of September 26, "continuing to make excellent time," Smith noted, "while obeying our precaution to avoid excessive and unsafe speed." They reached Benwood, 412 miles from Washington, on Sunday morning, September 27, "two hours less than our promise of forty-four hours through." By then 12,600 men, 33 cars of artillery, and 21 cars of baggage and horses had left Washington. The entire 11th Corps had passed Cumberland by that afternoon. Stanton advised Scott that "the whole force will be moving to-night." Prescott Smith also telegraphed Scott to give him "the rate of movement," as Scott could calculate his needs "better than anyone else."[32]

Garrett assigned the B&O's master of roads, John L. Wilson, and Alexander Diffey, the general supervisor of trains, to supervise the Ohio River crossing at Benwood. Passengers and freight normally crossed the river on ferries, but an unusually dry summer had left the river too low to float the shallow-draft ferries. On his own initiative, Wilson immediately organized engineers to build a temporary but "substantial and superior bridge of scows and barges, strongly connected" in less than two days.[33]

At 1:30 P.M. on September 28, Daniel McCallum shipped the last train for Chattanooga. His officers had shipped twenty-three thousand soldiers, their artillery, wagons, and equipment in three days, while continuing to supply the troops who remained with the Army of the Potomac. The lead units passed through Columbus, Ohio, as the last left Virginia.[34] The War Department had made the decision to rein-

31. McCallum to Stanton, September 26, 1863, *OR,* Ser. 1, 29, pt. 1:162; Smith to McCallum, ibid., 164.

32. Smith to Stanton, September 26, 1863, ibid., 162, 167; Stanton to Scott, September 27, 1863, ibid., 166.

33. Smith to Stanton, September 27, 1863, ibid., 167.

34. Ibid., 170–72.

force Chattanooga just four and one-half days earlier. The railroad men planned and assembled the rail movement in thirty hours, no more time than it took for the troops to march to the railheads. They successfully organized it in spite of having no experience with a movement of this magnitude and often having incorrect information about such basic matters as the number of soldiers involved.

The army had "greatly underestimated" the 11th Corps's strength. The railroads carried 20 percent more men and 50 percent more horses than expected within the original time schedule. They needed 460 cars to carry both corps (420 had been originally requested) and half the 11th Corps's 1,100 horses.[35] Even if most of the artillery had not ridden so far to use Alexandria's loading platforms, it seems unlikely that the railroad men could have started the movement any faster than they did.

General Robert E. Lee peered into the fog that soldiers call intelligence. He advised President Jefferson Davis on September 28 that the Union had possibly sent the 11th and 12th Corps to Tennessee to relieve General Rosecrans. Lee's lookouts reported "the disappearance of a large encampment east of Culpepper Courthouse" (probably part of the 11th Corps). He ordered cavalrymen General John D. Imboden and Major Harry W. Gilmor to break the B&O. Lee also suggested that Davis warn General Bragg to take "prompt action." But Lee could not be certain that these soldiers had in fact left the Army of the Potomac, much less to go to Tennessee. Meade might have sent them on a diversion. Lee recommended that Davis send "bold and reliable scouts" to patrol the Peninsula area east of Richmond, the scene of McClellan's failed campaign in 1862.[36]

Lee faced one of a commander's most vexing questions: could he believe his own intelligence reports? The next day, September 29, he received another report of an 11th and 12th Corps movement but still lacked corroboration. In fact, his scouts reported reinforcements heading *to* Meade. But they might be conscripts, raw troops. If, however,

35. Ibid., 171, 173.
36. Lee to Davis, September 28, 1863, *OR,* Ser. 1, 29, pt. 2:769, 753–54.

Meade had reinforced Rosecrans, "it shows that the enemy is not as strong as he asserts [in Virginia]."[37]

The Yankees did not make it easy. Brigadier General Benjamin Franklin Kelley, a former Baltimore & Ohio employee, commanded the troops guarding that railroad. General Henry Halleck ordered him to "Take all precautions to protect [the] road from rebel raids." General Imboden's four hundred cavalrymen found the B&O "too strongly defended to attack." Major Gilmor "made several attempts to break the railroad, but could accomplish nothing." General Kelley's troopers had done their job.[38]

"A scout, in whom I have not entire confidence," wrote Lee (the man had reported Meade's army moving to the Peninsula), confirmed the transfer of the 11th and 12th Corps on September 30. More evidence arrived on October 1. On October 3, Major William Norris, chief of the Confederate Signal Corps, gave Secretary of War James A. Seddon a dispatch "from a source which may be considered reliable." The note from an "A. Howell" in Washington, dated September 25, accurately outlined the 11th and 12th Corps movement. Confirmation, however, came too late. At 6:00 A.M. on Wednesday, September 30, the 55th Ohio Volunteer Infantry chugged into Bridgeport, Alabama, twenty-eight miles from Chattanooga. The first troops to arrive, they had left Manassas five days earlier.[39]

Crossing the Ohio River seemed like crossing the Jordan to the men in the 11th and 12th Corps; they thought they had reached the Promised Land. Two Pennsylvanians remembered the passage through Ohio as "a perfect ovation. All along our route of travel men cheered and fair women waved their handkerchiefs and bade us God Speed in the good cause." Farmers stood beside the tracks and tossed apples into the passing cars. "Indeed we met smiling faces everywhere," one sol-

37. Ibid., 756.

38. Halleck to Kelley, September 24, 1863, Ser. 1, 29, pt. 1:149; Lee to Davis, October 3, 1863, *OR,* Ser. 1, 29, pt. 2:769.

39. Lee to Davis, October 3, 1863, *OR,* Ser. 1, 29, pt. 2:757–59; Arrival in Bridgeport reported by Pvt. Alonzo Keeler, 55th Ohio, MHICB.

dier wrote. Strong for the Union, Ohioans believed that the army sent these soldiers to reinforce General Rosecrans, an Ohio man and a popular officer. Ten of the fifty-eight regiments in the 11th and 12th Corps came from Ohio, and two from Indiana. The word spread and crowds of citizens came out to greet them. They were local boys. They were heroes.[40]

Zanesville restaurants lowered their prices for soldiers; one man claimed to have gotten a free breakfast in Richmond, Ohio. The ladies of Columbus met the 147th Pennsylvania's train and gave them, one soldier wrote, "pies, cakes, and kinds of fruit, and a little smile and a kind word for each of us, which was so nice and we all appreciated it to the fullest extent." The 20th Connecticut remembered "women crowning the soldiers with garlands of flowers, and filling their haversacks so full of their 'goodies,'" that the soldiers regarded army rations with "utmost contempt." Ohio women represented "the choicest beauty on the face of the earth," wrote one soldier. Many gave soldiers "missives indicative of sympathy and sisterly regard . . . much correspondence grew out of these little favors."[41]

Men fresh from a northern Virginia landscape ravaged by two years of war found Ohio an agricultural paradise. A New Yorker described corn so high on the farms near Columbus that hogs could not reach the ears. Trees sagged with ripe apples before soldiers relieved them of the "great treat." Dr. Hubbard praised "the finest and most luscious specimens of the catawba [grape]." Ohio's prosperity, "in pleasing contrast with the desolate regions we have but recently occupied," confirmed to the doctor that "[t]he farther we get from the blighting influences of the accursed system of slavery the more evident are the smiles of Providence on human industry."[42]

40. Caldwell diary, October 2–5, 1863; David Nichol to his sister, October 10, 1863, HCWRT, MHICB.

41. Robert Hubbard Papers, September 29, 1863, MHICB; Sgt. Fergus Elliott, 109th Pennsylvania, diary, October 3, 1863, MHICB; Schroyer diary, September 29, 1863; Storrs, *20th Connecticut,* 112; Collins, *149th Regiment, New York,* 184.

42. Sgt. Sanford Eggleston, Co. D 150th New York Volunteers, October 13, 1863 letter from Tullahoma to David Eggleston of Millerton, Dutchess County,

Crowds mobbed the soldiers in Xenia, fifty miles west of Columbus. Sergeant Nichol remembered, "Every Lady had a Basket. It seemed to me like Pittsburgh & we were just returning home & all our friends were there to welcome us back." Happy 150th New Yorkers discovered that "Any number of Books Magazines and Papers were passed to us. . . . [N]one of the boys need want for Lady correspondents for nearly all the reading matter had an address." Others "were visited by a perfect avalanche of eatables."[43]

General Rosecrans, "preeminently the pride of his State among military notables," according to Dr. Hubbard, came from the Xenia area. According to Hubbard, "the fact that we are going to help 'Rosy' as they familiarly & affectionately call him lent not a little to the enthusiasm with which they received us." In Dayton, David Nichol reported, "the Odd Fellows formed a procession and marched past us headed by a fine brass Band."[44]

The "ovation" continued in Indiana, where the ladies of Indianapolis prepared hot meals for the soldiers. A captain in the 46th Pennsylvania reported, "I assure you ample Justice was done it by our brave boys. The ladies 'God Bless em' spent their night among the grim faced soldiers—some not quite so grim—serving them with whatever they needed and having a cheerful smile for every one." Sergeant Schroyer also felt the warmth: "The citizens treated us with the greatest kindness. Ladies would go along the train and exchange their names and addresses with the bashful boys. This, of course, resulted in many letters being written to the boys in blue, when we got to the front. . . . The railroad stations along our route were crowded with cheering men, women and children."[45]

Some stations offered even more interesting attractions. The 147th Pennsylvania's train stopped across the street from a saloon "with beer kegs on the pavement." The alert Pennsylvanians timed their strike

New York. Dutchess County Historical Society Collection, MHICB; Schroyer diary, September 29, 1863; Robert Hubbard Papers, September 29, 1863.

43. David Nichol to Annie, October 10, 1863; Peter Funk diary, undated.

44. Nichol to Annie, October 10, 1863; Hubbard to Nellie, September 30, 1863.

45. Caldwell diary, October 2–5, 1863; Schroyer diary, September 30, 1863.

perfectly. Waiting until the engineer gave the "all aboard" signal, they rushed the saloon and made off with the kegs as the train pulled out of the station. As Schroyer reported, "The saloon keeper, failing to recover the captured kegs, was mad, but the boys were happy." Ecstatic, apparently. Captain Krider, "who scarcely ever surprised his stomach with a drink of cold water, placed, as he said, the soberest man he had in his company to guard the beer." Before long most of the men in the car were fighting drunk, including the guard and the captain.[46]

Curious Ohio citizens asked the soldiers to display their regimental flags. The 149th New York's colors, "with its broken staff, splinter wrappings and scores of bullet holes . . . told plainer than words what the command had done and of the trying scenes through which it had passed." The people responded enthusiastically, and "By this demonstration of patriotic regard the courage of the men was renewed and their hearts made stronger for the trying ordeal of the many scenes which were to follow."[47]

The 27th Indiana felt "a joy and an inspiration, which will linger with us to the end of life . . . the warm-hearted expressions of sympathy and encouragement. . . . The beaming eyes, winsome smiles and brave cheering words, no less than the kindly deeds, of the loyal women and girls, not only rewarded us for what we had done, but made better soldiers of us in the time to come." General Howard agreed: "Nothing ever inspirited our men more. True, these lovely faces and these demonstrations were reminders of home; but with our soldiers generally such reminders . . . awakened them to fresh energy and exertion to struggle on, and to preserve to their children an unbroken heritage."[48]

Despite its citizens' warm greetings to the soldiers, Ohio struggled with a bitter gubernatorial race. Dr. Hubbard recalled that in Dayton, "A large concourse of people a majority of whom were ladies," welcomed the soldiers and "entertained us with patriotic & also political songs for politics here just now run high. [F]or this is the home of the traitor Vallandigham and political feeling extends even to the chil-

46. Schroyer diary, October 1, 1863.
47. Collins, *149th Regiment, N.Y.*, 184–85.
48. Brown, *27th Indiana*, 439–40; Howard, *Autobiography*, 1:453–54.

dren." The Republican-oriented Union Party tapped the Lincoln Democrat, "Honest" John Brough, to oppose former congressman Clement Laird Vallandigham. A Copperhead, or Peace Democrat, Vallandigham campaigned from exile in Canada. Federal troops had escorted him into Confederate lines in May 1863, but the Davis administration considered him a political liability and got rid of him through the blockade. The troops referred to Vallandigham simply as "the traitor." Sergeant William Tallman of the 66th Ohio recalled that "copperheads receive no mercy from the Soldier Boys." He found the soldiers from other states in his 12th Corps "more bitter in their hatred of Vallandighamers than the Ohio men." Soldiers covered the walls of the cars with Vallandigham graffiti.[49]

Some Ohio Copperheads heckled the soldiers, unmindful of the risks inherent in antagonizing armed men. Edmund Brown of the 27th Indiana wrote that when the train "was moving too fast to alight from it, yet not fast enough to prevent our hearing them, men would tantalize us by shouting for Vallandigham, and frequently for Jeff Davis. We had our guns, of course, but shooting under the circumstances was a more radical measure than seemed advisable." Sergeant Tallman's 66th Ohioans, however, felt a bit less constrained. Determined to square accounts with cheering Vallandighamers in Cambridge, Ohio, "A dozen or more fellows grabbed their guns and made after them . . . and the[y] loaded with blank cartridge and gave them a volley. They thought they were to be massacred sure and the[y] urged [their] horses to their greatest speed and were soon out of sight."[50]

The 27th Indiana also got revenge. They collected "a plentiful supply of David's favorite weapons, namely, 'Smooth stones from the brook.' It was most amusing to witness the result when the next group

---

49. Hubbard to Nellie, September 30, 1863; Tallman, *Recollections,* 79. One citizen called Vallandigham "a Treble tongued, Hidra headed, Cloven footed, Heaven forsaken, Hell begotten, Pucilanimous curse." Frank L. Klement, *The Limits of Dissent: Clement L. Vallandigham and the Civil War* (Lexington: University Press of Kentucky, 1970), 229, citing Clemens L. Clendenen to his sister, September 16, 1863, Clendenen Family Papers, Huntington Library, San Marino, Calif.

50. Brown, *27th Indiana,* 440; Tallman, *Recollections,* 78–80.

of men . . . began to shout their taunting hurrah's. How they did dodge and scamper, when it began to rain good-sized stones in their midst!" The 27th repeated the successful tactic "with the same laughable and gratifying results," Brown wrote, "until we finally passed out of Ohio." At Bellaire, seeing his men pelting a cheering Vallandighamer with rocks, General Geary cried out, " 'That's right, boys, give it to him, d—n him!' at which the miserable Copperhead beat a hasty retreat."[51]

The soldiers took great pleasure in ambushing unsuspecting Copperheads. A soldier jumped onto the station platform at Zanesville and urged his regiment to give three cheers for Vallandigham. According to Tallman, "a fellow that looked as if he might be Petroleum V. Nasby rushed up to grasp [the cheerleader's] hand, saying he knew all the boys had not lost [their] senses. That was enough for the Blue-coat and he yelled out, 'Heres a simon pure Copperhead! go for him boys,' and the next minute our Nasby friend was picking himself up and making tracks up the street with a crowd of yelling soldier boys at his heels."[52]

The issue had nothing to do with party labels in the soldiers' minds, rather a clear line between patriotism and treason. Many 27th Indianans voted as Democrats before the war. But as the historian of the 27th wrote, "we were all on the other side now. None of us could brook the idea of a man who had been convicted of being in secret alliance with [an] armed rebellion, being voted for governor of the great, loyal state of Ohio, much less elected to that office." One Pennsylvanian observed hopefully, "the enthusiasm seemed universal and from what I saw [and] learned from citizens Vallandigham stands a poor chance."[53]

A soldier of the 94th Ohio, an Army of the Cumberland regiment slowly starving in Chattanooga wrote, "How earnest is the soldiers' wish that people at home may be as firmly united in their support of the Union party as are the men here in the field fighting for their coun-

51. Brown, *27th Indiana*, 440; Richard Eddy, *History of the Sixtieth Regiment, New York State Volunteers* (Philadelphia: published by the author, 1864), 288.
52. Tallman, *Recollections*, 78–80.
53. Brown, *27th Indiana*, 440; Caldwell diary, October 2–5, 1863.

try." The 94th voted their opinions, 287 for Brough, 6 for Vallandigham.[54] Perhaps because Vallandigham ran less for governor than against the federal government, Brough crushed him by 100,000 votes.

General Hooker knew what could happen if the men thought they could stray from the trains. They had left home a long time ago, missed their families, and wanted to see their loved ones. They also knew that, considering their destination, they might never get another chance. The 27th Indiana's historian observed, "With all that we had been called upon to do and to witness, and with what, in all probability was yet to come, the impulse to stop was very strong, if only for the next train."[55] An enlisted soldier never asks for permission under these circumstances. Asking has two possible results, one of which is bad. Disobedience of a direct order risks harsh consequences. Knowing that he probably will not get caught and, if he does, he can seek forgiveness and promise not to do it again, the soldier sees no reason to ask permission.

No one thought to close the telegraph offices. When David Nichol's 1st Pennsylvania Light Artillery reached Benwood, "several of the Boys friends were [there] to see them." Nichol and another man from his battery went home to Pittsburgh to visit. When they returned, they found that their train had left. They took the next one and, after spending "a very hard night [where] there was not room for a man to lie down," caught up with the battery in Indianapolis. As luck would have it, Nichol wrote, "I saw the Capt nearly the first one [and] he asked me how I left all the folks (here) and said it was all right."[56]

Some 66th Ohioans telegraphed friends and families in Columbus, and "the hours were made the most of among those who had wives and sweethearts there to greet them." Sergeant William Tallman decided that "the hours allotted [were too] short to suit my ideas of a visit or allow time enough to do all the talking I wanted to" so, finding

54. *Record of the Ninety-fourth Regiment, Ohio Volunteer Infantry, in the War of the Rebellion* (Cincinnati: Ohio Valley, n.d.), 57.

55. Brown, *27th Indiana*, 441.

56. Nichol diary, September 30, 1863, and letter to Annie, October 10, 1863.

Hooker's order impractical, he ignored it. "When the train pulled out," Tallman wrote, "I was not there to go, because I was not ready, and I did not get ready until noon of the following day." Besides, "Those of us who stopped off knew that by taking a short cut by Passenger Trains we could overtake our Regt before crossing into Ky." They caught up at Seymour, Indiana.[57]

Isaac W. Gardner of the 1st Ohio Light Artillery did not go home because, he said, "it would cost considerable and I could not stay at home but a short time anyway" though a friend had been to see family in Cincinnati "and came back" to the train. A considerable number of those who could go home took advantage of the opportunity. Henry Henney of the 55th Ohio recorded, "Short call at Columbus— unsatisfactory to men—numbers fell behind." Colonel Ario Pardee, commanding the 147th Pennsylvania, wrote, "[L]ost about 100 men since I left the Rapidan. Most of them were left behind by accident but there will be many of them take advantage and desert. I expect a detach't of the stragglers today."[58]

Twenty-seventh Indianans passed through their home towns, but "only a limited number could stop off, even for a short time. . . . It called, therefore, for heroic self-denial on the part of some." They set priorities: married men went home before bachelors; those with sick parents before others. Their selflessness provided a powerful example of fraternal love. "Several of those who then saw home and friends, partly through the kindness and encouragement of officers and comrades, never saw them again," the regimental historian observed, "while some who then voluntarily denied themselves the opportunity, for the sake of others, never had the opportunity recur. . . . When these men crossed the Ohio River they were never to recross it in the body." Hard campaigning lay ahead of them and everyone in the 27th understood what that meant.[59]

57. Tallman, *Recollections*, 81.

58. Gardner to his parents, October 2, 1863; Ames diary, October 2, 1863; Pardee to "Dear Pa," October 11, 1863.

59. Brown, *27th Indiana*, 441–42. Brown credits Gen. Slocum for his "great kindness" in holding the regiment in Indianapolis so families could meet. This

The soldiers deserted neither Cause nor comrades. With a few exceptions, they returned to their regiments after visiting their families, a matter of significance and of incalculable importance for the Union. For this reason, the practical 11th and 12th Corps commanders turned a blind eye to what a later generation of soldiers would call "bugging out." The provost guards reasserted military law in Louisville, corralled the stragglers, and sent them on to their units. "This made it easy for those who stopped off at home to overtake us without serious detention . . . when they reached the corps, and nothing farther was said about it."[60] Serious business lay ahead. The army needed every fighting man. It had no time for military legalities.

The first trains reached Indianapolis in the afternoon of September 28, "followed in quick succession and excellent time by others." A gauge barrier between the 4-foot 10-inch–gauge Indiana Central and the standard-gauge Jeffersonville, Madison & Indianapolis railroads caused a bottleneck. This required offloading and reloading each train, even though the tracks paralleled each other. A local decision to feed the soldiers hot meals a mile across town at the Soldiers Home extended the delay, but the railroad men maintained firm control. Prescott Smith felt "such confidence now in affairs as to enable us to continue our promise of the best results." Anticipating the worst case, he added, "We are hurrying equipments back from west . . . to meet further emergencies or requisitions, should such be presented."[61]

They faced problems head on. The magnitude of the undertaking required that all trains adhere strictly to their schedules. The B&O station agent at Grafton, West Virginia, wired Smith that General Carl Schurz, commanding the Third Division of the 11th Corps, ordered him to hold all trains until Schurz arrived. It seems that the general wanted to ride at the head of his division. Advising Secretary Stanton that "this kind of thing will cripple your whole movement," Smith im-

---

seems highly unlikely, but it does reflect the regiment's affection for their corps commander.

60. Brown, *27th Indiana*, 442.

61. Smith to Stanton, September 28, 1863, *OR*, Ser. 1, 29, pt. 1:178. The *Official Records* have no other reports between Bellaire and Indianapolis, suggesting an unremarkable passage.

mediately issued a "peremptory order," which Stanton promptly confirmed. All trains would keep moving except by direct order from
Stanton himself; no one would interfere with the schedule without
risk. Stanton threatened to arrest the chagrined Schurz, who innocently explained that he had simply intended to restore order to his
regiments, which had become scrambled on the trains.[62]

By September 28 more than eight thousand men had crossed the
Ohio River at Bellaire, Ohio, 137 miles from Columbus. Traveling in
two hundred cars, five thousand passed through the Ohio capital that
afternoon. Stanton advised Scott that "the advance were at Columbus
at 3 o'clock today." As he wrote, they actually rolled two hours from
Louisville.[63] The movement had yet to complete its fifth day.

At least two serious train accidents marred the movement. Chaplain
Lyman Ames noted, "A collision, our train ran into the rear of another,
smashed two cars, hurt 7 men of 7 O.V.I. [7th Ohio Volunteer Infan-
try]." The 147th Pennsylvania's Sergeant Michael Schroyer experienced a rear-ender near Cumberland, Maryland, that left him "slightly
bruised, lay[ing] under the seat. The two rear cars were pushed on top
of the third one. . . . Thirteen soldiers were wounded, but none killed.
A splinter from one of the cars about eighteen inches long and about
as broad as a man's hand, pierced the thigh of one of the boys, produc-
ing a very painful wound."[64] Soldiers' letters and diaries, and official
correspondence, record breakdowns and at least one derailment, but
no other accidents. If only two accidents occurred, and no deaths resulted, then the 11th and 12th Corps enjoyed a very safe trip.

Once they dispatched the last group of soldiers, the railroad men
turned to the draft animals. Told that the Army of the Cumberland

62. Stanton and Smith, September 27, 1863, ibid., 167–69; Schurz to Stanton, September 28, 1863, ibid., 172. Schurz sent Stanton a long explanation from
Bridgeport, Alabama, on October 1, asking the Secretary "to withdraw the cen-
sure you have inflicted upon me." Hooker and Howard supported Schurz and the
matter died. Ibid., 181–82. Schurz's memoirs do not mention the incident or anything else about the rail movement.

63. Smith to Stanton, September 28, 1863, ibid., 173; Stanton to Scott,
ibid., 175.

64. Ames diary, September 30, 1863; Schroyer diary, September 29, 1863.

would supply horses and mules for the 11th Corps, Prescott Smith prepared to ship only the 12th Corps's animals. On Tuesday afternoon, September 29, he delivered every available car he had, 112 in all, "which is more than double the first requisition." The correspondence shows the railroad men's ability to adjust to changing circumstances. Smith intended to ship four hundred fifty 12th Corps horses still at Bealeton Station, Virginia, in cars returning from Benwood. He did not expect those cars for another day, however, so advised McCallum that he planned to "try to borrow or impress thirty (30) [cars] from Northern Central road." The Philadelphia, Wilmington & Baltimore also contributed eleven cars. Smith closed, "[T]he column at every point is moving onward in good order and with entire success."[65]

The Baltimore & Ohio officers thought that they could start winding down the Washington-Jeffersonville phase of the movement with the boarding of the last horses and mules on September 30. They planned to shut down operations completely by October 2. Prescott Smith told Stanton that the only place "where any real impediment has been threatened" was the "very tedious and difficult" change of cars in Indianapolis. He complained about inadequate sidings and the lack of familiarity "in that quarter with the details of such things on such a scale." His men had accomplished "wonders" in spite of the bottleneck; the delay averaged only six hours. Still, he remained "more than satisfied of the correctness of [his] judgment" in recommending a Cincinnati-by-rail and Louisville-by-water route. Smith took understandable pride in moving fifty-eight infantry regiments, ten artillery batteries with horses, and more than one hundred cars of baggage. They represented 35 percent "beyond the requisition and our expectations, and we only wonder that under such circumstances such results have been secured." He concluded that "even without previous notice, we feel ready to undertake it again, with all the anxiety and constant effort involved."[66] He would get the chance.

Events then conspired against Prescott Smith. John Devereux expected each car to carry fifteen horses. Quartermasters, however, found

65. Smith to McCallum, September 29, 1863, National Archives.
66. Smith to Stanton, September 30, 1863, *OR*, Ser. 1, 29, pt. 1:183–84.

themselves struggling to load ten. Some officers insisted on putting no more than four horses in a car, a practice that, if unchecked, would create an impossible demand for rolling stock. Then the railroads failed Smith. The Northern Central promised eighteen of thirty cars that he requested but sent only seven. Worse, in order to conserve stream water for boilers along the drought-stricken road, the B&O men kept trains moving west by holding up deadheading eastbounders, the very cars that Prescott Smith needed for shipping horses. The discouraged man observed that he had delivered twice the number of cars originally requested, but some of them "were not loaded to more than half their Capacity." Regardless, the last horses left Bealeton Station on October 2. The B&O men thought they had finished the job. They were wrong.[67]

On October 2, a ten-mile-long Union wagon train labored west of Waldens Ridge on the sixty-mile trail between Bridgeport and Chattanooga. Confederate cavalrymen commanded by the "War Child," General Joseph Wheeler, swept down on them. They destroyed 350 wagons and killed or drove away more than 400 animals. They also extinguished William Rosecrans' flickering career.[68]

Quartermaster General Montgomery Meigs telegraphed General Halleck from Chattanooga and urged him to ship any 11th and 12th Corps supply animals left in Alexandria "with all dispatch." Quartermasters had already reassigned the 11th's animals to other units, but Meade's chief quartermaster located the teams "intact" within hours. He rounded up the animals, wagons, and as many ambulances as the 12th Corps had turned in, informed Halleck of the animals' reassignment, and arranged to forward the animals and equipment to Hooker at once.[69]

67. Devereux to Smith, September 30, 1863, ibid., 180; Smith to Devereux and McCallum, September 30, 1863, National Archives.

68. McDonough, *Chattanooga,* 69–71; Lamers, *Edge of Glory,* 374. For a fascinating reminiscence by an Ohio cavalryman who pursued Wheeler, see William L. Curry, *Raid of the Confederate Cavalry* (1908; reprint, Birmingham, Ala.: Birmingham Public Library Press, 1987).

69. Meigs to Stanton, October 3, 1863, *OR,* Ser. 1, 29, pt. 1:186; Brig. Gen. Rufus Ingalls to Maj. Gen. Andrew A. Humphreys, Meade's chief of staff, ibid., 187.

Stanton carefully explained the obvious to John Garrett, "that the energy and skill that have thus far been manifested shall not be relaxed, but, on the contrary, that whatever experience may have improved shall be manifested now." Raising the specter of bad weather, Stanton begged Garrett "to bend yourself to this job." Garrett answered drily, "Appreciating the importance and urgency of the movement, on my arrival in Baltimore at 1 this A.M. I at once ordered a rapid movement eastward of the peculiar cars needed for this service from all parts of our line." His subordinates had the situation under control, he explained: "We are now making necessary alterations in house cars so as to fit them for horses and mules, and devoting every energy to concentrate equipment as rapidly as practicable at Washington." They loaded forty wagons and three hundred mules in the afternoon of October 4 and had "cars ready for 140 wagons and 650 mules. We hope to accomplish large work to-morrow." He added, "You may rely that no effort will be spared." He dismissed any problem in Indianapolis, saying, "Our principal officers are on duty at all points, working with thoroughness and energy to insure the best results, and I shall continue to give my most earnest and careful attention until the movement is completed."[70]

Stanton's nearly photographic memory recalled Prescott Smith's concern about the Indianapolis bottleneck. He asked Garrett to help Tom Scott "save this delay and trouble." Evidently unaware that a gauge barrier caused the problem, he then told Scott that "the evil should be cured immediately by connecting the roads," impressing the labor to do the work if necessary. The secretary stressed the urgency of shipping the 11th and 12th Corps animals, as if Scott needed reminding. Setting aside his pressing business in Kentucky and Tennessee, Scott hopped a train to Indianapolis, where he found the transfer running smoothly. Revealing a distressing tendency to micromanage, Stanton, remembering another of Smith's ideas, suggested that Scott might consider shipping troops by steamboat from Cincinnati to Louisville, if the river's depth permitted.[71]

70. Stanton to Garrett, Garrett to Stanton, October 4, 1863, ibid., 187–88.

71. Stanton to Garrett, October 4, 1863, ibid., 187–88; Stanton to Scott, October 4, 1863, ibid., 189; Scott to Stanton, October 5, 1863, ibid., 191.

John Garrett had no interest whatever in changing to the water route, or any route that did not involve the financial interests of the Baltimore & Ohio Railroad. Edward Hungerford describes Garrett as a man who could be brusque or charming, depending on the situation. He refers to Prescott Smith as Garrett's "man Friday," and one who would remain calm while bearing Garrett's wrath.[72] One wonders how calm Smith remained at their next meeting.

The railroad men went back to work, again showing superb managerial flexibility, sense of urgency, and excellent spirit of cooperation. They met head on the difficult and urgent tasks once more thrust upon them with no time to organize. Prescott Smith had enough cars to ship the 11th Corps's horses and mules, "and a few over," and expected to have enough for the 12th Corps's animals in the morning. He needed flatcars for the wagons and ambulances. "We are really Seriously put to it however for so Extraordinary a number of Gondolas and flats." He asked if McCallum could give him forty flatcars for the 11th Corps's wagons, adding, "We are scrapeing Everything together rapidly as possible for those of 12[th Corps] but have to bring most of the cars from the Ohio river over 400 miles."[73]

Smith offered to swap B&O gondola cars for USMRR flatcars if Devereux needed flats before Smith could return them. Suspicious that Smith might try to foist off "rotten and broken" cars for his good ones, Devereux suggested that McCallum tell Smith to use his own gondolas. He argued that they could perform the same functions as flatcars "and for artillery baggage men & wagons, a gondola is much the best." USMRR gondolas approached Washington as Devereux and McCallum considered the matter. A Captain Koontz told McCallum that they could "with energy" ship all the 11th Corps animals by midnight if he could have the USMRR gondolas in addition to thirty-seven boxcars he expected that evening. McCallum overruled Devereux. The B&O men got the flatcars and, starting in midafternoon, loaded nine hundred mules and one hundred wagons by 7:00 P.M.[74]

---

72. Hungerford, *History,* 1:330 and 2:27.

73. Smith to McCallum, October 4, 1863, National Archives.

74. Devereux to McCallum, October 5, 1863, National Archives; Koontz to McCallum, October 5, 1863, ibid.; also found in *OR,* Ser. 1, 29, pt. 1:190–91.

The loan allowed Prescott Smith to ship all the 11th Corps transportation by midnight on October 5. As the operation completed its twelfth day, the railroad men continued to demonstrate their resourcefulness. The B&O's Mount Clare maintenance shops reinforced passenger car floors to accommodate the animals' greater weight. They rounded up rolling stock from every possible source that could carry wagons. The Central Ohio Railroad pledged to cooperate "with dispatch." Garrett reported smooth operations to Stanton, and good route times on the B&O line, adding, "We are continuing to strain every energy to accomplish prompt movement."[75]

They finished their work in the early hours of October 8 with cars left over. In just four days, Prescott Smith's men shipped 416 six-mule teams, 150 two-horse ambulances, 3 spring wagons, and 150 four-horse teams, 719 vehicles and 3,396 animals in total, "with horses, harness, wagon-masters, assistant wagon-masters, and drivers, all in good order."[76] October 8 marked the start of the fifteenth day of the operation. The tail of the original movement had passed Indianapolis two days before the head of the animal movement crossed the Ohio River at Benwood.

Louis M. Cole, described by Prescott Smith as "one of [the B&O's] most experienced, practical officers," managed the transfer in Indianapolis. When some railroads declined to volunteer necessary manpower and equipment, he applied the stick of federal law without hesitation, securing "his requisitions . . . by impressment in some cases." The commandeered rolling stock and trainmen, Smith reported, assured that "full provision is at hand to effect our wants."[77]

John Garrett later congratulated Cole, saying, "Your energy and success in meeting the difficulties by which you have been surrounded command approval." He told Cole to prepare carefully for the approaching animals and to make sure that he had enough cars with rein-

75. Garrett to Stanton, October 5, 1863, ibid., 191.
76. Brig. Gen. Daniel H. Rucker, Chief Quartermaster's Office, U.S. Army, to Army of the Cumberland Chief Quartermaster Col. Henry C. Hodges, October 9, 1863, ibid., 194–95.
77. Smith to Stanton, September 29, 1863, ibid., 178.

forced floors and plenty of flatcars. Garrett, unaware that Cole had already used federal law to get equipment he needed, reminded him, "If necessary, exercise the power placed in your hands in securing such cars to the extent required, from as many roads as may be requisite to accomplish the object." If Cole needed relief crews to spell his exhausted men, Garrett instructed him to "order suitable and reliable men from connecting lines to work these trains through to Jeffersonville." Garrett closed by stressing the great importance of Cole's mission: "The necessity is imperative, and you must not fail in using any means that are necessary to obtain the required results."[78]

Daniel McCallum then showed the strain of two pressure-filled weeks by turning on Prescott Smith. "Great anxiety is manifested in the west," he wrote to Smith, and alleged, "Great delay is reported [in Washington] and principally upon your line." The equally exhausted Smith reminded McCallum that trying to cross the Ohio River at night on the makeshift bridge at Benwood exposed men and animals to unacceptable risks. The railroad men used the down time to feed, water, and rest the animals. He acknowledged two delays from broken axles that cost time but caused little damage, and he pointed out that neither car belonged to the B&O. "Everything though I do assure you is moving well," Smith concluded. He would shortly leave for Indianapolis, "to the neglect of urgent and important matters here," to relieve Cole and others "greatly over tasked by so long a pressure." McCallum apologized.[79] The last animals passed through Indianapolis on Wednesday, October 14, the operation's twenty-first day.

Tom Scott arrived in Louisville on September 26 to manage the final leg of the movement. He knew the condition of the Louisville & Nashville Railroad from his 1862 fact-finding trip. He had repaired the rail yards at Bowling Green at that time and improved the track well enough for the railroad to support General Don Carlos Buell's success-

78. Garrett to Cole, October 6, 1863, ibid., 193. Garrett's telegram is a model message from a chief executive to a trusted subordinate, thorough and precise, while supportive and encouraging. It speaks to Garrett's leadership.

79. McCallum to Smith, Smith to McCallum, October 9, 1863, National Archives; Garrett to Stanton, October 12, 1863, *OR*, Ser. 1, 29, pt. 1:195.

ful campaign for Nashville. His experience had turned Scott into a strong advocate for attacking the Confederacy through east Tennessee as the fastest, surest means of destroying the rebellion.[80] He would now set the stage to prove the soundness of that strategy.

Scott reported "Matters all right in Indianapolis; arrangements for ferriage here completed . . . everything ready for prompt work." The challenges he faced, however, would test even his exceptional ability. Its promoters had built the Louisville & Nashville on the cheap. Its tracks, completed just four years earlier, followed old roads, curved around farms, and meandered over hills. Primitive cuts and fills, steep grades, and sharp curves reflected cut-rate surveying and engineering. Some rails, including some original strap rails, lay on unprepared ground. Two years of hard war had left the L&N "pretty well used up."[81]

Compared to the Nashville & Chattanooga, however, the L&N looked good. Accidents happened all the time on the N&C, even with trains running at eight miles per hour. Daniel McCallum would find the N&C "in the worst condition. The track was laid originally on an unballasted mud roadbed in a very imperfect manner, with a light U-rail on wooden stringers, which were badly decayed, and caused almost daily accidents by spreading apart and letting the engines and cars drop between them."[82]

The soldiers agreed, describing the N&C south of Nashville as "a curiosity . . . built with considerable contempt of levels." Dr. Hubbard's train took 40 hours to travel the 124 miles from Nashville to Bridgeport, Alabama. "The grade most of the way is very heavy & the locomotives very inferior," he wrote. One steep hill required three engines to pull trains up it, needing "much time to get the three to pull together." One hill's blue limestone walls threatened "to tumble into the cuts." Because the army packed the cars with supplies, the troops

---

80. Kamm, *Scott*, 113, 117–18, citing *OR*, Ser. 1, 9, pt. 2:12–13.

81. Scott to Stanton and Hooker, September 26, 1863, *OR*, Ser. 1, 29, pt. 1:162–63; McKinney, *Education in Violence*, 175; Kamm, *Scott*, 167. Jaynes describes early railroad financing in his dissertation, "The Civil War and Northern Railroads: A Test of the Cochran Thesis," 141–50.

82. McCallum report of May 26, 1865, *OR*, Ser. 3, 5:982.

rode on the roofs, "having to hold on to one another like a swarm of bees to avoid being shaken off." Hubbard and his comrades "passed several wrecks with locomotives and cars upside down; and new-made graves, close by each, reminded us of the perilous ride we were not enjoying."[83]

The 149th New York "suddenly entered a tunnel a mile in length, then came the tug of war. The smoke settled down and was stifling, but the boys pulled the capes of their overcoats tightly over their heads and clung to the top of the cars with their hands." A chaplain prayed, "In darkness, we are tried. We are in trouble. We see no light. But God reigns. Have no fear, therefore." The 149th man agreed: "It was an experiment no one desired to repeat." The railroad plunged steeply from the plateau to the valley near Bridgeport, Alabama. The soldiers saw "grand and picturesque" scenery, "but few persons would desire to view it from the top of a freight car with an active memory of recent work by guerrilla bands in that vicinity, especially as the curves were frequently so sharp that it was impossible to see the length of the train." The men in the regiment did not breathe easily until the train reached the valley.[84]

Scott found twenty-five new five-foot-gauge, government-owned boxcars and eighteen flatcars in Jeffersonville. He promptly shipped them across the river to Louisville. Part of a regular 128-car military order for September, they show the strength of the northern manufacturing capability available to the Union war effort. Scott made a quick inspection trip to determine what he needed in order to ship the 11th and 12th Corps and to supply the Army of the Cumberland and other

83. Quint, *2nd Massachusetts*, 196; Hubbard to Nellie, October 5, 1863; Eddy, *60th Regiment, New York*, 290; Bryant, *3rd Wisconsin*, 217.

84. Collins, *149th Regiment, N.Y.*, 192; Alonzo Hall Quint (chaplain, 2nd Massachusetts), *The Potomac and the Rapidan: Army Notes from the Failure at Winchester to the Reinforcement of Rosecrans, 1861–1863* (Boston: Crosby and Nichols, 1864), 362. Interstate 24's eastbound descent from the plateau to the Tennessee Valley may be one of the most hazardous sections of the interstate highway system. Two runaway truck turnoffs, strict state police enforcement of a 40-m.p.h. truck speed limit, and a powerful stench of burning brake shoes make the descent a white-knuckle ride even for today's travelers.

Union forces headed toward Chattanooga or operating in Tennessee: three hundred boxcars, fifteen passenger cars, fifty flatbeds, and twenty-five locomotives, "The house cars [boxcars] to be constructed suitable for carrying horses, soldiers, and perishable stores. The passenger cars to be suitable for movement of officers, and for hospital cars." Cars from all over the northwest started rolling toward Louisville.[85]

General Robert Allen of the Quartermaster's Department in St. Louis immediately shipped twenty-five cars to Scott and ordered railroads in the area to change their cars to five-foot gauge. Allen learned that twenty cars supposedly nearing completion at Michigan City, Indiana, were "not so far advanced as the contract required." Told by the manufacturers that they could not deliver them before the end of October, Allen sent an officer "with instructions to push them forward night and day, and complete them if possible within ten days." The Union not only had great industrial power, it knew how to use it.[86]

Before leaving for his inspection trip, Scott recommended, and Stanton approved, changing the gauge on the Louisville & Lexington Railroad to five feet and connecting it to the L&N. By spending $18,000 to change the L&L's gauge to five feet, Scott integrated the tracks and rolling stock of all the Kentucky and Tennessee railroads. This removed the alleged obstacle that led to the selection of the longer route across Ohio and Indiana. Because work crews had to move the rails on only one side of the track, they completed the change in eight days, finishing the work on October 17. The government also paid the L&L $38,000 to change its cars' wheels to five-foot gauge. Scott also ran a rail spur from the L&N main line to the Louisville wharfs to speed cargo transfers and reduce waste, saving the government another $40,000.[87] The nimble Tom Scott simultaneously cre-

85. *OR*, Ser. 1, 29, pt. 1:166; Scott to Stanton, September 29, 1863, ibid., 181.

86. Allen to Assistant Secretary of War P. H. Watson, September 28–29, 1863, *OR*, Ser. 1, 29, pt. 1:176, 179.

87. Scott to Stanton, September 27, 1863, ibid., 166–67; Scott to Stanton, October 4, 1863, ibid., 188–89. Local interests stoutly resisted through traffic and immediately changed back to the old gauge after the war, and it so remained for another twenty years. The L&N would not complete its conversion to standard

ated an additional shorter, more direct route to the western armies through Cincinnati; increased the Kentucky and Tennessee railroads' available rolling stock and line capacity; and eliminated a bottleneck between the wharfs and the L&N's main line, all with minimal staff assistance while preparing to ship the 11th and 12th Corps soldiers, artillery, equipment, horses, and wagons.

One cannot find stronger evidence of the contrast in Union and Confederate railroad management than Tom Scott's generalship of the Kentucky and Tennessee railroads. He knew what he had to do, justified his requests, and issued the necessary orders. In turn, Secretary Stanton made sure that Scott got everything he needed to do the job. The resources that Scott could call on certainly stand in cruel comparison to the pitiful conditions Alexander Lawton and Frederick Sims faced. However, Scott's instant recognition of the facts of the situation and his problem assessment, establishment of priorities, and decisive actions reflect a managerial excellence shared by no one in the Confederacy, possibly excepting Josiah Gorgas. Further, John Garrett, Daniel McCallum, or William Prescott Smith could have managed the Kentucky-Tennessee phase of the 11th and 12th Corps movement as ably as Scott.

The first trains reached Louisville in the early hours of Monday, September 29. By then, all but a handful of the 11th and 12th Corps were chugging west. At Jeffersonville, Indiana, after sampling the fresh output of a government cracker factory, the 2nd Massachusetts soldiers once more crossed the Ohio River on "queer and aged" ferryboats to Louisville. Citizens' expressions of goodwill stopped at the river. Sergeant Schroyer found Kentucky "the enemy's country . . . not a smile or a kind word was given us." From then on, they would serve "entirely among enemies and in an enemy's country." Official orders prohibited soldiers from buying food from civilians amid rumors of poisonings. New Yorkers of the149th found Louisville "not over cordial. No letters, no hot coffee, and none of the thousand and one little

---

gauge until 1900. It perversely converted to four-foot *nine*-inch gauge during the great track standardization of May 31–June 1, 1886. Klein, *Louisville & Nashville,* 315–20.

courtesies which had been shown during the two or three preceding days." General Howard observed, "War had become a desolating curse and terror."[88]

Chaplain Ames of the 29th Ohio declared Louisville "a neat and proud city." David Nichol of the Pennsylvania Light Artillery sensed strong southern sympathies among the residents. Dr. Hubbard observed "melancholy evidences of the recent conflict in large numbers of wounded officers." He dismissed Nashville as "a corrupt dirty city both physically & morally." In Nashville Chaplain Ames found "Signs of war numerous. City looks hard. Country is hard. . . . Troops are gathering." Kentucky, on the other hand, looked familiar to the 27th Indiana, whose historian wrote, "War in one locality is much the same as in another."[89]

The seceded states did not impress the men in the 11th and 12th Corps. The 150th New York defended Decherd Station east of Nashville, which one soldier described as "a stopping place among the rocks and hills of Tennessee, but it was part of the Union and must be held, although I would not give $10 for 10 square miles of it." The 73rd Ohio in Alabama saw "abundant 'white trash,' which, though not the whitest, was yet the trashiest . . . such wretched, sallow, squalid, ragged and unclean starvelings as only a land of 'chivalry' could produce."[90]

Dr. Hubbard found Tennessee Unionists "a sorry looking people . . . in utter destitution driven from their homes by the persecutions of the rebels . . . wandering in the mountain vastnesses for months to avoid capture." Although their plight informed President Lincoln's determination to hold and relieve Chattanooga, Hubbard concluded, "They are wild and ignorant and would not be very submissive I apprehend to discipline for regular soldiers."[91]

Rosecrans ordered Scott to run his trains straight through to Bridgeport, Alabama, "infantry to move in advance; guns and horses

88. Quint, *2nd Massachusetts,* 193; Schroyer diary, October 1, 1863; Collins, *149th Regiment, N.Y.,* 186; Howard, *Autobiography,* 1:456.

89. Ames diary, October 2, 5, 1863; Nichol diary, October 6, 1863; Hubbard to Nellie, September 30, 1863; Brown, *27th Indiana,* 446.

90. Funk diary, undated; Hurst, *73rd Ohio,* 84.

91. Hubbard to Nellie, October 5, 1863.

follow." Promising Rosecrans that "no effort will be spared to hurry off all that arrive," Scott told him that the limited available rolling stock would require "several trips of all the equipments [locomotives and cars] . . . to move the entire forces." He impressed upon Rosecrans the absolute necessity of unloading and turning around the cars in Bridgeport as quickly as possible. Scott dispatched the first train at 5:30 A.M. on September 29. Others followed at 7:00 and 10:00 A.M., noon, 12:30 and 1:00 P.M. (The *Official Records* shows 11:00 P.M., a probable typo.) He advised Rosecrans, "Stream will now be continuous for the balance of the week." He actually shipped troops from Louisville faster than the B&O officers shipped them in. The L&N connected to the N&C tracks at Nashville. The first train passed at 7:00 P.M. They switched onto the Memphis & Charleston (also connected) at the N&C terminus at Stevenson, Alabama, and reached the Tennessee River at Bridgeport, "less than a half a dozen dilapidated shanties," at 6:00 A.M. on September 30, followed shortly by three more trains.[92] The movement ended at Bridgeport. The Confederates had burned the M&C bridge when Bragg retreated from Chattanooga, and they now controlled the east side of the river between the bridge and Chattanooga. The 11th and 12th Corps movement entered its sixth day.

Well-intentioned quartermasters and railroad men held up the 11th Corps at Louisville. Meaning to let the soldiers rest, they loaded soldiers, animals, and equipment without officers' supervision. The job took longer than expected, and they accidentally mixed together different regiments' gear. General Howard called the result "as destructive as fire" and unhappily looked forward to "unraveling this wretched entanglement when we reached our journey's end." The lesson learned: "It taught every officer . . . that each organization [must keep] the management of its own material to itself. Let the helpers help, but not control, particularly in such hurried transfers."[93]

The last companies of the 11th Corps reached the Bridgeport area on October 1 as the 12th Corps passed through Nashville. All ex-

92. Scott to and from Rosecrans and Stanton, September 29, 1863, *OR,* Ser. 1, 29, pt. 1:177–80; Hubbard to Nellie, October 5, 1863.
93. Howard, *Autobiography,* 1:454–55.

pressed delight with the progress, according to Secretary Stanton, except "the enemy, who only found out two days ago where [the 11th and 12th Corps] were gone." Twenty-one trains carried more than thirteen thousand Union soldiers and four artillery batteries through Tennessee as the movement concluded its eighth day.[94]

While Prescott Smith's men loaded animals and wagons in Washington, Tom Scott reported that everything had "gone forward" from Louisville, except for stragglers and "remains." Trouble loomed, however. Scott notified Stanton, "Things unfavorable for forwarding troops." Confederate cavalry "with artillery" had broken the railroad in at least two places south of Murfreesboro. This put the entire campaign at risk because the Union "armies farther south [might] have great trouble in getting sufficient supplies."[95]

Morning brought more bad news. Confederate cavalry raiders had captured Glasgow, Kentucky, and most of the Union soldiers stationed there. The town, 75 miles south of Louisville, lay only nine miles from the L&N tracks. All the 11th and 12th Corps infantry had reached or passed Nashville; only artillery remained in Louisville. Scott loaded the batteries on trains, "ready for movement" as soon as the infantry secured the railroad and restored the telegraph, which he expected "in the next few hours." The danger passed by evening with the railroad "still unmolested by the rebels." In the morning, Scott reported that Union forces "closely pursued" the enemy cavalry.[96]

Sergeant David Nichol's 1st Pennsylvania Light Artillery arrived in Louisville on October 5. Cavalry raids kept them there three days. Reaching Nashville on Thursday, October 8, the battery stopped fifteen minutes to change locomotives, then "pushed right on" to Murfreesboro to catch up to General John Geary's division defending the railroad.[97] If Nichol's battery brought up the rear, the railroad men completed the movement of the infantry in eleven days and the rest of

94. Hooker to Stanton, Stanton to Hooker, October 2, 1863, *OR,* Ser. 1, 29, pt. 1:184; Scott to Stanton, ibid., 185.

95. Scott to Stanton, citing Col. Innes' report, October 5, 1863, ibid., 191–92.

96. Scott to Stanton, October 6, 1863, and October 7, 1863, ibid., 193–94.

97. David Nichol to his sister, October 10, 1863.

the combat arms in fifteen days. The last troops left Virginia within three days of the first; the first troops reached Bridgeport on September 30. This means that enemy action, not the railroads, delayed some units by as long as four days.

Scott correctly anticipated the rail capacity necessary to supply the Army of the Cumberland and put together a workable plan, even as he shipped the 11th and 12th Corps to east Tennessee. An unfounded rumor prompted him to ask Stanton whether General Grant's army sailed toward Louisville, "as I intended to take seats out of a number of our troop cars to-morrow and turn them into carrying supplies to the army." He ordered one hundred cars from a Michigan City, Indiana, foundry "and assessed balance of equipment [that he needed] on Western roads, making it a light tax upon each." He expected to operate at full capacity within a month.[98]

Quartermaster General Montgomery Meigs praised Secretary Stanton's strategic decision to send the 11th and 12th Corps to Tennessee. He declined to predict the Confederates' plans, but he said, "I think their great effort of concentration has failed. The United States holds Chattanooga, and, I believe will hold it." He described Chattanooga's importance for Union strategy noting that "As a fortified base, it threatens the South and Southwest."[99]

The last trains reached their destinations on October 16, twenty-three days after James Garfield and Charles Dana proposed sending reinforcements to hold Chattanooga. Tom Scott could now run 140 cars a day directly from Louisville to Bridgeport, without stopping at Nashville. "With properly organized means to unload," Scott noted, "The cars could be sent back without delay."[100] Thinking, facilitating, constantly finding ways to unravel snags and move the freight, Tom Scott deserves his reputation as one of the premier business executives of nineteenth-century America. A company vice president at age thirty-seven, he was now forty.

98. Scott to Stanton, October 2, 1863, *OR*, Ser. 1, 29, pt. 1:185, 188–89.
99. Meigs to Stanton, October 3, 1863, *OR*, Ser. 1, 30, pt. 4:52.
100. Scott to Rosecrans, October 14, 1863, *OR*, Ser. 1, 29, pt. 1:335, 360–61.

In spite of its great strategic importance, the success of the 11th and 12th Corps movement passed almost without notice, though some soldiers would later remember it with high praise. No official message records its completion. No "Well done" telegrams survive, other than a telegram from Hooker congratulating Stanton with the words "you may justly claim the merit of having saved Chattanooga to us." McCallum did not mention the operation in his final report on the U.S. Military Railroads.[101] They all simply went home and back to their jobs.

Hope sprang that the reinforcements would end the war. A Marysville, Ohio, woman wrote to her brother in the 66th Ohio, "I see in the papers today some of the boys down South wanted to know who these men was that was comming with Stars and half moons on their hats. . . . I hope that Bragg will get discouraged and lay down his arms and go home and say that he is tired of the war."[102] It was a pleasant hope.

The perceptive Dr. Hubbard assessed the military situation for Darling Nellie. The Union army held the upper hand. The Confederates could not drive Rosecrans from Chattanooga unless raiders destroyed his railroad supply line. "If the enemy do not regain Chattanooga," he wrote, "their whole campaign is worse than a failure as their loss is fully equal to ours in men and material and they are not as well able to afford it." Rosecrans could hold Chattanooga until reinforced, "then will be able to assume the offensive." Hubbard expected the army to campaign toward Atlanta as soon as army engineers rebuilt the railroad bridge across the Tennessee River at Bridgeport. He predicted, "If Gen. Grant now would capture Mobile and march inland toward us we could cut the Confederacy in two again."[103]

His commander in chief agreed. Lincoln, the self-taught strategist, saw that Chattanooga was the key to controlling east Tennessee and one of the Confederacy's most important railroads. He believed Chat-

101. Hooker to Stanton, October 11, 1863, *OR,* Ser. 1, 29, pt. 4:291; McCallum report, *OR,* Ser. 3, 5:974–1005.

102. Lt. John N. Rathburn Papers, MHICB. The 11th Corps selected a crescent moon for its insignia, the 12th Corps a five-pointed star.

103. Hubbard to Nellie, October 5, 1863.

tanooga "so vital" that the Confederates must try to recapture the city, thus drawing the enemy out, "and saving us the labor, expense, and hazard of going further to find him." If Rosecrans could hold, "the rebellion can only eke out a short and feeble existence, as an animal sometimes may with a thorn in its vitals." He urged Rosecrans to stand firm. "You and Burnside now have him by the throat," Lincoln wrote, "and he must break your hold or perish." Hubbard told Nellie, "When we add to this the blockade of their ports and the loss of ne- groes who are rapidly being armed and used against them their pros- pect is by no means an encouraging one."[104]

The relief of Chattanooga depended on the Union's maintaining an intact Nashville & Chattanooga Railroad. Cavalry raids forced the Union command at first to assign most of the 11th and 12th Corps to guard the railroad on which they depended as much as did the Army of the Cumberland. At least one man thought that they had been sent to Tennessee for that specific purpose. The 147th Pennsylvania, ex- pecting action, left Nashville with loaded weapons to guard the Duck River railroad bridge, sixty miles southeast of Nashville. Confederate cavalry had destroyed "quite a lot of railroad," putting several isolated regiments at risk. "It was cause enough," one wrote, "to place our commanding officer [Col. Ario Pardee] on the alert." The soldiers welcomed the change after the "tedious ride of seven days on the cars." They wanted to "stretch out full length and have a good night's rest" after the fatigue, overcrowding, uncomfortable seating, and boredom generally broken only by twice-a-day stops to eat and stretch. The 147th Pennsylvania enjoyed returning to the routine of garrison life, in between raids, at their "pleasant camp."[105]

The Army of the Potomac had strict standing orders against "forag- ing." The 27th Indiana discovered that the only rule in Tennessee was to avoid getting caught. They needed little encouragement and raided

104. Lincoln to Halleck, September 21, 1863, in Basler, *Collected Works of Abraham Lincoln,* 470–71; Lincoln to Rosecrans, October 12, 1863, *OR,* Ser. 1, 29, pt. 1:306; Hubbard to Nellie, October 5, 1863.

105. Orlando White, 154th New York, to Gowanda, New York, *Reporter,* Oc- tober 11, 1863, Michael Winey Collection, MHICB; Schroyer diary, October 7, 1863.

the offerings of the local farms. Sergeant Schroyer's 147th Pennsylvanians also "visited the hen roosts, found no chickens but came back lousy from head to foot." Some 147th men then tried to "clean" a sutler at Decherd Station but some cavalrymen and Colonel Pardee stopped them. Unknown parties uncoupled Pardee's car from the train that evening, an act "not discovered until we had gone a number of miles, when we were sidetracked and an engine sent back for the Colonel's car." Pardee, "'raving mad does not tell half the tale,' tried but never discovered 'the guilty party.'" When they reached Stevenson, Alabama, "Hardly had the train come to a standstill until the boys of the regiment spied a sutler and in a few moments his tent was looted of everything he had in the eating line."[106]

Warehouses bulged with supplies in Louisville and Nashville, but quartermasters struggled to feed and supply the soldiers south of Nashville. Supply problems reduced the Cumberlanders in Chattanooga to bare survival on half, then quarter, rations. The supreme strategic importance of holding Chattanooga, however, outweighed concerns for the soldiers' personal comfort or well-being.

Confederate cavalrymen tried to break Rosecrans' supply line with repeated strikes against the L&N and the mule trains between Bridgeport and Chattanooga. They almost succeeded. The Cumberlanders steadily weakened from short rations, a direct consequence of Rosecrans' failure to secure his line of communication. Regimental histories describe men literally too weak to fight. Some claimed that no one thought of abandoning Chattanooga, but others recognized that starvation nearly defeated the army. The 11th and 12th Corps men, also placed on reduced rations, shared the Cumberlanders' privation.[107]

Few in the Union high command truly understood the Cumberlanders' desperate condition at first. The stark reality of General

106. Brown, *27th Indiana*, 446; Schroyer diary, October 20, 26, 1863.

107. *Record of the Ninety-fourth Regiment, Ohio Volunteer Infantry, in the War of the Rebellion* (Cincinnati, Ohio: Ohio Valley, n.d.), 56; Dr. David Lathrop, *The History of the Fifty-ninth Regiment Illinois Volunteers* (Indianapolis: Hall & Hutchinson, 1865), 220–21; George H. Puntenney, *History of the Thirty-seventh Regiment of Indiana Infantry Volunteers* (Rushville, Ind.: Jacksonian, 1896), 64; Bennett and Haigh, *36th Regiment Illinois*, 498.

Thomas' "hold until we starve" telegram became clear to General
Grant when he arrived in Chattanooga in October. "It looked, indeed," Grant wrote,"as if but two courses were open: one to starve,
the other to surrender or be captured." With enough ammunition for
less than one day's fighting, Grant believed that had the Cumberlanders retreated "it is not probable that any of the army would have
reached the railroad as an organized body, if followed by the enemy."
Even after the Yankees drove Bragg's army back into Georgia in November and secured Chattanooga from a military standpoint, supply
remained a major problem for several months. When describing his
supply deficit to Grant in February 1864, General Thomas said, "My
only hope is that we can stand it longer than the enemy."[108]

Archer Jones argues that Rosecrans' desperate condition in October
gave Bragg the confidence to divide his command and send Longstreet's corps on a fool's errand to recapture Knoxville. Great commanders, such as Ulysses S. Grant and Robert E. Lee, can throw away
the rule book by dividing their armies in the face of superior enemies
and get away with it, but Braxton Bragg did not qualify as one of them.
In spite of clear evidence of the Yankee buildup, Bragg chose to weaken
his army, suffering and depleted nearly as much as Rosecrans', in order
to dispose of a rival he considered a more important enemy—
Longstreet.[109]

The Armies of the Potomac and the Cumberland looked each other
over suspiciously. The Cumberlanders thought themselves fighters
who won battles, while the Army of the Potomac seemed cowed by
General Lee. They considered the easterners effete "paper collar soldiers" until Longstreet's hard-nosed fighters gave them a new point of
view at Chickamauga. The men of the 11th and 12th Corps took pride
in smart soldiering. The Cumberlanders' disdain for military propriety
and perverse pride in looking like a rabble impressed Colonel Ario Pardee as "mighty loose and negligent." Dr. Hubbard thought them

108. Grant, *Memoirs,* 312; Thomas to Grant, February 8, 1864, *OR,* Ser. 1,
32, pt. 2:352.
109. A. Jones, *Command and Strategy,* 179; McDonough, *Chattanooga,*
100, 205.

"less efficient, more disorderly & more corrupt . . . and I am disposed much to doubt the superior fighting qualities with which they are credited." He found them "wild and rough . . . a kind of barbarous society for which I have no taste."[110] Both Union armies would soon learn a great deal more about each other.

The 27th Indiana considered itself well qualified to resolve the amicable friction. As westerners in the Army of the Potomac, the 27th suffered everyone's slings and arrows. They were proud of the Army of the Potomac. As Edmund Brown wrote, "We all believed in it, heart and soul, and we all gloried in being identified with its history." They rejected disparaging characterizations of the Army of the Potomac as "a 'paper-collar,' 'soft-bread,' 'feather-bed,' 'review and dress-parade' army . . . that . . . would not fight." On the contrary, "their numerous uncalled-for defeats, and their repeated buffetings and disappointments . . . the exposures they endured and the privations they suffered" had toughened them. They could stand the test.[111]

The 72nd Indiana Cumberlanders eyed the 4th New Jersey with disdain, "fresh from the Army of the Potomac, where they had been well supplied with everything that soldiers need, and had never missed a ration since in the service, and were complaining bitterly of their present hardships. This was fun for us, who had not seen a hard-tack for ten days, and who knew that the army at Chattanooga was on the point of starvation." The 4th stood picket duty that night. The New Jersey men "took some pains in describing some of the terrible sufferings endured since leaving the Potomac, and among other things said they had not had a bit of butter for a week." The Indianans "told them it was pretty rough to be without butter to grease the hard-tack so it could be swallowed without cutting the throat in furrows, but their failure to get it was, no doubt, owing to the fact that they were so constantly on the move," adding mordantly that "when they got to Chattanooga they would 'get dead loads' of butter."[112]

110. Ario Pardee letters, October 10, 1863; Hubbard to Nellie, October 5, 11, 1863.

111. Brown, *27th Indiana*, 437–38.

112. Benjamin F. Magee, *History of the Seventy-second Indiana Volunteer Infantry of the Mounted Lightning Brigade* (Lafayette, Ind.: S. Vater, 1882), 212.

The soldiers good-naturedly needled each other. When Cumberlanders said that Potomac men could not fight, the men of the 123rd
New York would "tell them that when we was in the Army of the Potomac we used to draw Sweet Cake, Butter, Cheese, Potatoes, soft Bread
and that once a Week we had a batch of Pies sent to us from Washington, then [the] Western man would swear & say he knew we was having good living & doing nothing down there." The Cumberlanders
could think whatever they wished, a New Yorker concluded, "but
when they saw the 2nd Division of our Corps fight [at Wauhatchie] it
changed some of their minds."[113]

They saw the faces of their enemy soon enough. The 27th Indiana
pursued Confederate cavalrymen trying to burn the Duck River bridge
near Murfreesboro. Contemplating the wisdom of men on foot chasing men on horses, they wondered "Whether we had brought this spe-
cies of lunacy with us, or whether it was indigenous in the West, as well
as East." Heading back to the railroad after ending the fruitless chase,
the 66th Ohio "concluded to show the Western fellows what we knew
about marching." They stepped up the pace and called on the 102nd
Ohio in front "to pull out or get out of the way." After a time the
Cumberlanders began dropping out. The 66th kept marching hard
until they reached camp, and "In the early morning the 102d came
into camp looking as if they had experienced a bad night."[114]

Soldiers in the Army of the Potomac wore corps patches, an innovation formalized by General Hooker. A crescent moon identified the
11th Corps, a five-pointed star the 12th. The Cumberlanders did not
wear and had not seen unit patches before the Potomac regiments arrived in Tennessee. A sentinel, seeing a 12th Corps orderly's star, presented arms. As the regiment came by, he saluted and saluted until,
"seeing that all wore stars, brought down his piece in disgust. 'They
are *all* brigadier-generals.'" The western soldiers gave as good as they
got. A man in General Sherman's corps approaching Chattanooga
broke ranks to warm himself at a 12th Corps campfire. Seeing their

113. John C. Gourlie to his brother, November 8, 1863, Civil War Miscellaneous Collection, MHICB.
114. Brown, *27th Indiana*, 445; Tallman, *Recollections,* 81–84, MHICB.

patch, he asked if they were all brigadier generals. After some discussion, the Potomac men asked about the 15th Corps's badge. According to Sherman, the soldier replied, "Why . . . forty rounds in the cartridge-box, and twenty in the pocket!" Sherman says that General John Logan later used the story as the basis for choosing a cartridge box and the number "20" for the 15th Corps patch.[115]

The Cumberlanders flaunted their contempt for military formalities, but the Potomac men taught them the purpose and value of discipline. After the Confederates captured several Cumberland picket guards, General Geary took charge, and thereafter "Guard-mounting took place with much pomp and style." Army of the Potomac officers rigorously inspected the guards, but the Cumberlanders "were a nondescript lot and so there were some heart-burnings and internal swearing." The Confederates, however, never captured another picket, "and in the end the Western officers gave due credit for the benefits received from the discipline."[116]

The three-hundred-mile supply line sorely tested the Union's ability to supply its soldiers. The importance of reinforcing Chattanooga took priority over sustaining the soldiers adequately when they got there. It seemed to the 29th Ohio that the army sent their rations straight to Chattanooga, "leaving us with scarcely anything to eat." Hungry Yankees fought hungry Confederates for the miserable gleanings from a cornfield; they boiled their prizes "to allay in part the bitter pangs of hunger." When they began receiving regular rations, however, the 29th started trading coffee for tobacco with their enemy, "each forgetting for the time the hate engendered over the fight for corn."[117]

Potomac men became as hungry on half rations as the besieged Cumberlanders. They began to share a comradeship of suffering. The Potomac men learned the Soldier's Blessing, "Three crackers for four of us, Thank the Lord there are no more of us." A Cumberland regiment from Michigan shared its food with the nearby 2nd Massachu-

115. Quint, *2nd Massachusetts*, 196; Sherman, *Memoirs*, 391–92.

116. Collins, *149th Regiment*, *N.Y.*, 189.

117. John H. SeCheverall, *Journal History of the Twenty-ninth Ohio Veteran Volunteers, 1861–1865: Its Victories and Its Reverses* (Cleveland: n.p., 1883), 84.

setts that had exhausted its rations. The Massachusetts men offered to pay but the Wolverines refused to take any money. At the time a hard-tack biscuit brought a dollar in Chattanooga.[118]

Men weaken quickly on half rations. Ninety-fourth Ohioans on a work detail in Chattanooga "were easily fatigued, and could do but little work." Several described "mouldy and condemned crackers" that hungry soldiers ate "with avidity." Soldiers followed wagons carrying corn for the animals. "Parched corn is a luxury and in great demand. The men take rations of corn issued to mules and horses, leaving them to starve." Desperate men "picked up and converted into hominy the undigested grains of corn, which had passed through the intestines of the mules," the 75th Indiana regiment's historian noted, adding, "The writer has had the satisfaction of eating some of this hominy; but not until he had gone three days without eating anything else." It came down to priorities: "Food must be brought to the soldiers if all the horses starve."[119]

The army stationed armed guards to prevent hungry soldiers from stealing the draft animals' corn, but the animals suffered terribly from lack of forage. Artillery horses, "entirely deprived of food . . . would stand until exhausted and fall to rise no more." The 82nd Indiana sent four 6-mule teams on a wood-gathering detail, but only "two mules and one empty wagon came back to camp, twenty-two mules having died during the day." Deteriorating roads and animals weakened by starvation greatly reduced the number of wagons and weight of their loads with each trip. Mules struggled to climb Waldens Ridge, "so steep that a heavy army wagon was almost a load going up." Rain-soaked roads became "so soft and cut up that a lightly loaded wagon

118. Schroyer diary, October 26, 1863, at "Camp Starvation"; Quint, *2nd Massachusetts*, 197.

119. *94th Ohio*, 56; Rev. David Biddle Floyd, *History of the Seventy-fifth Regiment of Indiana Infantry Volunteers, Its Organization, Campaigns, and Battles, 1862–65* (Philadelphia: Lutheran Publication Society, 1893), 202; William Sumner Dodge, *A Waif of the War; or, The History of the Seventy-fifth Illinois Infantry* (Chicago: Church and Goodman, 1866), 102; *One Hundred Fifty Years of Freedom, 1811–1961: August 9–13, 1961* (Freedom, N.Y.: Freedom Sesquicentennial Committee, 1962).

would sink up to the axles." One man recalled seeing a wagon sunk in the mud up to its bed, its tough, hard-bitten teamster weeping in frustration. More than ten thousand animals starved to death in Chattanooga.[120]

Union and Confederate soldiers alike hunkered down in east Tennessee's fall weather. The dry spell ended with a vengeance as autumn arrived "in one of her most savage moods." A southern newspaperman reported, "The picturesque has become puddlesome . . . and the saucy wind, sharp as Shylock's knife, searches to the very crannies of our bones." The cold, wet weather made hungry and exhausted men "melancholy, misanthropic, and miserable." One of Longstreet's staff officers, "about as uncomfortable as a man can be," wrote to his wife, "The rain is coming down in such torrents that it not only puts the fire out, but washes the wood away." He added, "I hear no news except that our corps, from its head down, wants to go back to Virginia." Rain meant mud—and misery for exhausted mule teams and men. The 72nd Indiana, driving horses to Nashville, "looked like a lot of men and horses that had been made of mud and were running away from the factory before dried and baked." As Major Benjamin Magee explained, "The only reason that we were not smothered in mud is that a deluge of rain would pour upon us now and then and wash it off."[121]

The 11th and 12th Corps secured the railroad from Nashville while Hooker's engineers rebuilt the railroad bridge at Bridgeport. On October 27, eighteen hundred Cumberlanders quietly boarded barges in Chattanooga. They launched a daring predawn amphibious assault and established a beachhead at Browns Ferry, then secured Raccoon Mountain, on the south (or east) bank of the Tennessee River, west of Chattanooga. The successful mission eliminated the Waldens Ridge obstacle and shortened General Thomas' supply route by one third; a

120. Edwin W. High, *History of the Sixty-eighth Regiment Indiana Volunteer Infantry, 1862–1865* (Metamora[?], Ind.: n.p., 1902), 122; J. S. Fullerton, "The Army of the Cumberland at Chattanooga," *Century* 34 (May 1887), 137.

121. "Personne" (Felix G. deFontaine), Charleston *Courier*, October 22, 1863, quoted in J. Cutler Andrews, *The South Reports the Civil War* (Princeton: Princeton University Press, 1970), 362; Blackford, *Memoirs*, 146–48; Magee, *72nd Indiana*, 211–12.

"cracker line" ran from Jasper across Moccasin Bend to Chattanooga.[122]

General Hooker marched the 11th and 12th Corps into Lookout Valley to link up with the Cumberlanders. The 73rd Ohio enthusiastically greeted them; "hereafter our fortune and destiny were to be linked with the great army of the West," one wrote. Hooker left General Geary's fifteen-hundred-man division in an exposed position at Wauhatchie, to the Cumberlanders' horror, as well as Geary's. His brigade commander, Major General George Sears Greene, ordered his men to sleep with their boots on, their loaded weapons beside them. In the early hours of October 29 Longstreet's men pounced on Geary's undefended rear in a sharp, if disorganized, night attack. Men fired at muzzle flashes in the blackness. While "the 2nd Division got rather severely used . . . they had not got them whiped." Knap's battery paid a heavy price. Both officers fell dead, including Geary's son, Edward, "cut down in the bud of his usefulness." Twenty of the 48 men in the battery were killed or wounded, and 37 of the battery's 48 horses died. Its 4 cannons fired 224 rounds; 2 remained in action at the end. John Gourlie overheard a Cumberland cavalryman say "that he never saw men fight like them . . . like tigers."[123] The Potomac men had passed the final exam.

The 11th and 12th Corps soldiers first helped to secure the Cumberlanders' line of communication, then to shorten it by almost half, then to relieve Chattanooga. In late November, General Sherman arrived with fifteen thousand men; George Thomas' biographer described Sherman's average six-mile days as "The slowest relief march in American history."[124] The combined armies won stunning victories

122. Peter Cozzens, *The Shipwreck of Their Hopes: The Battles for Chattanooga* (Urbana: University of Illinois Press, 1994), 59–61.

123. Hurst, *73rd Ohio,* 85–86; Boyle, *111th Pennsylvania,* 164; John Pugh Green, *The Movement of the 11th and 12th Corps from the Potomac to the Tennessee* (Philadelphia: Allen, Lane & Scott's, 1892), 13; William A. Blair, ed., *A Politician Goes to War: The Civil War Letters of John White Geary* (University Park: Pennsylvania State University Press, 1995), 131; John C. Gourlie, 123rd New York, letter to his brother, November 8, 1863, MHICB.

124. Garfield to Salmon Chase, September 30, 1863, *OR,* Ser. 1, 30, pt. 3:792; McKinney, *Education in Violence,* 278.

at Lookout Mountain and Missionary Ridge on November 24 and 25 and drove the Confederates headlong from Tennessee. They relieved Chattanooga and proved the wisdom of Stanton's vision that led to the 11th and 12th Corps movement.

General Grant believed that Bragg squandered his victory at Chickamauga on two counts. Had Bragg pursued Rosecrans vigorously, "It would have been a victory to have got [Rosecrans'] army away from Chattanooga safely." Holding the city and defeating Bragg gave the Union a "manifold greater" victory. Confederate General William W. Loring considered the loss of Chattanooga a mortal blow to the Confederacy. "As long as we held it," he declared, "it was the closed doorway to the interior of our country. When it came into your [Union] hands the door stood open, and however rough your progress in the interior might be, it still left you free to march inside."[125]

Victory alone, however, did not solve the problem of sustenance. In December, General Halleck sent Daniel McCallum to take charge of the army's western railroad operations. Army engineers rebuilt the Memphis & Charleston bridge over the Tennessee River at Bridgeport as McCallum's 285-man Military Railroad Construction Corps reconstructed 29 miles of M&C track to Chattanooga in three weeks. They reopened the section on January 14, 1864. In February his men began to rebuild almost the entire distressed N&C line from Nashville to Bridgeport. According to McCallum, "About 115 mile of track were relaid with new iron, cross-ties and ballast. . . . Sidings were put in at intervals to be not more than eight miles apart, each capable of holding from five to eight long freight trains, and telegraph stations were established at most of them. In all, nineteen miles of new sidings were added to this road and forty-five new water tanks erected."[126]

In the meantime, McCallum designed a circular route to increase

125. Sorrel, *Recollections,* 196; Grant in *Battles and Leaders of the Civil War* (New York: Century, 1884, 1888), 3:711; Loring interview in J. Cutler Andrews, *The North Reports the Civil War* (Pittsburgh: University of Pittsburgh Press, 1955), 462–63.

126. Albert Castel, *Decision in the West: The Atlanta Campaign of 1864* (Lawrence: University Press of Kansas, 1992), 16–18, 91–92; Turner, *Victory,* 323; McCallum report, *OR,* Ser. 3, 5:987.

line capacity and improve safety. Trains ran from Nashville to Chattanooga via Stevenson and Bridgeport. The return trains ran through
Bridgeport and Stevenson on the Memphis & Charleston to Decatur,
Alabama. Retreating Confederates had completely destroyed the Tennessee & Alabama, the final leg from Decatur to Nashville. The postwar builder of the Union Pacific Railroad, General Grenville N.
Dodge, marching with General Sherman, organized construction
crews. Equipped only with "axes, picks, and spades," Dodge's pioneers rebuilt 102 miles of the T&A, including 182 bridges, in 40 days.
Soon, four 10-car trains left Nashville for Chattanooga four times a
day, carrying sixteen hundred tons of supplies.[127] Although the soldiers
would not return to full rations until February 1864, the specter of
starvation ended.

McCallum had two other problems. First, he had only 39 locomotives and 400 freight cars running on 292 miles of track between Nashville, Chattanooga, Knoxville, and other Tennessee and Alabama
outposts. In Virginia, his USMRR had forty locomotives and eight
hundred cars to supply the Army of the Potomac over only seventy
miles of Orange & Alexandria Railroad tracks. McCallum also found
John B. Anderson, superintendent of Military Railroads in the Division
of the Mississippi, unable to "comprehend the magnitude" of the task
involved in supporting the armies, much less the mission that General
Sherman would shortly undertake to Atlanta. Grant gave the job to
McCallum, who promptly ordered two hundred locomotives and three
thousand cars.[128]

Northern foundries and mills responded. They delivered fifty-three
locomotives to McCallum between February and May 1864 "and kept
up the latter rate as long as he called for them." On March 23, 1864,

127. Weber, *Northern Railroads,* 188–89, 197. Dodge's achievement made a
great impression on Gen. Grant (Grant, *Memoirs,* 322–23). It also earned Dodge
a corps command.

128. Castel, *Decision,* 18. George Turner says that McCallum had seventy locomotives and six hundred freight cars (*Victory Rode the Rails,* 323). Maury Klein
finds proof of Anderson's suspected southern sympathies "strong but entirely cir-
cumstantial. The evidence of his inefficiency was convincing" (*Louisville & Nashville,* 40).

Stanton preempted locomotives under construction for other railroads and ordered them sent to McCallum. Twelve new locomotives arrived in Nashville in April, twenty-four more in both May and June, and twenty-six more in July. McCallum acquired a total of 140 new locomotives in 1864. He also added an average of 202 new cars each month. He borrowed 14 engines and 120 cars from the L&N and 2 locomotives and 60 cars from the Kentucky Central, evidence of Scott's foresight in converting the Louisville & Lexington Railroad to five-foot gauge. McCallum had his two hundred locomotives and three thousand cars by the end of 1864. In addition, USMRR maintenance shops in Nashville repaired one hundred locomotives and one thousand cars each month. General Grant gave McCallum permission to build a rolling mill in Chattanooga. His construction crews built it as time allowed, then rerolled rails for one-third the cost of new. The army literally remade Chattanooga, including creating a reservoir and building a bridge across the Tennessee River.[129]

General Sherman constantly monitored his supply requirements during the Atlanta campaign. Ever mindful of the vulnerability of his line of communication, he stuffed Chattanooga's warehouses with enough supplies to keep his army well stocked in spite of the diligent efforts of Confederate raiders. The USMRR seized the Western & Atlantic Railroad from the state of Georgia and operated the road in support of Sherman's armies. McCallum's men rebuilt eleven bridges and laid seventy-five miles of track during the Atlanta campaign. A month after Sherman's great victory at Atlanta, General John Hood's raiders destroyed 35.5 miles of track and 455 feet of bridges. McCallum's Construction Corps repaired the damage within thirteen days, beginning the work even as the bridges burned.[130]

Cumberlanders, Potomac men, and Sherman's soldiers became part of what today's soldiers call an army group, commanded by General

129. Carl R. Fish, "The Northern Railroads, 1861," *American Historical Review* 22 (1917): 789–90; Weber, *Northern Railroads*, 194–95; McCallum report, May 26, 1866, *OR*, Ser. 3, 5:996–98.

130. Castel, *Decision*, 91–92; McCallum report, May 26, 1866, *OR*, Ser. 3, 5:988; Weigley, *Meigs*, 291.

Sherman. In May 1864 the Armies of the Cumberland, the Ohio, and the Tennessee set out to destroy the Confederacy. Capturing Atlanta in September, they cut the Confederacy in two for a second time and deprived it of a major manufacturing city and rail center. Sherman's March to the Sea in November helped to break the Confederacy's will to fight. Sherman's ranks as one of the finest fighting armies in the history of warfare. General Joseph Johnston considered Sherman's the greatest army since the legions of Julius Caesar.[131]

131. McPherson, *Battle Cry of Freedom,* 828, quoting Jacob D. Cox, *Military Reminiscences of the Civil War* (New York, 1900), 2:531–32.

6

The Failure of Confederate War Management

‡+++‡

> All our sacrifices of life and all our successes lead to no decisive
> result. . . . Is this owing to our inferior numbers, or to want of
> solidarity in the commands, or, finally, to want of genius in our
> commanders?
>
> —Josiah Gorgas

Generations of myth, romance, and historical perspective have left
many Americans with the impression that Union victory in the Civil
War was inevitable. Historians cite the Union's vastly greater industrial
resources and population four times larger than the southern whites',
the Union navy's strangling blockade, a flawed Confederate military
strategy, and to some critics, the allegedly limited strategic vision of
General Robert E. Lee. This sense of inevitability, however, escaped
the people who lived through the experience.

On August 23, 1864, a weary and discouraged Abraham Lincoln
took stock of the war. General Grant, in spite of a summer of constant
fighting with horrifying casualties, had neither defeated Lee nor captured Richmond. General Sherman maneuvered outside Atlanta, unable to get a bear hug on General John Hood's army. The president
reflected, then wrote a personal memo, sealed it in an envelope, and
had his cabinet members sign their names across the seal. The memo

read: "This morning, as for some days past, it seems exceedingly probable that this Administration will not be re-elected. Then it will be my duty to so co-operate with the President-elect as to save the Union between the election and the inauguration; as he will have secured his election on such ground that he cannot possibly save it afterward."[1]

Abraham Lincoln had possibly the surest feel for the American political pulse of any president in the history of the Republic. His despair calls into question the Civil War's "inevitable" outcome.

Eight days after Lincoln wrote the memo, Sherman took Atlanta and broke the Confederacy's back. The victory assured Lincoln's re-election, with the rebellion crushed, its slave-based society destroyed, and the Union preserved. America would face the future as one nation indivisible, although thousands more Americans would have to die before the fighting stopped. Had Confederate arms denied Sherman his prize for another ten weeks, Lincoln's memo might have proved prescient.

Some historians claim that the Confederacy's smaller population, limited manufacturing and railroad assets, lack of a navy, and modest financial resources condemned the Cause to defeat from the start. James A. Huston states that "ultimate victory has generally gone to the side having the greater economic strength and thus the greater logistical potential." Richard N. Current argues, "It is hard to believe, and impossible to prove, that the Southerners did a worse job with economic affairs than Northerners would have done in the same circumstances." He believes that, because of the Union's significantly greater economic resources, Confederate managers "would have had to be *several times* as able, man for man, as those of the North" (emphasis added). He concludes that northern industry only had to perform as efficiently as southern for the Union to win the war.[2]

One respectfully disagrees. Rebellions by definition fight from positions of weakness—those in power have no need to rebel. Successful

1. Basler, *Collected Works of Abraham Lincoln*, 7:514.
2. Huston, *Sinews of War*, 159; Richard N. Current, "God and the Strongest Battalions," in Donald, *Why the North Won the Civil War*, 15.

rebels, as George Washington, Mao Tse-tung, and Ho Chi Minh at-test, find ways to compensate for their limitations and capitalize on their strengths while neutralizing the enemy's strengths and exploiting its weaknesses. Many rebel causes, such as the colonial Americans, Chinese Communists, and Vietnamese, to be sure, received valuable aid from sponsor governments hostile to their adversaries, while the Confederacy did not. British merchants, however, sold a war-sustaining volume of supplies on credit to the Confederacy, which blockade runners delivered through the aquatic equivalent of the Ho Chi Minh Trail. This suggests that capitalist greed exerts as powerful an appeal as liberty or socialism.

For all its limitations, the Confederacy enjoyed some significant advantages that directly influenced logistical considerations. First, it was huge. The states east of the Mississippi River embraced a land area almost as large as France, Germany, and the Low Countries combined. In addition, the armies fought in Texas, Louisiana, and Arkansas. The Union also maintained what amounted to an army of occupation in Missouri during an ugly mini–civil war. Many southerners believed that the Confederacy's size conferred a significant advantage. Secretary of State George W. Randolph wrote to his wife, Molly, "They may overrun our frontier States and plunder our coast but, as for conquering us, the thing is an impossibility. There is no instance in history of a people as numerous as we inhabiting a country so extensive as ours being subjugated if true to themselves."[3]

Some historians believe that the huge southern land mass, coupled with the advantage of interior lines, should have made the Confederacy invulnerable to military conquest. One group of prominent historians cite a study by Carl von Clausewitz that estimated that an enemy would need a 600,000-man army to conquer just one third of France. The Confederacy should have won the Civil War, they argue, because the Union should not have been able to conquer a territory more than

3. George W. Randolph to Molly Randolph, October 10, 1861, Molly Randolph Edgehill-Randolph Papers, University of Virginia Library, Charlottesville, cited in Hattaway and Jones, *How the North Won*, 18.

five times larger than the France of Clausewitz's example.[4] Clausewitz, however, died in 1831 and may never have heard of railroads, much less had the opportunity to theorize about their potential in war a generation later.

Union invaders snatched the fruits of critical food-producing areas from Confederate stomachs, to be sure, but paid a terrible price. Many southerners believed that the Confederacy could not—and did not need to—defend every part of its territory. Glenn Tucker argues that the cost to the Union of its gains in Mississippi and Tennessee demonstrated the impossibility of total conquest. Even after the Yankees relieved the Cumberlanders in Chattanooga and secured the city for good, "The Southerners clearly did not consider the odds against a stand-off war hopeless."[5]

Second, the Confederacy also enjoyed a strategic advantage in its war aims. The Lincoln administration struggled with the political reality that the Union had to physically subjugate most of the Confederacy, in a multifront war of unprecedented scale, in order to suppress the rebellion. The Confederacy almost certainly could not have defeated the Union militarily, in the conventional meaning of victory. But it did not have to win, it only had to avoid losing. It might well have won simply by resisting until it exhausted the Union's will to persist.[6]

4. G. F. R. Henderson argues the size advantage in *Stonewall Jackson and the American Civil War* (London: Longmans, Green, 1898), 130–35; Beringer et al. conclude that the Confederacy lost the Civil War due to a lack of will in *Elements of Confederate Defeat*, 12–13. The argument labors beside the fact that one in five southern white males of military age died in the conflict.

5. Hattaway and Jones, *How the North Won*, 488; Tucker, *Chickamauga*, 90. Charles H. Wesley in *Collapse of the Confederacy* (Washington, D.C.: Associated, 1937), 170, and Paul Gates in *Agriculture*, 111, cite the loss of territory in limiting the Confederacy's food-producing capacity. Thomas Connelly makes a strong argument to this effect in *Army of the Heartland*.

6. James M. McPherson summarizes the different arguments in his essay, "American Victory, American Defeat," in *Why the Confederacy Lost*, ed. Gabor S. Boritt (New York: Oxford University Press, 1992), 17–42. The five essays in the collection conclude that military success led to victory; putting it another way, Gen. George E. Pickett observed, "I've always thought the Yankees had something

As the weaker contestant, the Confederacy had to carefully organize and shrewdly allocate its limited resources. It did not do so. Southern disdain for commerce and manufacturing ("they suit not the genius of our people, our institutions or our government," one newspaper wrote)[7] produced too few men with the vision, experience, and skill necessary to address and solve the war's complex problems. A business school truism says that good decisions come from experience and experience comes from bad decisions. More significant than their lack of preparedness for the war they found themselves fighting, the Confederate leaders did not learn from their mistakes. They do not in fact appear to have recognized, much less understood, the problems that handicapped their war effort in the first place. Managerial incompetence thus emerges as a more important factor than perhaps previously allowed in understanding why the Confederacy lost a war that it might have won.

An earlier generation of historians believed that the Confederacy's philosophy of weak central government and strong states' rights explains its failure to organize its war-making resources efficiently. Current historical thinking has moved beyond the states' rights argument, which, in any event, does not explain Confederate mismanagement. Emory M. Thomas sees differences between the thrust for secession and the evolution of the Confederate government. The southern states supposedly seceded to preserve the slave-based culture's beloved traditions. The Civil War, however, "revolutionized that way of life." Thomas says that the Davis government bore a "striking resemblance" to the federal system that secessionists had supposedly spurned.[8]

George Edgar Turner believes that mistaken ideas, selfish interests,

---

to do with it" (19). See also Williamson Murray, "What Took the North So Long?" in *America at War: An Anthology of Articles from MHQ: The Quarterly Journal of Military History,* ed. Calvin L. Christman (Newport: Naval Institute Press, 1995), 87–96.

7. Augusta *Chronicle and Sentinel,* May 12, 1861, cited in DeCredico, *Patriotism for Profit,* 52.

8. Current, "God and the Strongest Battalions," in Donald, *Why the North Won,* 15; Vandiver, *Rebel Brass,* 6; Black, *Railroads of the Confederacy,* 63; Thomas, *Revolutionary Experience,* 56–59.

and succumbing to local politics and favoritism show how "faintly the [Confederate] government understood the ventures on which it had embarked." Charles H. Wesley attributes the failure of Confederate war management to a lack of "industrially minded leadership." Frank Vandiver calls its railroad policy "demoralized." He points out that war is about command and command about planning. He argues that the Confederate leadership never understood the nature of command, that it could delegate, but not abdicate, authority. He concludes that Confederate leaders never understood the totality of modern war's demands.[9]

John Stover attributes the Confederacy's defeat, in part, to its failure to provide "effective supervision over its inferior railroad system." He adds, however, "In the North, where the basic vitality of the railway network made strong regulation less necessary, Lincoln's government was more willing to act," underestimating the importance of strong regulation that helped ensure good rail service. Allen Trelease notes that, for all the contingencies that it could not control, the Confederate government had the opportunity to organize the southern railroads into a more coherent system. It did not, and because it did not, "few things within its power handicapped the Confederacy's war effort more seriously." Thomas G. Ziek Jr. argues that the Confederacy had lost the advantage of interior lines by 1863. As a result of poor management, southern railroads steadily declined for want of maintenance and replacement equipment. Soldiers and civilians alike went hungry at times while food rotted elsewhere for lack of transportation. Deterioration led inexorably to collapse; Confederate armies gradually became immobilized in a war of mobility.[10]

General Winfield Scott's winning Union strategy, the Anaconda Plan, itself dependent on excellent logistics support, recognized that the Confederacy could not withstand constant pressure simultaneously

9. Turner, *Victory Rode the Rails,* 234–35; Wesley, *Collapse of the Confederacy,* 46; Vandiver, *Rebel Brass,* 20–21.

10. Stover, *American Railroads,* 57; Trelease, *North Carolina Railroad,* 179; Ziek, "Effects of Southern Railroads."

exerted on several fronts. President Lincoln, however, spent three long, bloody years before Generals Grant and Sherman emerged as commanders who both understood the strategy and knew how to execute it. The Union's prolonged inability to execute the Anaconda strategy gave the rebellion a large gift of time and figured prominently in the Confederacy's ability to conduct the Longstreet movement. But once Grant and Sherman made contact with Lee and Johnston in May 1864, they never let go. They kept up a grinding pressure that made it impossible for the Confederacy to consider shifting troops between theaters. They made certain that their enemy would attempt no more Longstreet-type movements. Scott's Anaconda strategy then proved itself.

The underdog must fight a clever war. Its sheer bulk, the potential advantage of interior lines, political aims, and Yankee strategic ineptitude, however, certainly provided substantial equalizers and, possibly, the edge, if the Confederacy had intelligently exploited these assets. Victory therefore did not depend on leadership "several times as able, man for man" as the Union's, even if such genius ever existed. Competent planning and management could have overcome many of the Confederacy's handicaps, perhaps enough to achieve the final victory.

The Confederate leadership, however, neither planned nor efficiently managed the war effort. Rather, it squandered its natural advantages of sheer mass and interior lines by failing to organize its railroads to fight a war of mobility along interior lines. Its assets became liabilities as declining mobility turned the Confederacy's territory into a quagmire. The heroic efforts necessary to conduct the Longstreet movement do not obscure the cumulative effect of bad decisions.

A government justifies its existence by delivering efficient services. It achieves efficiency through planning. Richard D. Goff says Confederate inefficiency resulted directly from its leaders' failure to use central planning as a management tool. He adds that the absence of planning precludes one from defining the Confederacy as a central government. Concluding that the "accidental accumulation" of some attributes of a central government means nothing without planning, Goff dismisses the Davis government as "planless, uncoordinated, tardy, and impotent."[11]

Good managers analyze problems, even though they are sometimes handicapped by incomplete or inaccurate information and hindered by externally imposed time constraints. They use their experience and skill, regardless of obstacles, to make decisions that solve those problems. Planning enables well-managed organizations to anticipate many problems and opportunities. It reduces the frequency of having to make hasty decisions under pressure. War is chaos gone mad and hidden in fog. By failing to organize its war effort through formal central planning, so critical to a coherent railroad policy, the Confederacy denied itself any measure of control over the challenges it faced.

Its leaders had never fought a war increasingly driven by logistics, but that was the war they found themselves fighting. One cannot fault them for their failure to anticipate the unknown. One can criticize them for their failure to respond to the new environment. Indecision at the higher levels of the Confederate government suggests leaders who did not know what to do. The Confederate leadership remained curiously blind in its failure to recognize obvious problems or to learn from its mistakes. Well-educated and financially successful men filled the Davis cabinet. Although few had business backgrounds, many had practiced law. Lawyers tend to learn a lot about business by addressing their business clients' legal problems. Many cabinet members had served in the Congress, which considers such economic issues as tariffs and trade, internal improvements, and military procurement. Congress, however, does not deal with the types of operational problems that businesses face, such as the sometimes mundane but necessary steps that a product takes between manufacturer and consumer. Maury Klein makes a perceptive observation about the managerial mind-set of the original Confederate cabinet. In its blind pursuit of its goal to represent all seceding states in its cabinet, the Confederate government ignored candidates' practical qualifications for their jobs. It appointed only one man with any experience in his area of responsibility: Secre-

11. Richard D. Goff, *Confederate Supply* (Durham: Duke University Press, 1969), 229, 243.

tary of the Navy Stephen Mallory, a Floridian, once chaired the U.S. Senate's Naval Affairs Committee.[12]

All the Davis cabinet members owned slaves. They may have shared the negative perception of commerce and industry embraced by many planters, the southern political elite. If so, these attitudes suggest possible clues to the basis of the Confederacy's wretched management performance. Many believed that a grasping North wanted to keep the South in the Union only so that it could continue to gorge itself on the South's treasure. Some worked up figures to prove that secession would save the southern states $47 million, or $105 million, or $231 million.[13]

Stuart Bruchey argues that a society that defined itself by, and celebrated its dependence on, the forced labor of others would naturally tend to belittle the notion of an inherent value to labor. He further notes that many planters had completely removed themselves from the market process by selling their raw cotton to factors who arranged insurance, shipping, and sale—more reason to disdain commerce. As a result, Bruchey finds the "resource of entrepreneurship" a seriously "underemployed" attribute among southerners.[14]

Fred Bateman and Thomas Weiss also find stunted entrepreneurship in the antebellum South. They examine the general failure of southerners to invest in industrial development in spite of, they argue, more attractive potential returns than found in cotton planting. Investing in regional manufacturing businesses also would have provided diversification from the vagaries of the cotton market. Only 6 percent of planters who held twenty or more slaves (a sign to Bateman and Weiss of wealth, thus investment capital) actually made such investments. They conclude that "southern investors were exceptionally averse to risk, were not knowledgeable about the benefits of diversification, failed to

12. Maury Klein, *Days of Defiance: Sumter, Secession, and the Coming of the Civil War* (New York: Alfred A. Knopf, 1997), 293.

13. Patrick, *Davis and his Cabinet*, 8. The purported savings included $5 million in salaries paid to northerners teaching in the South, according to the Richmond *Examiner*.

14. Stuart Bruchey, *The Roots of American Economic Growth, 1607–1861: An Essay in Social Causation* (New York: Harper & Row, 1965), 40.

alter their expectations in the light of accumulating evidence on the greater profitability of manufacturing, or attached unagreeably high social costs to industrial diversification."[15]

Bruchey also finds it significant that many southerners seemed proudly indifferent to the value of education. In 1840, Bruchey notes, 5.72 percent of southerners attended school, compared with 18.41 percent of northerners, figures admittedly skewed by the slave population. The southern states had half the North's population but one third as many schools, one fourth as many pupils, one twentieth as many libraries, and one sixth as many books in them. He sees a gap created by the North's "investment in human capital" that widened with improved transportation and finds that education in the North nurtured an "intense work psychology" driven by the "cult" of the self-made man. Bateman and Weiss see only "a difference in degree" between northerners' and southerners' attitudes toward risk taking and entrepreneurship. They acknowledge, however, that southern industrialization fell further behind after the Civil War, suggesting that "the roots of retardation" possibly existed before the war.[16]

Education elevates the imagination. It enhances one's ability to see patterns and possibilities. Addressing a range of different problems in any calling generally makes one a more confident decision maker, i.e. a risk taker. The British recognized education's contribution to what they called "the American system of manufacture," especially "The skill of hand that comes of experience . . . rapidly following the perceptive power so keenly awakened by early industrial training." They attributed to education Americans' broad base of entrepreneurial endeavor and their ability to exploit a wide range of areas, which also showed in the quality of labor and risk-taking talent.[17]

---

15. Fred Bateman and Thomas Weiss, *A Deplorable Scarcity: The Failure of Industrialization in the Slave Economy* (Chapel Hill: University of North Carolina Press, 1981), 123, 161.

16. Bruchey, *Roots,* 192, 195, 197; Bateman and Weiss, *Deplorable Scarcity,* 163, 23.

17. North, *Economic Growth,* 174, citing Joseph Whitworth and George Wallis, *The Industry of the United States in Machinery, Manufactures, and Useful and Ornamental Arts* (London: George Routledge, 1854), ix.

Planters, however, enjoyed a great comparative advantage in cotton production. Cotton made money, a lot of it. Even better, it conveyed prestige and high status to the planter, so southerners, as rational beings, understandably concentrated on planting cotton. Many felt no compulsion whatever to change direction. They gave lip service to the need to diversify but the smart money went with cotton. Kenneth M. Stampp notes that the Panic of 1857 touched the agricultural South but lightly, proof to planters that cotton provided "a more stable foundation than the commercial economy of the North."[18] It may have—in peace time.

If they shied from investing in manufacturing, southern planters demonstrated sound managerial instincts and a bias toward risk taking in the business of growing cotton. And in fact, James Oakes notes, unstable cotton prices and the high cost of acquiring slaves exposed planters to significant risks. But better plows, seed, and organization significantly improved productivity, according to Paul Gates. A slave worked an average of five acres and picked sixty pounds of cotton a day in 1810; by 1850 the average slave worked ten acres and picked one hundred pounds per day. During the same period, yields improved from between 800 and 1,000 ginned pounds per hand to between 2,000 and 2,500.[19]

Southerners, then, demonstrated entrepreneurial initiative in those enterprises that they valued. Unfortunately for the Confederacy, they spurned those endeavors that would have taught them the variety of talents most needed to fight a war of logistics. Excellence in managing cotton plantations does not seem to have given them adequate transferable skills for war management. In any event, the southern economy produced too few people with management experience adequate for the trials the Confederacy faced. The mismanagement of southern railroads offers a prime example.

A few exceptional managers served the Confederacy. Ordnance

18. Kenneth M. Stamp, *America in 1857: A Nation on the Brink* (New York: Oxford University Press, 1990), 187, 230.

19. James Oakes, *The Ruling Race A History of American Slaveholders* (New York: Vintage, 1983), 123–26; Gates, *Agriculture,* 14.

Chief Josiah Gorgas, a Pennsylvanian and ordnance officer, graduated from West Point in 1841. Married to the daughter of a former Alabama governor, he worked miracles in turning "ploughshares into swords." Today's soldiers would admiringly call him a "scrounger," a man who makes things happen and gets things done. His ammunition factories made three million lead Minié musket balls per month in 1862 and 1863 in spite of a severe lead shortage. Window weights from Charleston homes provided one third of the metal; most of the rest came from unused water mains that Gorgas' officers found in Mobile. The Confederacy lost its only source of copper, critical for making cartridges and bronze cannons, when the Yankees captured Chattanooga and east Tennessee. Gorgas' agents made up for the loss by purchasing 130,000 pounds of copper whiskey and turpentine stills.[20]

Gorgas performed an invaluable role as ordnance chief, but his managerial talent could have performed a still greater service. The Confederacy would have served its interests better by putting Gorgas in charge of all areas of logistics, from raw materials procurement to food, clothing, and weapons production. His broad duties should have included logistics' distribution function, from the blockade running program to railroads. A well-planned and coordinated logistics program, the absence of which so hindered the war effort, may have represented the one area that could have bought the Confederacy the time necessary to win the war. No one apparently thought of promoting Gorgas, however, so his government limited his considerable talent to arms production.

Joseph Anderson, the Tredegar Iron Works' managing partner, also showed the potential ability to adapt to the war's new requirements. Intelligent, resourceful, and popular, he enjoyed extensive business contacts throughout the southern states. He bartered with railroads during the war to carry his cotton and other freight; they traded their scrap iron for his finished products. Tredegar sold the Virginia Central several locomotive wheels in 1864, although Charles Dew says that Tredegar did not have enough iron to make the program practical by that stage of the war. A man with Anderson's intellect would have un-

20. Vandiver, *Ploughshares*, 199, 201, 222.

derstood the need for, and benefits of, central planning. He could have organized a program to coordinate and improve iron procurement, and allocate it for maximum iron production. He also enjoyed the stature among southern businessmen and railroad leaders to carry it out successfully. Instead, a lack of iron limited Tredegar (and presumably others) to operating at one-third capacity throughout the war. His near death in combat while leading the Tredegar Battalion may be the ultimate example of the Confederacy's misuse of human resources.[21]

New Hampshire–born William M. Wadley, arguably "the ablest railroad man" in the Confederacy, could have become the strong overseer to coordinate southern railroads for the Cause. A blacksmith by training, Wadley had lived in the South since 1834, oversaw early railroad construction, and rose through the ranks to superintendent of the Central of Georgia Railroad by the time of the war, to become its president after the war. The Davis administration appointed the abrasive Wadley to create a "quasi-independent" Railroad Bureau in December 1862. It gave him the rank of colonel but authority over neither the army nor the railroads, which resisted all attempts to control them. Powerless, Wadley resigned after only seven months, when the Confederate Senate succumbed to railroad managers' complaints and declined to confirm him.[22]

Frederick W. Sims, "endowed with a happy ability to endure frustration," replaced Wadley and served until the end of the war. The Confederate Congress finally gave Sims the power to control the railroads on March 9, 1865, too late to make any difference. Robert Black dismisses Sims as "accomplish[ing] nothing of lasting consequence,"[23] overlooking his very capable performance in organizing and conducting the Longstreet movement. Wadley and Sims could have organized the integrated rail system that Confederate arms needed, but the government ignored them, while at the same time ignoring, in the condi-

21. Dew, *Ironmaker*, 271, 288; Black, *Railroads of the Confederacy*, 215.

22. Black, *Railroads of the Confederacy*, 121–22, 292.

23. DeCredico, *Patriotism for Profit*, 75; Black, *Railroads of the Confederacy*, 292; Black, "War on Rails," in Davis and Wiley, *Photographic History of the Civil War*, 855–57.

tion of its railroads, a problem that it absolutely had to solve if it
expected to win the war.

The much-maligned Lucius Northrop suffered the outrageous fortune of responsibility for the flawed commissary-subsistence system.
Others unfairly attributed mistakes and errors to him, including matters clearly beyond his control. Northrop recognized early in the war
that "the two matters of subsistence and transport are ultimately inter-
twined" in railroads. He also understood that distance from collection
points and transportation limited the application of the flawed tithe-
in-kind, the tax on food. The success of Confederate subsistence and,
unfortunately for him, his reputation depended on efficient railroads.[24]

These four men possessed solid managerial talents that the Confederacy could have put to better use but did not. All four, interestingly,
understood the role of railroads better than anyone in Richmond.

Jefferson Davis demonstrated his readiness to take strong measures
for the Cause. The conscription of men and impressment of food immediately come to mind. Paul D. Escott argues convincingly that
Davis believed in an important role for federalism in a states' rights
Confederacy. He says that Davis vigorously used his presidential powers to create a central government strong enough to fight the war. He
asked for extensive war powers, and the Confederate Congress gave
them to him. He had to exercise those powers forcefully for the Confederacy to win, however, and he did not.[25]

Why did Davis hesitate to use the power he had to force the railroads to cooperate? Paul Escott suggests that Davis, like Abraham Lincoln, believed that railroad men could run the railroads better than
government personnel. Fearing a reaction to the strong centralizing
measures his government had already taken, Escott adds that Davis
may have hoped that the states would secure the railroads' cooperation. Frank Vandiver agrees that Davis may have thought that he had
pressed the railroads—and states' rights—as far as he could.[26]

24. J. Moore, *Confederate Commissary General*, xii, 203. This very credible
work rebuts many popular criticisms of a man in a job that probably no one could
have performed successfully under the circumstances.

25. Escott, *After Secession*, 54–55.

26. Vandiver, conversation with the author, April 4, 1996; Escott, conversation with the author, April 12, 1996.

One struggles with these answers; war is not a time for shyness. One seeks in vain for evidence that southern railroad executives defied either Jefferson Davis or his subordinates who laid down the law. One hears whining and complaints and objections. One sees railroad officers expressing contempt for Confederate authority. One does not find outright refusal to obey a law imposed and backed by the full authority and police power of the Confederate government. The Lincoln administration secured northern railroads' cooperation with carrot and stick. The Jefferson Davis government never made a serious try with either. The great philosopher and bank robber Willie Sutton once observed that one gets farther with a kind word and a gun than with a kind word alone. Davis had all the guns he needed to enforce the cooperation of southern railroads. He never used them.

William C. Davis finds the seeds of defeat in the personality of Jefferson Davis himself. A fascinating individual in a period filled with them, the Confederate president was a West Pointer, Mexican War hero, secretary of war in the Franklin Pierce administration, and United States Senator from Mississippi. Possessed, however, of a rigid personality, he was an abysmal judge of character and had miserable administrative skills. A perfectionist, he had a distressing tendency to bury himself in minutiae. His procrastination seemed to correlate directly with the seriousness of the problem. Calling him a "demonstrably" poor manager, historian Davis attributes President Davis' indecisiveness to profound insecurity and concludes, "Taking into consideration his manifest disabilities for the job, . . . Davis emerges as more successful than could have been expected in the administrative aspects of his presidency." The president's personality may have rendered him incapable of bringing himself to demand the railroads' cooperation. George Edgar Turner says that railroad men warned Davis about the roads' decline on several occasions. Davis' "senseless resentment of advice," however, caused him to turn a deaf ear to their concerns. Indecision is a fatal weakness in a manager, especially one at war. Jefferson Davis' image would no doubt shine brilliantly today had the Confederacy won the war. Unfortunately for him, it sank on his watch.[27]

27. *Jefferson Davis: The Man and His Hour* (New York: Harper Collins, 1991), 390–92, 689–96; Turner, *Victory Rode the Rails*, 313.

When the war expected to be short and glorious turned out otherwise, the federal government expertly marshaled its industrial resources, including the cooperation of its railroads. Excellent war management ensured adequate logistical support to the Union armies. Railroads made an important contribution to victory. The Confederacy, nonetheless, could have prevailed by exhausting the Union's will to keep fighting. His memo shows that Lincoln believed that the Union had reached that point.

The Confederate government, however, never positioned itself to successfully prosecute a war so heavily influenced by logistics. It never understood the nature of the war it found itself fighting. To take maximum advantage of its strengths and minimize its limitations as the weaker combatant, it had to plan and organize its war effort carefully and manage it effectively. But it did not plan. It did not organize. It did not manage. As a result, it neither capitalized on its strengths nor overcame its weaknesses. It did not use its railroads to exploit the advantage of interior lines. It wasted resources and made poor use of the potential opportunity in blockade running. It squandered its best opportunities for victory.

The Union learned how to exploit its ability to rapidly reposition large numbers of soldiers. In late January 1865, the army shipped General John M. Schofield's eleven-thousand-man Army of the Ohio from Tennessee to Washington in eleven days. It then loaded them onto ships and inserted them at Morehead City, North Carolina, to link up with General Sherman's army in the war's closing days. The Confederacy could not react to the Union's speed of movement at that point, even if it had had the manpower.[28]

Analyzing the Longstreet movement strips away part of the romantic fiction of the Lost Cause. When compared with the 11th and 12th Corps movement, it starkly reveals the great difference in the quality of Union and Confederate war management. Longstreet's five brigades and his battlefield leadership made an invaluable contribution to the tactical victory at Chickamauga, but Bragg may have squandered the opportunity to achieve a stunning strategic victory by pursuing and de-

---

28. Weber, *Northern Railroads,* 212–14, citing *OR,* Ser. 1, 47:216–83.

stroying Rosecrans. Had Bragg pursued Rosecrans and driven him across the Tennessee River toward Nashville, with or without Longstreet's absent three brigades, he might have changed the outcome of the war. Longstreet urged Bragg to advance, to "move instantly against Rosecrans's rear to destroy him," adding, "Should we fail, we can put him in retreat, and then clear East Tennessee of Burnside and the Union forces."[29] If General Sherman had had to fight his way back across the river and retake Chattanooga before invading Georgia, one questions whether he could have captured Atlanta—the event that reversed Abraham Lincoln's political fortune and saved the Union—before the federal elections of 1864.

In this light, the Confederacy's inability to get all of Longstreet's troops to Chickamauga in time, a direct result of its failure to organize the southern railroads for war, and also allowing them to deteriorate, may loom larger than generally acknowledged. In contrast, the 11th and 12th Corps movement shows the genius of Secretary Stanton's determination to reinforce the Army of the Cumberland by rail, and its successful completion had a profound impact on the war's outcome.

Rock Benning's brigade reached Atlanta in four days, on September 12. Those at the end of the movement took eleven to twelve days. In spite of Jefferson Davis' glacial decision-making process, the entire Longstreet complement almost certainly could have reached the Chickamauga battlefield in time to fight had the Confederacy efficiently organized its railroads. The available rolling stock of each mainroute railroad controlled the rate of troop flow. Getting the railroads "organized" need have involved little more than the simple step of joining the same-gauge tracks of different railroads. This would have

29. Historians disagree whether Bragg's troops had the strength to conduct an aggressive pursuit. Thomas Connelly says it would have been impossible because of supply constraints (*Autumn of Glory*, 232). Peter Cozzens believes that Bragg wasted an opportunity on September 21 but says that he still had a good chance even after Grant arrived in Chattanooga (*This Terrible Sound*, 390). Cozzens also notes that Gen. Nathan Bedford Forrest urged a vigorous pursuit of the defeated Yankees, the cavalry genius adding brightly that Bragg could solve his supply problems with the Yankees' stores in Chattanooga (519–20).

permitted neighboring railroads to lend their rolling stock to the main roads in order to increase their troop-carrying capacity.

The inability of the main roads' neighbors to lend them locomotives and cars caused major delays that might otherwise have been avoided. Private Robert Moore's 17th Mississippi, for example, spent more than two days in stations simply waiting for trains to carry them forward to Chickamauga; it took the regiment 43 hours to travel one 208-mile stretch.[30] In contrast, though the Baltimore & Ohio did not own nearly enough rolling stock to handle the 11th and 12th Corps movement, John Garrett and Prescott Smith made up the shortfall by borrowing from the same-gauge—and connected—Philadelphia, Wilmington & Baltimore; Northern Central; and U.S. Military railroads.

The relief of the Cumberlanders at Chattanooga demonstrates the superb management practiced by northern railroads in the 1860s. Daniel McCallum, John Garrett, Tom Scott, and Prescott Smith planned the entire operation with no more lead time than it took for the troops to reach the railheads. They moved twenty-three thousand infantrymen thirteen hundred miles in ten and one-half days and all of their artillery in four more days and shipped the balance of the two corps' equipment and transportation in another eight days, twenty-three days in all. Tom Scott managed the movement through the final three hundred miles of unfriendly territory on disintegrating southern railroads. The total elapsed time included shutting down an operation that the railroad men thought they had completed, then had to restart because the army misjudged the availability of wagons and animals in Tennessee.

An impressive logistical accomplishment, the 11th and 12th Corps railroad movement to Chattanooga demonstrated management skill and technical expertise that would soon elevate America to world economic supremacy. Even after almost eight years of study, this writer is struck with admiration for the seeming ease with which Garrett, McCallum, Scott, and Smith made it happen, on the fly, with no time for preparation, and without a hitch, glitch, or error. Their experience and competence showed in the confidence and speed with which they made decisions and responded to problems. Competition had honed

30. R. Moore, *Diaries,* 164–66.

their skills. They showed how outstanding managers influence outcomes.

Because they and their associates' management skill enabled the 11th and 12th Corps movement to flow smoothly and efficiently, some historians dismiss the accomplishment as a competent administrative effort, to be sure, but otherwise unremarkable because the Union had the means. Bruce Catton accepts the Union-as-hewers-of-wood-and-drawers-of-water stereotype: "In a way [the 11th and 12th corps movement] was less remarkable than the Confederate transfer of Longstreet's men, because the Confederacy had so much less to work with." Catton then adds, "but as a demonstration of the power of the North it was most impressive; it showed a smoothly running machine, directed by able technicians, delivering what was needed promptly and without lost motion."[31] Catton backhandedly acknowledges the importance of expert management and, in so doing, puts his finger on an important reason the Union won, and the Confederacy lost, the Civil War.

James Huston observes that the Confederacy did not have a Lincoln or a Stanton to demand the creation of an integrated southern railroad system. It had no Haupts or McCallums to assure coordinated army-railroad operations. It had no John Garretts or Tom Scotts or Prescott Smiths to arrange a Longstreet movement as skillfully as an 11th and 12th Corps movement.[32] Perhaps it did not, but it did not develop them, either. It did not make the attempt.

The Longstreet movement reveals a seriously deteriorated railroad system that Alexander Lawton and Frederick Sims patched together to make the operation possible. It means, according to Thomas Ziek, that the Confederacy could act but not react. In comparison with the 11th and 12th Corps movement, the Confederacy sent half the number of troops with no equipment or transportation, and limited artillery, three-quarters of the distance, all in friendly territory, in approximately the same length of time. Only half arrived in time to address the threat their government sent them to meet.[33]

31. Catton, *Never Call Retreat,* 256.
32. Huston, *Sinews of War,* 210–11.
33. Ziek, "Effects of Southern Railroads."

The high level of cooperation that the federal government achieved with northern railroad managers contrasts sharply with systemic southern railroad problems highlighted in the Longstreet movement. Brigadier General Henry A. Wise, the former Virginia governor, found the supervision of the trains so deficient as to raise the question, who was in charge, the government or the railroads?[34] The answer was no one. That Wise asked the question speaks to the Confederacy's flawed management of its basic war resources.

Still-developing southern railroads ran over shorter routes and carried less traffic at higher cost. Perhaps their executives had less experience than northern managers, but they had also insulated themselves from the rigors of the marketplace. This left them unable, in Mary DeCredico's opinion, "to respond creatively to the challenge of wartime mobilization."[35] While her assessment is credible, it is also astounding when one considers that it describes a people supposedly fighting a desperate war for independence.

War management, as seen in the railroads, made positive, but relative, contributions to victory and defeat. The Confederacy's bid for independence might have been successful had it used its railroads effectively; it almost won even with incompetent management. The Union could not have won the war without excellent use of its railroads; it almost lost in spite of it. In the end, Confederate mismanagement of its railroads and other resources hobbled its drive for independence. The Union's skillful use of railroads, combined with overall excellence in logistics, helped it suppress the rebellion. The Confederate government failed to manage the war well enough to buy the time needed to frustrate the Union, to exhaust its will to keep on. As it happened, it fell short by perhaps only ten weeks.

The Confederates, under the superb leadership of Robert E. Lee and others, fought with a ferocity and tenacious courage that inspire Americans to this day. The fighting spirit and stubborn determination of a brave and proud people proved extremely resistant to defeat. Even

34. Wise to Samuel Cooper, September 16, 1863, John D. Whitford Papers, Raleigh, N.C.
35. DeCredico, *Patriotism for Profit,* 72.

though support for the Cause was far from universal in the South, Glenn Tucker observes that by the summer of 1863 two Union soldiers had died for each Confederate, and the federal government had spent fifty thousand dollars for each Confederate soldier killed. The deliberate destructiveness of Sherman's March to the Sea in November 1864 introduced civilians to the hard hand of war and gave the world a glimpse of the war of the future. In spite of Sherman, many southerners sustained the war in the face of adversity. With a white population only one fourth that of the North, the Confederacy lost 40 percent more senior officers than the Union; by the war's end, seventy-two Confederate general officers had died for the Cause, its fighting leadership bled white.[36] The Confederacy fought until it no longer had anything to fight with.

The element of contingency could have fallen differently. In spite of the courage, determination, and suffering of a great nation, it took the Union four terrible years to suppress the rebellion. Victory was not assured—quite the contrary. With moderately competent management of its war effort, the Confederacy might very well have succeeded. As it was, it came close.

The quality of war management pervades the Union and Confederate war economies. Comparing their railroads and their governments' approaches to achieving maximum effectiveness from them, however, shows clearly that the Union addressed its problems and solved them. The Confederacy in contrast ignored, tried to finesse, or mismanaged its problems. It was the Confederacy's war to win. It managed to lose it.

36. Tucker, *Chickamauga,* 90; Bruce Catton, *This Hallowed Ground: The Story of the Union Side in the Civil War* (Garden City, N.Y.: Doubleday, 1956), 371; Francis Trevelyan Miller, editor in chief, *The Photographic History of the Civil War,* 10 vols. (New York: Review of Reviews, 1911), 1:129–57.

APPENDIX

Units of Longstreet's Corps and the 11th and 12th Corps

MAJ. GEN. LAFAYETTE MCLAWS'
DIVISION

Brig. Gen. Joseph B. Kershaw's Brigade
2nd South Carolina, Lt. Col. Franklin
Gailliard
3rd South Carolina, Col. James D. Nance
7th South Carolina, Lt. Col. Elbert Bland,
Maj. John S. Hard, Capt. E. J. Goggans
8th South Carolina, Col. John W. Henagan
15th South Carolina, Col. Joseph F. Gist
3rd South Carolina Battalion, Capt. Joshua
M. Townsend

*Brig. Gen. Benjamin G. Humphrey's
Brigade*
13th Mississippi, Lt. Col. Kennon McElroy
17th Mississippi, Lt. Col. John C. Fiser
18th Mississippi, Capt. W. F. Hubbard
21st Mississippi, Lt. Col. D. N. Moody

*Brig. Gen. William T. Wofford's
Brigade*[a]
16th Georgia
18th Georgia
24th Georgia
3rd Georgia Battalion Sharpshooters
Cobb's (Georgia) Legion
Phillips (Georgia) Legion

Brig. Gen. Goode Bryan's Brigade[a]
10th Georgia
50th Georgia
51st Georgia
53rd Georgia

MAJ. GEN. JOHN B. HOOD'S
DIVISION

Brig. Gen. Micah Jenkins' Brigade[a, b]
1st South Carolina
2nd South Carolina Rifles
5th South Carolina
6th South Carolina
Hampton Legion

*Brig. Gen. Evander McIver Law's
Brigade*
Col. James L. Sheffield
4th Alabama, Col. Pinckney D. Bowles
15th Alabama, Col. W. C. Oates
44th Alabama, Col. William F. Perry
47th Alabama, Maj. James N. Campbell
48th Alabama, Lt. Col. William M.
Hardwick

*Brig. Gen. Jerome B. Robertson's
Brigade*[c]
3rd Arkansas, Col. Van H. Manning
1st Texas, Capt. J. R. Harding
4th Texas, Lt. Col. John P. Bane, Capt.
R. H. Bassett
5th Texas, Maj. J. C. Rogers, Capt. J. S.
Cleveland, Capt. T. T. Clay

*Brig. Gen. George T. Anderson's
Brigade*[a]
7th Georgia
8th Georgia
11th Georgia
59th Georgia

Brig. Gen. Henry L. Benning's Brigade
2nd Georgia, Lt. Col. William S. Shepherd
Maj. W. W. Charlton
15th Georgia, Col. Dudley M. DuBose
17th Georgia, Lt. Col. Charles W. Matthews
20th Georgia, Col. J. D. Waddell

CORPS ARTILLERY, COL. E. PORTER ALEXANDER[a]

Fickling's (South Carolina) Battery
Jordan's (Virginia) Battery
Moody's (Louisiana) Battery
Parker's (Virginia) Battery
Taylor's (Virginia) Battery
Woolfolk's (Virginia) Battery

Source: Adapted from *OR,* Ser. 1, 30, pt. 2:17–18.
[a] Did not arrive in time to participate in the Battle of Chickamauga.
[b] Assigned to the division September 11, 1863.
[c] Served part of the time in Johnson's provisional division, Army of Tennessee.

11TH ARMY CORPS[a]
MAJ. GEN. OLIVER O. HOWARD

HEADQUARTERS
1st Indiana Cavalry, Companies A and B, Capt. Abram Sharra
8th New York (independent company), Capt. Hermann Foerster

SECOND DIVISION
BRIG. GEN. ADOLPH VON STEINWEHR

First Brigade, Col. Adolphus Buschbeck[b]
134th New York, Lt. Col. Allan H. Jackson
154th New York, Maj. Lewis D. Warner
27th Pennsylvania, Lt. Col. Lorenz
  Cantador
73rd Pennsylvania, Col. William Moore

Second Brigade, Col. Orlando Smith
33rd Massachusetts, Col. Adin B.
  Underwood
136th New York, Col. James Wood Jr.
168th New York, Col. William R. Brown
55th Ohio, Col. Charles B. Gambee
73rd Ohio, Maj. Samuel H. Hurst

THIRD DIVISION
MAJ. GEN. CARL SCHURZ

First Brigade, Col. George von Amsberg
82nd Illinois, Col. Frederick Hecker
45th New York, Maj. Charles Koch
143rd New York, Col. Horace Boughton
61st Ohio, Lt. Col. William H. H. Bown
82nd Ohio, Lt. Col. David Thomson

Second Brigade, Col. Wladimir
  Kryzanowski
58th New York, Capt. Michael Esembaux
68th New York, Col. Gotthilf Bourry
119th New York, Col. John T. Lockman
141st New York, Col. William K. Logie
75th Pennsylvania, Maj. August Ledig
26th Wisconsin, Col. William H. Jacobs

Artillery, Maj. Thomas W. Osborn
1st New York Light, Battery I, Capt. Michael Wiedrich
New York Light, 13th Battery, Capt. William Wheeler
1st Ohio Light, Battery I, Capt. Hubert Dilger
1st Ohio Light, Battery K, Lt. Columbus Rodamour
4th United States, Battery G, Lt. Eugene A. Bancroft

Source: Adapted from *OR,* Ser. 1, 29, pt. 2:126–27.
[a] The First Division transferred to Department of the South
[b] The 173rd Pennsylvania mustered out.

12th Army Corps,[a]
Brig. Gen. Alpheus S. Williams

HEADQUARTERS
10th Maine (four companies), Capt. John D. Beardsley

FIRST DIVISION
BRIG. GEN. JOSEPH F. KNIPE

First and Second Brigades,
Col. Samuel Ross[b]
5th Connecticut, Col. Warren W. Packer
20th Connecticut, Lt. Col. William B.
Wooster
3rd Maryland, Col. Joseph M. Sudsburg
123rd New York, Col. Archibald L.
McDougall
145th New York, Col. Edward L. Price
46th Pennsylvania, Col. James L. Selfridge

Third Brigade, Col. Ezra A. Carman
27th Indiana,[d] Col. Silas Colgrove
2nd Massachusetts,[d] Col. William Cogswell
13th New Jersey, Lt. Col. John Grimes
107th New York, Col. Nirom M. Crane
150th New York, Col. John H. Ketchum
3rd Wisconsin,[d] Col. William Hawley

SECOND DIVISION
BRIG. GEN. JOHN W. GEARY

First Brigade, Col. Ario Pardee Jr.
5th Ohio,[c] Col. John H. Patrick
7th Ohio,[c] Col. William R. Creighton
29th Ohio,[c] Col. William T. Fitch
66th Ohio,[c] Lt. Col. Eugene Powell
28th Pennsylvania, Capt. John Flynn
147th Pennsylvania, Maj. John Craig

Second Brigade, Col. George A.
Cobham Jr.
29th Pennsylvania, Col. William Rickards Jr.
109th Pennsylvania, Capt. Frederick L.
Gimber
111th Pennsylvania, Maj. John A. Boyle

Third Brigade, Brig. Gen. George S.
Greene
60th New York, Capt. Jesse H. Jones
78th New York, Lt. Col. Herbert von
Hammerstein
102nd New York, Col. James C. Lane
137th New York, Lt. Col. Koert S. Van
Voohis
149th New York, Maj. Winslow M. Thomas

ARTILLERY, MAJ. JOHN A. REYNOLDS

1st New York Light, Battery M, Lt. Charles E. Winegar
Pennsylvania Light, Battery E, Capt. Charles A. Atwell
4th United States, Battery F, Lt. Edward D. Muhlenberg
5th United States, Battery K, Lt. David H. Kinzie

Source: Adapted from *OR,* Ser. 1, 29, pt. 2:126–27.
[a] In temporary absence of Maj. Gen. Henry W. Slocum.
[b] Temporarily consolidated.
[c] On duty in New York, under command of Col. Charles Candy.
[d] On duty in New York.

Bibliography

++

Manuscripts

Ames, Chaplain Lyman Daniel. Diary. *Civil War Times Illustrated* Collection, Military History Institute, U.S. Army War College, Carlisle Barracks, Pennsylvania (hereinafter cited as MHICB).

Brent, George William. Diary. Braxton Bragg Papers, MS 2000, Western Reserve Historical Society, Cleveland, Ohio.

Brigham family. Papers. Small Collection, Tennessee State Library and Archives, Nashville.

Chase, Salmon P. Papers. National Archives, Washington, D.C.

Cheves, Rachel Susan B. Papers. Special Collections Library, Duke University, Durham, N.C.

Coon, Steuben H. Letters. Civil War Miscellaneous Collection, MHICB.

Eggleston, Sgt. Sanford. Letters. Dutchess County [N.Y.] Historical Society Collection, MHICB.

Elliott, First Sgt. Fergus. Diary. *Civil War Times Illustrated* Collection, MHICB.

Funk, Peter W. Diary. Red Hook *Advertiser* (Dutchess County, N.Y.). Civil War Miscellaneous Collection, MHICB.

Gardner, Isaac W. Letters. Harrisburg Civil War Round Table Collection, MHICB.

Garfield, James A. Papers. Library of Congress, Washington, D.C.

Gourlie, John C. Letters. Michael Winey Collection, MHICB.

Griswold, Capt. John C. Letters. Michael Winey Collection, MHICB.

Hanks, O. T. "History of Captain B. F. Beton's Company, 1861–1865." Frederick A. Eiserman Research Collection, Carlisle, Pa.

Harper, William D. Reminiscences. Michael Winey Collection, MHICB.

Henney, Henry. "The Faithful Diary and Letters of an Unterrified Patriot." *Civil War Times Illustrated* Collection, MHICB.

Houghton, Charles A. Papers, MHICB.

Hubbard, Dr. Robert. Letters. MHICB.

Keeler, Pvt. Alonzo. Diary. Civil War Miscellaneous Collection, MHICB.

Lawton, Quartermaster General Alexander R. Receipt Book. Huntington Library, San Marino, Calif.

Mark, Pvt. John T. Diary. Susan Boardman Collection, MHICB.

Mason, George J. Letters. Michael Winey Collection, MHICB.

McConnell, John Daniel family. Papers. Winthrop University Manuscript Collection. Rock Hill, S.C.

Mesnard, Luther B. Reminiscences. Civil War Miscellaneous Collection, MHICB.

Nichol, Sgt. David. Letters. Harrisburg Civil War Round Table Collection, MHICB.

Pardee, Lt. Col. Ario. Letters. MHICB.

Rathburn, Lt. John N. Papers. MHICB.

Schroyer, Michael S. Diary. Susan Boardman Collection, MHICB.

Shaffner, Dr. J. F., Sr. Diary. North Carolina State Archives, Raleigh.

Simpson, Samuel Robert. Papers. Tennessee State Library and Archives, Nashville.

Sims, Frederick W. Letterbook. Huntington Library, San Marino, Calif.

Titus, Capt. Richard. Letters. Dutchess County [N.Y.] Historical Society Collection, MHICB.

U.S. Army Quartermaster Corps. Official Records and Telegrams, 1861–1865. National Archives, Washington, D.C.

Whitford, John D. Papers. North Carolina State Archives, Raleigh.

Books

Alexander, E. Porter. *Military Memoirs of a Confederate*. New York: Charles Scribner's Sons, 1912.

Alger, John I. *Definitions and Doctrine of the Military Art: Past and Present.* Wayne, N.J.: Avery, 1985.

Ambrose, Stephen E. *Halleck: Lincoln's Chief of Staff.* Baton Rouge: Louisiana State University Press, 1962.

Anderson, Bern. *By Sea and by River: The Naval History of the Civil War.* New York: Alfred A. Knopf, 1962.

Andrews, J. Cutler. *The North Reports the Civil War.* Pittsburgh: University of Pittsburgh Press, 1955.

———. *The South Reports the Civil War.* Princeton: Princeton University Press, 1970.

Armytage, W. H. G. *A Social History of Engineering.* Cambridge: M.I.T. Press, 1961.

Athearn, Robert G., ed. *Soldier in the West: The Civil War Letters of Alfred Lacey Hunt.* Philadelphia: University of Pennsylvania Press, 1957.

Barringer, Graham Andrew. "The Influence of Railroad Transportation on the Civil War." In *Studies in American History, Inscribed to James Albert Woodburn . . . Professor Emeritus of American History in Indiana University, by His Former Students.* Bloomington: Indiana University, 1926.

Basler, Roy P., ed. *The Collected Works of Abraham Lincoln.* 9 vols. New Brunswick: Rutgers University Press, 1953–1955.

Bateman, Fred, and Thomas Weiss. *A Deplorable Scarcity: The Failure of Industrialization in the Slave Economy.* Chapel Hill: University of North Carolina Press, 1981.

Bates, David Homer. *Lincoln in the Telegraph Office: Recollections of the United States Military Telegraph during the Civil War.* New York: Century, 1907.

Battles and Leaders of the Civil War. 4 vols. New York: Century, 1884, 1888.

Bensel, Richard Franklin. *Yankee Leviathan: The Origins of Central State Authority in America, 1859–1877.* New York: Cambridge University Press, 1990.

Beringer, Richard E., et al. *The Elements of Confederate Defeat.* Athens: University of Georgia Press, 1988.

Billington, David P. *The Tower and the Bridge: The New Art of Structural Engineering.* Princeton: Princeton University Press, 1983.

Black, Robert C., III. *The Railroads of the Confederacy.* Chapel Hill: University of North Carolina Press, 1952.

Blackford, Susan Leigh, comp. *Memoirs of Life in and out of the Army in Virginia during the War between the States.* 2 vols. Annotated and edited by Charles Minor Blackford. Lynchburg: J. P. Bell, 1894–1896.

Blair, William A., ed. *A Politician Goes to War: The Civil War Letters of John White Geary*. University Park: Pennsylvania State University Press, 1995.

Bond, Natalie Jenkins, and Osmun Latrobe Coward, eds. *The South Carolinians: Colonel Asbury Coward's Memoirs*. New York: Vantage, 1968.

Boritt, Gabor S., ed. *Why the Confederacy Lost*. New York: Oxford University Press, 1992.

Briggs, Asa. *The Power of Steam: An Illustrated History of the World's Steam Age*. London: Michael Joseph, 1982.

Bruchey, Stuart. *The Roots of American Economic Growth, 1607–1861: An Essay in Social Causation*. New York: Harper & Row, 1965.

———. *The Wealth of the Nation: An Economic History of the United States*. New York: Harper & Row, 1988.

Caldwell, Robert Granville. *James A. Garfield: Party Chieftain*. New York: Dodd, Mead, 1931.

Calhoun, Daniel H. *The American Civil Engineer: Origins and Conflict*. Cambridge: Technology Press (MIT), 1960.

———. *The Intelligence of a People*. Princeton: Princeton University Press, 1973.

Castel, Albert. *Decision in the West: The Atlanta Campaign of 1864*. Lawrence: University Press of Kansas, 1992.

Catton, Bruce. *Glory Road*. Garden City, N.Y.: Doubleday, 1952.

———. *This Hallowed Ground: The Story of the Union Side in the Civil War*. Garden City, N.Y.: Doubleday, 1956.

———. *Never Call Retreat: The Centennial History of the Civil War*. 3 vols. Garden City, N.Y.: Doubleday, 1965.

———. *Grant Takes Command*. Boston: Little, Brown, 1968.

Chandler, Alfred D., Jr. *The Railroads: The Nation's First Big Business*. New York: Harcourt, Brace & World, 1965.

———. *The Visible Hand: The Managerial Revolution in American Business*. Cambridge, Mass.: Belknap, 1977.

———, ed. *The Railroads: Pioneers in Modern Management*. New York: Arno, 1979.

Chase, Salmon P. *Inside Lincoln's Cabinet: The Civil War Diaries of Salmon P. Chase*. Ed. David Donald. New York: Longmans, Green, 1954.

———. *The Salmon P. Chase Papers*. Vol. 1, *Journals, 1829–1872*. Ed. John Niven, James P. McClure, and Patrick Delana. Frederick, Md.: University Publications of America, 1987.

Clark, William H. *Railroads and Rivers: The Story of Inland Transportation*. Boston: L. C. Page, 1939.

Cochran, Thomas C. *Railroad Leaders, 1845–1890: The Business Mind in Action.* Cambridge: Harvard University Press, 1953.

———. "Did the Civil War Retard Industrialization?" In *The Economic Impact of the American Civil War,* ed. Ralph Andreano. Cambridge, Mass.: Schenkman, 1967. First published in *Mississippi Valley Historical Review* 48, no. 3 (September 1961): 197–210.

Coe, Lewis. *The Telegraph: A History of Morse's Invention and Its Predecessors in the United States.* Jefferson, N.C.: McFarland, 1993.

Collier, Calvin L. *"They'll Do to Tie To": The Story of the Third Regiment, Arkansas Infantry, C. S. A.* Little Rock: Pioneer, 1959.

Connelly, Thomas Lawrence. *Army of the Heartland: The Army of Tennessee, 1861–1862.* Baton Rouge: Louisiana State University Press, 1967.

———. *Autumn of Glory: The Army of Tennessee, 1862–1865.* Baton Rouge: Louisiana State University Press, 1971.

Cooper, Norman Lee. *A Confederate Soldier and His Descendants.* Bowie, Md.: Norm Cooper Associates, 1982.

Corliss, Carlton J. *Main Line of Mid-America: The Story of the Illinois Central.* New York: Creative Age, 1950.

Countryman, Edward. *Americans: A Collision of Histories.* New York: Hill and Wang, 1996.

Cozzens, Peter. *This Terrible Sound: The Battle of Chickamauga.* Urbana: University of Illinois Press, 1992.

———. *The Shipwreck of Their Hopes: The Battles for Chattanooga.* Urbana: University of Illinois Press, 1994.

Curry, William L. *Raid of the Confederate Cavalry.* 1908. Reprint, Birmingham, Ala.: Birmingham Public Library Press, 1987.

Dana, Charles A. *Recollections of the Civil War.* New York: D. Appleton, 1898.

Davis, William C. *Jefferson Davis: The Man and His Hour.* New York: Harper Collins, 1991.

Davis, William C., and Bell I. Wiley, eds. *Civil War Times Illustrated Photographic History of the Civil War: Fort Sumter to Gettysburg.* National Historical Society, 1981–1982. Reprint, New York: Black Dog & Leventhal, 1994.

Dawson, Francis W. *Reminiscences of Confederate Service, 1861–1865.* Ed. Bell I. Wiley. Baton Rouge: Louisiana State University Press, 1981.

DeCredico, Mary A. *Patriotism for Profit: Georgia's Urban Entrepreneurs and the Confederate War Effort.* Chapel Hill: University of North Carolina Press, 1990.

Dennett, Tyler, ed. *Lincoln and the Civil War in the Diaries and Letters of John Hay.* New York: Dodd, Mead, 1939.

Dew, Charles B. *Ironmaker to the Confederacy: Joseph R. Anderson and the Trede-gar Iron Works.* New Haven: Yale University Press, 1966.

Dickert, David A. *History of Kershaw's Brigade.* Newberry, S.C.: Elbert H. Aull, 1899.

Dilts, James D. *The Great Road: The Building of the Baltimore and Ohio, the Nation's First Railroad, 1828–1853.* Stanford: Stanford University Press, 1993.

Donald, David, ed. *Why the North Won the Civil War.* Baton Rouge: Louisiana State University Press, 1960.

Dozier, Howard D. *A History of the Atlantic Coast Line Railroad.* Boston: Houghton Mifflin, 1920; reprint: New York: Augustus M. Kelley, 1971.

Durkin, Joseph T., S.J. *Stephen R. Mallory: Confederate Navy Chief.* Chapel Hill: University of North Carolina Press, 1954.

Escott, Paul D. *After Secession: Jefferson Davis and the Failure of Confederate Nationalism.* Baton Rouge: Louisiana State University Press, 1978.

Esposito, Vincent J., ed. *The West Point Atlas of American Wars.* New York: Praeger, 1959.

Finch, James Kip. *Engineering and Western Civilization.* New York: McGraw-Hill, 1951.

Fishlow, Albert. *American Railroads and the Transformation of the Antebellum Economy.* Cambridge: Harvard University Press, 1965.

Flower, Frank Abiel. *Edwin McMasters Stanton: The Autocrat of Rebellion, Emancipation, and Reconstruction.* New York: Western H. Wilson, 1905.

Fogel, Robert W. *Railroads and American Economic Growth: Essays in Econometric History.* Baltimore: Johns Hopkins Press, 1964.

Förster, Stig, and Jörg Nagler, eds. *On the Road to Total War: The American Civil War and the German Wars of Unification, 1861–1871.* Washington, D.C.: German Historical Institute; Cambridge: Cambridge University Press, 1997.

Freeman, Douglas Southall. *Lee's Lieutenants.* Vol. 3. New York: Charles Scribner's Sons, 1944.

Furgurson, Ernest B. *Ashes of Glory: Richmond at War.* New York: Alfred A. Knopf, 1996.

Gallagher, Gary W. *The Confederate War: How Popular Will, Nationalism, and Military Strategy Could Not Stave Off Defeat.* Cambridge: Harvard University Press, 1997.

———, ed. *Fighting for the Confederacy: The Personal Recollections of General Edward Porter Alexander.* Chapel Hill: University of North Carolina Press, 1989.

———, ed. *The First Day at Gettysburg: Essays on Confederate and Union Leadership.* Kent: Kent State University Press, 1993.

———, ed. *The Second Day at Gettysburg: Essays on Confederate and Union Leadership.* Kent: Kent State University Press, 1993.

———, ed. *The Third Day at Gettysburg and Beyond.* Chapel Hill: University of North Carolina Press, 1994.

———, ed. *Lee the Soldier.* Lincoln: University of Nebraska Press, 1996.

Gates, Paul W., *Agriculture and the Civil War.* New York: Alfred A. Knopf, 1965.

Giles, Val C. *Rags and Hope: The Recollections of Val C. Giles, Four Years with Hood's Brigade, Fourth Texas Infantry, 1861–1865.* Ed. Mary Lasswell. New York: Coward-McCann, 1961.

Glatthaar, Joseph T. *Partners in Command: The Relationships between Leaders in the Civil War.* New York: Free Press, 1994.

Goff, Richard D. *Confederate Supply.* Durham: Duke University Press, 1969.

Gorham, George C. *Life and Public Services of Edwin M. Stanton.* 2 vols. Boston: Houghton Mifflin, 1899.

Grant, U. S. *Personal Memoirs of U. S. Grant.* New York: Da Capo, 1982.

Green, John Pugh. *The Movement of the 11th and 12th Corps from the Potomac to the Tennessee.* Philadelphia: Allen, Lane, & Scott's, 1892.

Hagerman, Edward. *The American Civil War and the Origins of Modern Warfare: Ideas, Organization, and Field Command.* Bloomington: Indiana University Press, 1988.

Hallock, Judith Lee. *Braxton Bragg and Confederate Defeat.* Vol. 2. Tuscaloosa: University of Alabama Press, 1991.

Hamilton, Sgt. D. H. *History of Company M, First Texas Volunteer Infantry, Hood's Brigade.* Groveton, Tex.: n.p., 1925.

Hattaway, Herman, and Archer Jones. *How the North Won: A Military History of the Civil War.* Urbana: University of Illinois Press, 1983.

Haupt, Herman. *Reminiscences of General Herman Haupt. . . .* Milwaukee: Wright & Joys, 1901.

Hebert, Walter H. *Fighting Joe Hooker.* New York: Bobbs-Merrill, 1944.

Henderson, G. F. R. *Stonewall Jackson and the American Civil War.* London: Longmans, Green, 1898.

Hill, Forest G. *Roads, Rails, and Waterways: The Army Engineers and Early Transportation.* Norman: University of Oklahoma Press, 1957.

Hoobler, James A. *Cities under the Gun: Images of Occupied Nashville and Chattanooga.* Nashville: Rutledge Hill, 1986.

Horn, Stanley F. *The Army of Tennessee.* New York: Bobbs-Merrill, 1941.

Hounshell, David. *From the American System to Mass Production, 1800–1932.* Baltimore: Johns Hopkins University Press, 1984.

Howard, Oliver Otis. *Autobiography of Oliver Otis Howard, Major General, United States Army.* 2 vols. New York: Baker & Taylor, 1907.

Hungerford, Edward. *The Story of the Baltimore and Ohio Railroad, 1827–1927.* 2 vols. New York: G. P. Putnam's Sons, 1928.

Huston, James A. *The Sinews of War: Army Logistics 1775–1953.* Washington, D.C.: Office of the Chief of Military History, United States Army, 1966.

Jensen, Oliver. *American Heritage History of Railroads in America.* New York: American Heritage, 1975.

Jones, Archer. *Confederate Strategy from Shiloh to Vicksburg.* Baton Rouge: Louisiana State University Press, 1961.

———. *Civil War Command and Strategy: The Process of Victory and Defeat.* New York: Free, 1992.

Jones, John B. *A Rebel War Clerk's Diary. . . .* 2 vols. Ed. Howard Swiggert. New York: Old Hickory Bookshop, 1935.

Jordan, William C. *Some Events and Incidents during the Civil War.* Montgomery, Ala.: Paragon, 1909.

Kamm, Samuel Richey. *The Civil War Career of Thomas A. Scott.* Philadelphia: University of Pennsylvania, 1940.

Klein, Maury. *The Great Richmond Terminal: A Study in Businessmen and Business Strategy.* Charlottesville: University Press of Virginia, 1970.

———. *History of the Louisville and Nashville Railroad.* New York: Macmillan, 1972.

———. *Unfinished Business: The Railroad in American Life.* Hanover, N.H.: University Press of New England, 1994.

———. *Days of Defiance: Sumter, Secession, and the Coming of the Civil War.* New York: Alfred A. Knopf, 1997.

Klement, Frank L. *The Limits of Dissent: Clement L. Vallandigham and the Civil War.* Lexington: University Press of Kentucky, 1970.

Koistinen, Paul A. C. *Beating Plowshares into Swords: The Political Economy of American Warfare, 1606–1865.* Lawrence: University Press of Kansas, 1996.

Lamers, William Mathias. *The Edge of Glory: A Biography of General William S. Rosecrans, U.S.A.* New York: Harcourt, Brace and World, 1961.

Lane, Mills, ed. *"Dear Mother: Don't Grieve about Me. If I Get Killed, I'll Only Be Dead": Letters from Georgia Soldiers in the Civil War.* Savannah: Beehive, 1972.

Lash, Jeffrey N. *Destroyer of the Iron Horse: General Joseph E. Johnston and Confederate Rail Transport, 1861–1865.* Kent: Kent State University Press, 1991.

Lebergott, Stanley. *The Americans: An Economic Record.* New York: W. W. Norton, 1984.

Leech, Margaret, and Harry J. Brown. *The Garfield Orbit.* New York: Harper & Row, 1978.

Lewis, Lt. Richard. *Camp Life of a Confederate Boy.* News and Courier Book Presses, 1883.

Licht, Walter. *Working for the Railroad: The Organization of Work in the Nineteenth Century.* Princeton: Princeton University Press, 1983.

Life and Reminiscences of Jefferson Davis. By Distinguished Men of His Times. N.p.: Eastern, 1890.

Lind, Michael. *The Next American Nation: The New Nationalism and the Fourth American Revolution.* New York: Free, 1995.

Longstreet, James. *From Manassas to Appomattox: Memoirs of the Civil War in America.* Philadelphia: J. B. Lippincott, 1896.

Lord, Francis A. *Lincoln's Railroad Man: Herman Haupt.* Teaneck, N.J.: Fairleigh Dickinson University Press, 1969.

Luvaas, Jay. *The Military Legacy of the Civil War: The European Inheritance.* Lawrence: University Press of Kansas, 1988.

Macksey, Kenneth. *For Want of a Nail: The Impact on War of Logistics and Communications.* London: Brassey's, 1989.

Magruder, Carter B. *Recurring Logistic Problems As I Have Observed Them.* Washington, D.C.: U.S. Army Center of Military History, 1991.

Martin, Albro. *Railroads Triumphant.* New York: Oxford University Press, 1992.

McDonough, James Lee. *Chattanooga: A Death Grip on the Confederacy.* Knoxville: University of Tennessee Press, 1984.

McGivney, Francis F. *Education in Violence: The Life of George H. Thomas and the History of the Army of the Cumberland.* Detroit: Wayne State University Press, 1961.

McPherson, James M. *Ordeal by Fire: The Civil War and Reconstruction.* New York: Alfred A. Knopf, 1982.

———. *Battle Cry of Freedom: The Civil War Era.* Oxford: Oxford University Press, 1988.

McWhiney, Grady. *Braxton Bragg and Confederate Defeat.* Vol. 1, *Field Command.* New York: Columbia University Press, 1969.

Meade, George Gordon. *The Life and Letters of George Gordon Meade.* 2 vols. New York: Charles Scribner's Sons, 1913.

Miller, Francis Trevelyan, ed. *The Photographic History of the Civil War.* New York: Review of Reviews, 1911. 10 vols.

Modelski, Andrew M. *Railroad Maps of North America: The First Hundred Years.* Washington, D.C.: Library of Congress, 1984.

Moore, Jerrold Northrop. *Confederate Commissary General: Lucius Bellinger Northrop and the Subsistence Bureau of the Southern Army.* Shippensburg, Penn.: White Mane, 1996.

Moore, Robert A. *A Life for the Confederacy as Recorded in the Pocket Diaries of Pvt. Robert A. Moore.* Ed. James W. Silver. Jackson, Tenn.: McCowat-Mercer, 1959.

Murray, Williamson. "What Took the North So Long?" In *America at War: An Anthology of Articles from MHQ: The Quarterly Journal of Military History*, ed. Calvin L. Christman, 87–96. Newport: Naval Institute Press, 1995.

Nicolay, John G., and John Hay. *Abraham Lincoln: A History.* 10 vols. New York: Century, 1890.

North, Douglass C. *The Economic Growth of the United States, 1790–1860.* Englewood Cliffs, N.J.: Prentice Hall, 1961.

Oakes, James. *The Ruling Race: A History of American Slaveholders.* New York: Vintage, 1983.

Oates, William C. *The War between the Union and the Confederacy and Its Lost Opportunities.* New York: Neale, 1905.

One Hundred Fifty Years of Freedom, 1811–1961: August 9–13, 1961. Freedom, N.Y.: Freedom Sesquicentennial Committee, 1962.

Patrick, Rembert W. *Jefferson Davis and His Cabinet.* Baton Rouge: Louisiana State University Press, 1944.

Perman, Michael, ed. *Major Problems in the Civil War and Reconstruction: Documents and Essays.* Lexington: D. C. Heath, 1991.

Peskin, Allan. *Garfield.* Kent: Kent State University Press, 1978.

Piston, William Garrett. *Lee's Tarnished Lieutenant: James Longstreet and His Place in Southern History.* Athens: University of Georgia Press, 1987.

Plum, William R. *The Military Telegraph during the Civil War in the United States.* 2 vols. Chicago: Jansen, McClurg, 1882.

Pratt, Edwin A. *The Rise of Rail Power in War and Conquest, 1833–1914.* Philadelphia: J. B. Lippincott, 1916.

Quint, Chaplain Alonzo Hall. *The Potomac and the Rapidan: Army Notes from the Failure at Winchester to the Reinforcement of Rosecrans, 1861–1863.* Boston: Crosby and Nichols, 1864.

Rable, George A. *The Confederate Republic: A Revolution against Politics.* Chapel Hill: University of North Carolina Press, 1994.

Randall, James G. *Constitutional Problems under Lincoln.* Urbana: University of Illinois Press, 1926, 1951.

Rostow, Walt Whitman. *The Stages of Economic Growth: A Non-Communist Manifesto.* 2nd ed. Cambridge: Cambridge University Press, 1971.

Rowland, Dunbar, ed. *Jefferson Davis, Constitutionalist: His Letters, Papers, and Speeches.* 10 vols. Jackson, Miss.: J. J. Little & Ives, 1923.

Sanger, Donald Bridgman, and Thomas Robson Hay. *James Longstreet.* Baton Rouge: Louisiana State University Press, 1952.

Savas, Theodore P., and David A. Woodbury, eds. *The Campaign for Atlanta and Sherman's March to the Sea: Essays on the American Civil War in Georgia, 1864.* Campbell, Calif.: Savas Woodbury, 1994.

Schofield, John M. *Forty-six Years in the Army.* New York: Century, 1897.

Schurz, Carl. *The Reminiscences of Carl Schurz.* 3 vols. New York: McClure, 1908.

Sears, Stephen W. *George B. McClellan: The Young Napoleon.* New York: Ticknor & Fields, 1988.

Sherman, William T. *Memoirs of Gen. W. T. Sherman.* 2 vols. New York: Charles L. Webster, 1891.

Simpson, Harold B. *Gaines' Mill to Appomattox: Waco and McLennan County in Hood's Texas Brigade.* Waco: Texian, 1963.

Slocum, Charles E. *The Life and Services of Major General Henry Warner Slocum.* Toledo: Slocum Publishing, 1913.

Smith, Theodore Clarke. *The Life and Letters of James Abram Garfield.* 2 vols. New Haven: Yale University Press, 1925.

Sorrel, Gen. G. Moxley. *Recollections of a Confederate Staff Officer.* New York: Neale, 1917. Reprint, Dayton, Ohio: Morningside Bookshop, 1978.

Stampp, Kenneth M. *America in 1857: A Nation on the Brink.* New York: Oxford University Press, 1990.

Stover, John F. *The Railroads of the South, 1865–1890.* Chapel Hill: University of North Carolina Press, 1955.

———. *The Life and Decline of the American Railroad.* New York: Oxford University Press, 1970.

———. *Iron Road to the West: American Railroads in the 1850s* New York: Columbia University Press, 1978.

———. *American Railroads.* Second edition. Chicago: University of Chicago Press, 1997.

Sullivan, James R. *Chickamauga and Chattanooga Battlefields National Park Service Historical Handbook.* Series No. 25. Washington, D.C.: n.p., 1956.

Summers, Festus P. *The Baltimore and Ohio in the Civil War.* New York: G. P. Putnam's Sons, 1939. Reprint, Gettysburg: Stan Clark Military, 1993.

Talley, Robert. *One Hundred Years of the "Commercial Appeal."* Memphis: Memphis Publishing, 1940.

Tallman, Sgt. William H. H. *Recollections of a Private in the War for the Union, 1861–1865.* New York: Century, 1884, 1888.

Taylor, George Rogers. *The Transportation Revolution, 1815–1860.* New York: Holt, Rinehart and Winston, 1951.

Taylor, George Rogers, and Irene D. Neu. *The American Railroad Network, 1861–1890.* Cambridge: Harvard University Press, 1956.

Taylor, John M. *Garfield of Ohio: The Available Man.* New York: W. W. Norton, 1970.

Thomas, Benjamin P., and Harold M. Hyman. *Stanton: The Life and Times of Lincoln's Secretary of War.* New York: Alfred A. Knopf, 1962.

Thomas, Emory M. *The Confederacy as a Revolutionary Experience.* Englewood Cliffs, N.J.: Prentice Hall, 1971. Reprint, Columbia: University of South Carolina Press, 1991.

———. *Robert E. Lee: A Biography.* New York: W. W. Norton, 1995.

Thomas, Wilbur. *General George H. Thomas: The Indomitable Warrior.* New York: Exposition, 1964.

Thompson, Julian. *The Lifeblood of War: Logistics in Armed Conflict.* London: Brassey's, 1991.

Todd, George T. *First Texas Regiment.* Waco: Texian, 1963.

Trelease, Allen W. *The North Carolina Railroad, 1849–1871, and the Modernization of North Carolina.* Chapel Hill: University of North Carolina Press, 1991.

Tucker, Glenn. *Chickamauga: Bloody Battle in the West.* New York: Bobbs-Merrill, 1961.

Turner, George Edgar. *Victory Rode the Rails.* New York: Bobbs-Merrill, 1953.

U.S. War Department. *The War of the Rebellion: A Compilation of the Official Records of the Union and Confederate Armies.* 128 vols. Washington, D.C., 1899.

Vale, Joseph G. *Minty and the Cavalry: A History of the Western Armies.* Harrisburg: Edwin K. Meyers, 1886.

van Creveld, Martin L. *Supplying War: Logistics from Wallenstein to Patton.* London: Cambridge University Press, 1977.

Vandiver, Frank E. *Ploughshares into Swords: Josiah Gorgas and Confederate Ordnance.* Austin: University of Texas Press, 1952.

———. *Rebel Brass: The Confederate Command System.* Baton Rouge: Louisiana State University Press, 1956.

———, ed. *The Civil War Diary of General Josiah Gorgas.* Tuscaloosa: University of Alabama Press, 1947.

von Clausewitz, Carl. *On War.* Ed. Michael Howard and Peter Paret. Princeton: Princeton University Press, 1984.

Ward, James A. *That Man Haupt: A Biography of Herman Haupt.* Baton Rouge: Louisiana State University Press, 1973.

————. *Railroads and the Character of America, 1820–1887.* Knoxville: University of Tennessee Press, 1986.

Weber, Thomas. *The Northern Railroads in the Civil War.* New York: King's Crown, 1952.

Weigley, Russell F. *Quartermaster General of the Union Army: A Biography of M. C. Meigs.* New York: Columbia University Press, 1959.

————. *The History of the United States Army.* Bloomington: Indiana University Press, 1967.

Welles, Gideon. *The Diary of Gideon Welles, Secretary of the Navy under Lincoln and Johnson.* 2 vols. Boston: Houghton Mifflin, 1911.

Wert, Jeffry D. *General James Longstreet: The Confederacy's Most Controversial Soldier—A Biography.* New York: Simon & Schuster, 1993.

Wesley, Charles H. *Collapse of the Confederacy.* Washington, D.C.: Associated, 1937.

Williams, Frederick D., ed. *The Wild Life of the Army: Civil War Letters of James A. Garfield.* Lansing: Michigan State University Press, 1964.

Williams, Kenneth P. *Lincoln Finds a General: A Military Study of the Civil War.* Vol. 2. New York: Macmillan, 1949.

Williams, T. Harry. *Lincoln and His Generals.* New York: Alfred A. Knopf, 1952.

Wise, Stephen R. *Lifeline of the Confederacy: Blockade Running during the Civil War.* Columbia: University of South Carolina Press, 1988.

Woodward, C. Vann, ed. *Mary Chesnut's Civil War.* New Haven: Yale University Press, 1981.

Woodworth, Steven E. *Davis and Lee at War.* Lawrence: University Press of Kansas, 1995.

Yearns, W. B., and John G. Barrett, eds. *North Carolina Civil War Documentary.* Chapel Hill: University of North Carolina Press, 1980.

Younger, Edward, ed. *Inside the Confederate Government: The Diary of Robert Garelick Hill Kean, Head of the Bureau of War.* New York: Oxford University Press, 1957.

NEWSPAPERS

Augusta *Constitution.* September 10, 1863.
Daily Southern Guardian. Columbia, S.C., September 19, 1863.
Richmond *Daily Dispatch.* September 12, 1863.
Richmond *Enquirer.* September 18, 1863.

ARTICLES

Chandler, Alfred D., Jr. "The Railroads: Pioneers in Modern Corporate Management." *Business History Review* 39 (1965): 16–40.

Coxe, John. "Chickamauga." *Confederate Veteran,* August 30, 1922: 291–94.

Fish, Carl R. "The Northern Railroads, 1861." *American Historical Review* 22 (1917), 778–93.

Fullerton, J. S. "The Army of the Cumberland at Chattanooga." *Century* 34 (May 1887), 136–50.

Gies, Joseph. "Mr. Eads Spans the Mississippi." *American Heritage* 20, no. 5 (August 1969): 16–21, 89–93.

Hagerman, Edward. "Field Transportation and Strategic Mobility in the Union Armies." *Civil War History* 34 (1988): 143–71.

Halley, R. A. "A Rebel Newspaper's War Story: Being a Narrative of the War History of the Memphis *Appeal.*" *Tennessee Historical Society Quarterly* 8 (1903): 124–53.

Harrison, Lowell H., ed. "The Diary of an 'Average' Confederate Soldier." *Tennessee Historical Quarterly* 29 (1970): 256–71.

Hoole, W. Stanley, ed. "The Letters of Captain Joab Goodson." *Alabama Review* 10 (April 1957): 126–53.

Hudson, Patricia L. "The Old Anderson Road: Lifeline to Chattanooga." *Tennessee Historical Quarterly* 42 (1983): 165–78.

Kime, Marlin G. "Sherman's Gordian Knot: Logistical Problems in the Atlanta Campaign." *Georgia Historical Quarterly* 70 (1986): 102–10.

Lash, Jeffrey N. "Joseph E. Johnston and the Virginia Railroads, 1861–62." *Civil War History* 35 (1989): 4–27.

———. "Civil War Irony: Confederate Commanders and the Destruction of Southern Railways." *Prologue* (Spring 1993): 35–47.

Lebergott, Stanley. "Why the South Lost: Commercial Purpose in the Confederacy, 1861–1865." *Journal of American History* 70: 1 (June 1983): 58–74.

Ramsdell, Charles. "The Confederate Government and the Railroads." *American Historical Review* 22 (1917): 794–810.

Snow, Richard F. "Not the Brooklyn Bridge." *American Heritage* 34, no. 6 (November–December 1983): 96–101.

Spiller, Roger J. "The Real War: An Interview with Paul Fussell." *American Heritage* 40, no. 7 (November 1989): 126–138.

Stuart, Meriwether. "Samuel Ruth and General R. E. Lee: Disloyalty and the Line of Supply to Fredericksburg, 1862–1863." *Virginia Magazine of History and Biography* 71, no. 1 (June 1963): 35–109.

Trelease, Allen W. "A Southern Railroad at War: The North Carolina Railroad and the Confederacy." *Railroad History* 164 (1991): 5–41.

Vaughan, Turner. "Diary of Turner Vaughan, Co. 'C' 4th Alabama Regiment, CSA." *Alabama Historical Quarterly* 18 (1956): 595–96.

Williams, Frank B., Jr., ed. "From Sumter to the Wilderness: Letters of Sergeant James Butler Suddath, Co. E, 7th Regiment, S.C.V." *South Carolina Historical Magazine* 63 (1962): 93–104.

Wood, W. Kirk. "U. B. Phillips and Antebellum Southern Rail Inferiority: The Origins of the Myth." *Southern Studies* 26 (1987): 173–87.

Regimental Histories
(Arranged alphabetically by state and numerically within each state.)

Marvin, Edwin E. *The Fifth Regiment Connecticut Volunteers.* Hartford: Wiley, Waterman & Eaton, 1889.

Storrs, John W. *The Twentieth Connecticut: A Regimental History.* Ansonia, Conn.: Press of the Naugatuck Valley Sentinel, 1886.

Bennett, L. G., and William M. Haigh. *History of the Thirty-sixth Regiment Illinois Volunteers.* Aurora, Ill.: Knickerbocker & Hodder, 1876.

Lathrop, Dr. David. *The History of the Fifty-ninth Regiment Illinois Volunteers.* Indianapolis: Hall & Hutchinson, 1865.

Society of the Seventy-fourth Illinois Volunteer Infantry. *Reunion Proceedings and the History of the Regiment.* Rockford, Ill.: W. P. Lamb, 1903.

Dodge, William Sumner. *A Waif of the War; or, The History of the Seventy-fifth Illinois Infantry.* Chicago: Church and Goodman, 1866.

The Committee. *Ninety-second Illinois Volunteers.* Freeport, Ill.: Journal Steam, 1875.

Calkins, William Wirt. *The History of the 104th Regiment of Illinois Volunteer Infantry.* Chicago: Donohue and Henneberry, 1895.

Brown, Edmund R. *The Twenty-seventh Indiana Volunteer Infantry in the War of the Rebellion.* Washington, D.C.: n.p., 1899.

Puntenney, George H. *History of the Thirty seventh Regiment of Indiana Infantry Volunteers.* Rushville, Ind.: Jacksonian, 1896.

High, Edwin W. *History of the Sixty-eighth Regiment Indiana Volunteer Infantry, 1862–1865.* Metamora[?], Ind.: n.p., 1902.

Magee, Benjamin F. *History of the Seventy-second Indiana Volunteer Infantry of the Mounted Lightning Brigade.* Lafayette, Ind.: S. Vater, 1882.

Floyd, Rev. David Biddle. *History of the Seventy-fifth Regiment of Indiana Infantry Volunteers, Its Organization, Campaigns, and Battles, 1862–65.* Philadelphia: Lutheran Publication Society, 1893.

Hunter, Alfred G. *History of the Eighty-second Indiana Volunteer Infantry, its Organization, Campaigns and Battles.* Indianapolis: Wm. B. Burford, 1893.

Gould, John M., and Rev. Leonard G. Jordan. *History of the First–Tenth–Twenty-*

ninth Maine Regiment, In Service of the United States from May 3, 1861, to June 21, 1866. By Major John M. Gould. With the History of the Tenth Maine Battalion, by Rev. Leonard G. Jordan. Portland: Stephen Berry, 1871.

Quint, Chaplain Alonzo Hall. *The Record of the Second Massachusetts Infantry.* Boston: James P. Walker, 1867.

Boies, Andrew J. *Record of the Thirty-third Massachusetts Volunteer Infantry, from August 1862 to August 1865.* Fitchburg, Mass.: Sentinel, 1880.

Underwood, Col. Adin Ballou. *Three Years Service of the 33rd Regiment Massachusetts Volunteers, 1862–1865.* Boston: A. Williams, 1881.

Toombs, Samuel. *Reminiscences of the War: Comprising a Detailed Account of the Experiences of the 13th New Jersey Volunteers.* Orange, N.J.: Journal, 1878.

Eddy, Richard. *History of the Sixtieth Regiment, New York State Volunteers.* Philadelphia: published by the author, 1864.

Collins, George K. *Memoirs of the 149th Regiment, New York Volunteer Infantry. . . .* Syracuse: published by the author, 1891.

Cook, Stephen W., and Charles E. Benton, eds. *The Dutchess County Regiment: The 150th Regiment of New York Volunteer Infantry in the Civil War.* Danbury, Conn.: Danbury Medical, 1907.

Wood, George L. *The Seventh Regiment: A Record* [Ohio Volunteer Infantry]. New York: James Miller, 1865.

Canfield, Capt. Silas S. *History of the 21st Regiment Ohio Volunteer Infantry in the War of the Rebellion.* Toledo: Vrooman, Anderson & Bateman, 1893.

SeCheverall, John H. *Journal History of the Twenty-ninth Ohio Veteran Volunteers, 1861–1865: Its Victories and Its Reverses.* Cleveland: n.p., 1883.

Keil, Frederick W. *Thirty-fifth Ohio: A Narrative of Service from August, 1861 to 1864.* Fort Wayne, Ind.: Archer, Housh, 1894.

Osborn, Hartwell, et al. *Trials and Triumphs: The Record of the Fifty-fifth Ohio Volunteer Infantry.* Chicago: A.C. McClurg, 1904.

Wallace, Frederick Stephen. *The 61st Ohio Volunteers, 1861–1865.* Marysville, Ohio: published privately by Theodore Mullen, 1902.

Hurst, Samuel H. *Journal-History of the Seventy-third Ohio Volunteer Infantry.* Chillicothe, Ohio: n.p., 1866.

Record of the Ninety-fourth Regiment, Ohio Volunteer Infantry, in the War of the Rebellion. Cincinnati: Ohio Valley, n.d.

Boyle, John Richards. *Soldiers True: The Story of the 111th Pennsylvania Veteran Volunteer Infantry, 1861–1865.* New York: Eaton & Mains, 1903.

Bryant, Edwin E. *History of the Third Regiment of Wisconsin Veteran Volunteer Infantry, 1861–1865.* Madison: Veteran Association of the Regiment, 1891.

UNPUBLISHED DISSERTATIONS AND THESES

Ducker, James Howard. "Men of the Steel Rails: Workers on the Atchison, Topeka and Santa Fe Railroad, 1869–1900." Ph.D. diss., University of Illinois at Urbana-Champaign, 1980.

Eiserman, Frederick A. "Longstreet's Corps at Chickamauga: Lessons in Intertheater Deployment." Master's thesis, U.S. Army Command and General Staff College, Fort Leavenworth, Kansas, 1985.

Jaynes, Peter Harold. "The Civil War and Northern Railroads: A Test of the Cochran Thesis." Ph.D. diss., Boston University, 1973.

McGehee, Charles Stuart. "The Detachment of Longstreet: The First Corps Reinforces Bragg." Undergraduate honors thesis, University of Tennessee at Chattanooga, 1979.

———. "Wake of the Flood: A Southern City in the Civil War, Chattanooga, 1838–1873." Ph.D. diss., University of Virginia, 1985.

O'Connell, Charles Francis, Jr. "The United States Army and the Origins of Modern Management, 1818–1860." Ph.D. diss., Ohio State University, 1982.

Ziek, Thomas G., Jr. "The Effects of Southern Railroads on Interior Lines during the Civil War." Master's thesis, Texas A&M University, 1992.

misuse of, 58–62, 72, 113; and quartermasters, 58–59, 62; soldiers' vandalism of, 59, 97; destruction of, 60, 61, 75, 76, 114, 119, 132, 133, 210; and Longstreet movement, 88–89, 92–98, 103–9, 113–14, 116–17, 229–30; conditions of, in 1863, 91; and troop capacity, 94–95, 104, 107, 108, 109; overcrowding on, 97–98; and damaged locomotives, 104–5, 106; and accountability, 105; difficulties in coordinating arrivals and departures, 107–8; and congestion, 113–14; accidents on, 114–15; and water tank with broken pump, 114. *See also* Longstreet movement; and specific railroads

Confederate war management: failure of, 21, 27, 31, 73, 217–33; and railroads, 24, 39–47, 62, 72–73, 92–93, 103–9, 113–14, 116–17; and hoarding of supplies, 27; and interior lines advantage, 28, 30–31, 44, 124–26, 215, 218; and conscription, 54–55, 56; and manpower problems, 55–57; importing of war supplies from Europe, 68–69, 70, 72; and decision on Longstreet movement into Georgia, 78–87; and western strategy, 80–81, 82; and communication flaws, 89, 106, 108–9, 122; and artillery in Longstreet movement, 115–17; and intelligence assessment, 118–20, 174–75; reasons for mismanagement, 217–23; and Confederate Cabinet, 220–21; and exceptional

managers, 223–26; and Davis presidency, 226–28. *See also* Confederate railroads; Longstreet movement

Connecticut, *20th,* 176

Connelly, Thomas Lawrence, 30n4, 83n18, 122, 123, 216n5, 229n29

Conscription, 54–55, 56, 57, 164

Cooper, Samuel, 111, 115n67

Copperheads, 80, 179–80

Corinth, Miss., 5, 30, 124n86

Corning, Erastus, 8

Cotton production and shipments, 10–11, 69, 70, 223

Covington & Lexington Railroad, 151

Coxe, John, 99, 100, 106, 112–13, 114

Cozzens, Peter, 229n29

Current, Richard N., 214

Dalton, Ga., 97, 113, 114

Dana, Charles A., 142, 144–47, 198

Daniel, Peter V., Jr., 58–59

Darwin, Charles, 73

Davis, Jefferson: weaknesses of administration of, 21, 24, 73, 217, 219–20, 226–28; and railroads, 24, 32, 41–43, 45–47, 72, 226–27; and blockade running, 69, 71–72; and Longstreet, 73, 83, 84, 85–87, 122, 126; and Day of National Fasting, Humiliation, and Prayer, 78; and Lee, 78, 80, 85–86, 120, 174; and western strategy, 80, 121; on Burnside in Knoxville, 89, 91; and Confederate soldiers' lawlessness in Raleigh, 110–11; and artillery in Longstreet movement, 115; and Union intelligence on Longstreet

of Kentucky, 34; at Petersburg siege, 45, 138; and Lee, 52, 213, 219; and railroad operations, 61; and Enfield muskets from Britain, 68n84; and Vicksburg campaign, 68n84, 77, 86, 144; 1864 campaign of, 71, 126, 213; and Mobile, 77, 81, 199; on George H. Thomas, 142n1; at Iuka, 144; and Lincoln, 144; Rosecrans' criticism of, 144; promotion of, to commander of western armies, 145; and Slocum, 158; and Scott's railroad operations, 198; in Chattanooga, 202, 211; on Battle of Chickamauga, 209; and Dodge, 210n127; and Anaconda Plan, 219

Greene, George Sears, 208

Greensboro, N.C., 45, 96

Guthrie, James, 33, 38

Halleck, Henry W.: and capture of rail junction at Corinth, Miss., 30; and railroad operations, 61, 65, 175; and Haupt, 64, 65; and Union versus Confederate troop strength, 76–77; and Rosecrans, 119, 120; and Battle of Chickamauga, 142; and meeting on troop movement to Chattanooga, 146–47; noncombat management skills of, 148n10; and 11th and 12th Corps movement, 154, 158, 164; and Hooker, 155, 158; and Slocum, 158; and transporting horses, 186

Hamilton, D. H., 84n20

Hanks, O. T., 103

Harper, William D., 167

Harpers Ferry, 37, 131

Hartford & New Haven Railroad, 54n53

Hattaway, Herman, 23, 122, 216n5

Haupt, Herman, 5–6, 36n18, 62–65, 149

Hebert, Walter H., 155n22

Hecker, W. F., 153n17

Helm, Benjamin Hardin, 145

Henderson, G. F. R., 216n4

Henney, Henry, 162, 163, 168, 182

Henry, G. A., 81

Hill, Ambrose P., 82, 118, 119

Holden, William W., 110, 112

Hood, John Bell "Sam," 61, 117, 123, 140, 145–46, 211, 213; division of, in Longstreet movement, 83, 84, 94, 95, 106–7, 119

Hooker, Joseph: and bridge construction, 136, 207; and alcohol abuse, 155; at Antietam, 155; at Chancellorsville, 155; as commander of 11th and 12th Corps movement, 155, 156, 199; Lincoln on, 155; and Slocum, 157–58; and food supply, 158; resignation of, from military, 158; and secrecy of 11th and 12th Corps movement, 163; and need for discipline in 11th and 12th Corps movement, 164–65, 181–82; and railroad arrangements for 11th and 12th Corps movement, 167; on railroad accidents, 169; and Schurz, 184n62; and transporting horses, 186; and corps patches for 11th and 12th Corps, 204

Horn, Stanley, 119

Horses and mules, 115–17, 115–

16*n*67, 158, 166, 167, 173, 174, 184–90, 206–7
Houghton, Charles A., 169
Howard, Oliver Otis: on train speed, 34; Meade's order to, for 11th and 12th Corps movement, 154; battles fought by, 156–57, 157*n*25; as commander of 11th Corps, 156–57; wounding of, 156; as commander of Army of Tennessee, 157; personality of, 157; and secrecy of 11th and 12th Corps movement, 163; and need for discipline in 11th and 12th Corps movement, 164; and alcohol use by soldiers, 165–66; on railroad accidents, 169; and civilians' good-will toward soldiers, 178; and Schurz, 184*n*62; on warfare as curse, 195; and problems in Louisville, 196; and officers in 11th Corps, 237
Hubbard, Robert, 155, 157, 163, 164, 169, 171, 176–78, 191–92, 195, 199–200, 202–3
Hungerford, Edward, 15, 188
Hurlbut, Stephen A., 118
Huston, James A., 31, 231
Huston, John A., 214

Illinois Central Railroad, 15–16
Imboden, John D., 174, 175
Indiana Central Railroad, 151, 183
Indiana units: *27th,* 178, 179–82, 195, 200–201, 203, 204; *72nd,* 203, 207; *75th,* 206
Indianapolis, 151, 177, 181, 183, 185, 187, 189, 190–91
Industry. *See* Manufacturing

Inflation, 39, 40, 52–53
Injuries. *See* Deaths and injuries
Insignia for corps patches, 199, 199*n*102, 204–5
Intelligence assessment, 118–20, 174–75
Interior lines of communication, 28, 30–31, 44, 124–26, 215, 218
Iron production, 6*n*8, 45, 49–50, 56, 66–67, 66*n*81
Ironclad fleet, 66–68
Isom, William, 102

Jackson, Stonewall, 32, 37, 65, 156, 171
Jaynes, Peter Harold, 53–54, 54*n*53
Jeffersonville, Madison & Indianapolis Railroad (JM&I), 15, 151, 183
Jenkins, Micah, 83, 84, 85, 108, 109
Jewett, Hugh J., 166–67
JM&I. *See* Jeffersonville, Madison & Indianapolis Railroad (JM&I)
Johnston, Joseph E., 28, 44, 60–62, 81, 85, 86, 118, 144, 212
Jones, Archer, 4, 23, 28, 122, 123, 202, 216*n*5
Jones, John B., 62, 75

Kamm, Samuel Richey, 154*n*19
Keller, William, 165
Kelley, Benjamin F., 164, 175
Kentucky, 33–34, 38, 80, 150, 153, 193–95. *See also* specific cities
Kentucky Central Railroad, 211
Kershaw, Joseph B., 97, 98, 107, 108, 113, 114
Kimber, John, 91
King, John B., 39–40

Wilderness campaign, 82; wounding of, 82; and command of Army of Tennessee, 83, 83*n*18; and Georgia campaign, 83–87; departure of, from Richmond, 107; departure of, from Wilmington, 108; at Chickamauga, 122, 123, 141; and recapture of Knoxville, 202; attack on Geary's troops by, 208; on Bragg's possible pursuit of Rosecrans after Chickamauga, 229; units of corps of, 238. *See also* Longstreet movement

Longstreet movement: accomplishment of, 1, 122–24, 126; attempt to recapture Knoxville, 1; and Chickamauga campaign, 1, 41, 87, 117, 121–26, 141, 228–29; and track gauge barriers, 46, 89; delays in, 47, 92, 95–98, 104–6, 113–14, 116–17, 125, 230; and vandalism of railroads, 59, 97; and Davis, 73, 122, 126; and decisions on Georgia campaign, 73, 83–87; officers for, 83–86, 238; Lee's fears about, 85–86, 88, 91; order for Georgia campaign, 87, 126; and direct route to Chattanooga, 88–89; Bragg's lack of awareness of, 89; and communication flaws, 89, 106, 108–9, 122; map of, 90; route of, 90, 91–94, 103–9, 113–14; number of troops in, 93, 94–95, 104, 107, 108, 109; and soldiers' feelings on leaving Fredericksburg, 94; and soldiers traveling light, 94; and unconnected tracks, 95–96, 107, 126; number of days and mileage for, 97, 104, 105,

117, 122, 230; and overcrowding on railroads, 97–98; civilians' goodwill toward, 98–103; and food for soldiers, 98–101; and women's good wishes for soldiers, 99–102, 103; and families of soldiers, 102–3; and desertions by soldiers, 103; and damaged locomotives, 104–5, 106; difficulties in coordinating arrivals and departures, 107–8, 120–21; and lawlessness of soldiers, 109–13; and destruction of private property by soldiers, 112–13; and railroad congestion, 113–14; and problems with Union destruction of Confederate railroad tracks and bridges, 114; and railroad accidents, 114–15; and water tank with broken pump, 114; artillery in, 115–17, 121; and leaky security and good Union intelligence, 118–20; and arrival at Bragg's headquarters, 120–21; criticisms of, 121–22; responses of Army of Tennessee to arrival of troops, 121–22; difficulty of generally, 123–24; and interior lines advantage, 125–26, concluding comments on, 228–31

Lord, Francis A., 65–66*n*80
Loring, William W., 209
Louisville, Ky., 33, 37, 149–51, 153, 183, 187, 192–98, 201
Louisville & Lexington Railroad (L&L), 151, 153, 193, 197, 211
Louisville & Nashville Railroad (L&N), 15, 33, 34, 36–38, 151, 190–91, 193–94, 193–94*n*87, 196, 211
Lynchburg, Va., 88–89, 91, 118

transporting horses and mules, 188, 190; and Nashville & Chattanooga Railroad, 191; and lack of praise for success of 11th and 12th Corps movement, 199; and army's western railroad operations, 209–11, 210*n*128

McClellan, George B., 150, 174

McConnell, John, 102

McCook, Alexander M., 120

McGowan, Dr., 91

McLaws, Lafayette, 83, 85, 94–95, 114, 118

McPherson, James B., 157, 158

McPherson, James M., xiii, 25*n*44, 45*n*35, 216*n*6

Meade, George G., 76–77, 80, 82, 85–88, 118–19, 125, 126, 154–55, 157, 174–75, 186

Meigs, Montgomery C., 22, 22*n*38, 32*n*8, 35–36, 69, 146, 186, 198

Memphis & Charleston Railroad (M&C), 147, 196, 209, 210

Mesnard, Luther B., 169–70

Minty, Robert H. G., 120

Mississippi, *17th,* 95–97, 99, 230

Mississippi River, 18, 22, 46, 74

Mitchell, S. P., 116*n*67

Mobile, Ala., 30, 77, 81, 199

Moore, J., 226*n*24

Moore, Robert, 95–97, 99, 230

Murfreesboro (Stones River), Battle of, 91, 124*n*86, 141

N&C. *See* Nashville & Chattanooga Railroad (N&C)

Nasby, Petroleum V., 180

Nashville, 34, 37, 142*n*1, 149, 151, 195–97, 201, 211

Nashville & Chattanooga Railroad (N&C), 2, 28, 143, 151, 191–92, 200, 209

Navy. *See* Confederate navy; Union navy

NCRR. *See* North Carolina Railroad (NCRR)

Neely, Mark E., Jr., 25*n*44

Neu, Irene D., 18, 19, 45*n*35

New Orleans, 10, 15, 68

New York & New Haven Railroad, 53

New York Central Railroad, 8, 12, 15, 16, 38–39

New York units: *123rd,* 204; *149th,* 165, 167–68, 172, 178, 192, 194–95; *150th,* 34, 167, 168, 171, 177, 195; *154th,* 167; 141st, 169

Nichol, David, 162, 167, 177, 181, 195, 197

Norris, William, 175

North Carolina. *See* specific cities

North Carolina, *26th,* 110

North Carolina Railroad (NCRR), 40, 43, 45, 47, 52, 56, 70, 93, 108*n*48

Northern Central Railroad, 18, 39, 54, 154, 185, 186, 230

Northern railroads. *See* Railroads; Union railroads

Northrop, Lucius Bellinger, 27, 31, 44, 226

O&A. *See* Orange & Alexandria Railroad (O&A)

Oakes, James, 223

O'Connell, Charles Francis, 11

Ohio, 175–81

Ohio River, 15, 16, 22, 34, 37, 46, 150, 151, 153, 153*n*17, 164, 167, 173, 175, 182, 184, 189, 190, 194

11th and 12th Corps movements, 149–54, 150*n*14, 230; and U.S. Military Telegraph, 149; and Garrett, 160; and schedule of 11th and 12th Corps movement, 173, 184, 195–96; and steamboats as alternative to rail travel, 187; and transporting horses and mules, 187; and management of 11th and 12th Corps movement, 190–94, 197–98, 211, 230

Scott, Winfield, 77, 87, 218–19

Seaboard & Roanoke Railroad, 51

Seago, E. M., 112

Secession, 217, 221

Seddon, James A., 51, 62, 76, 78, 175

Seven Days' Battles, 28, 56, 110

Seward, William H., 146, 147

Shaffner, J. F., 108

Sharp, J. R., 92, 108

Sharp, Thomas R., 37

Shash(?), Thomas R., 109

Sheridan, Philip H., 157

Sherman, William T.: and Atlanta campaign, 2, 5, 37, 61, 139, 210, 211–12, 214; supply line for, 37; destruction of railroads by, 60; and Vicksburg campaign, 60; 1864 campaign of, 71, 126, 213; "what if" questions on, 124, 229; movement of, toward Chattanooga, 147; and Hooker, 155, 158; in Tennessee, 208–9; and March to the Sea, 212, 228, 233; and Hood, 213; and Anaconda Plan, 219

Shipping costs, 6–7, 18, 35–36

Simpson, Samuel Robert, 122

Sims, Frederick W., 58, 89, 89*n*3, 91–95, 97, 107–9, 108*n*48, 124, 194, 225–26, 231

Slaves, 55–56, 176, 221, 223

Sleeping on trains, 168–69

Slocum, Henry Warner, 154, 156, 157–58, 182–83*n*59

Smith, Prescott William, xiii, 23, 123, 129, 149–54, 166, 170–73, 183–86, 188–90, 194, 197, 230

Sorrell, G. Moxley, 86, 88, 97, 99, 103, 120–21, 125–26, 142*n*1

South Carolina. *See* specific cities

South Carolina Railroad, 93, 109

South Carolina units: *2nd,* 99, 100, 106, 112–13; *4th,* 74–75; *5th,* 97–98, 102

South Side Railroad, 88, 89

Southern Railroad, 50

Southern railroads. *See* Confederate railroads; Railroads

Stampp, Kenneth M., 223

Stanton, Edwin M.: and 11th and 12th Corps movement, 34, 144–50, 150*n*14, 154, 156, 158–59, 160, 166, 173, 183–85, 187, 194, 197, 198, 199, 229; expertise of, concerning railroads, 35, 158–59; and military control of railroads, 43, 156; and conscription exemptions, 57; and recruitment of railroad men into Union army, 62; and intelligence on Bragg's army, 91; and Dana, 142; and Schurz, 184, 184*n*62; and transporting horses and mules, 187, 189; and Grant's movements, 198; and army's western railroad operations, 211. *See also* Union War Department

Van Creveld, Martin, 3
Vance, Zebulon B., 46, 110–11
Vandalism of railroads, 59, 97, 167–68
Vandiver, Frank E., 3, 23, 27, 55, 218, 226
Vicksburg, Miss., 44, 60, 68n84, 74, 77, 82, 86, 144
Virginia. *See* specific cities
Virginia & East Tennessee Railroad, 75, 91
Virginia & Tennessee Railroad (V&T), 89
Virginia Central Railroad, 52, 58, 88, 224

W&A. *See* Western & Atlantic Railroad (W&A)
Wadley, William M., 105, 225
Wallace, Frederick Stephen, 157n25
Walton, J. B., 116n67
War management. *See* Confederate war management; Union war management
Warner, Bill, 168
Washington Artillery, 115
Weapons: ammunition for, 3–4, 202, 224; manufacturing of, 32, 66, 66n82, 68; British-made Enfield muskets, 68, 68n84; blockade running of, by Confederacy, 71, 72
Webb, Thomas, 40
Weber, Robert, 32, 39, 62

Weber, Thomas, xiii, 5, 19, 24, 54, 57
Weigley, Russell F., 22, 22n38
Weiss, Thomas, 221, 222
Weldon, N.C., 92, 93, 96, 104, 107
Wellington, Duke of, 59
Wert, Jeffrey, 83n18
Wesley, Charles H., 216n5, 218
Western & Atlantic Railroad (W&A), 97, 107, 113–15, 117, 211
Wheeler, Joseph, 186
Whitcomb, W. D., 58
Whitford, John D., 93, 95, 107–8
Whiting, William H. C., 76
Wilder, John T., 78n9
Williams, Kenneth P., 2
Williams, T. Harry, 61
Wilmington, N.C., 71, 76, 92, 93, 106–10, 117, 119
Wilmington & Baltimore Railroad, 18
Wilmington & Manchester Railroad, 51, 93, 117
Wilmington & Weldon Railroad, 46, 92, 93, 104–5
Wilson, John L., 173
Wise, Henry A., 103–5, 232
Wise, Stephen, 69, 71
Withers, Col., 115n67
Wofford, William T., 107, 109
Wood, W. Kirk, 42

Younge, George, 93

Ziek, Thomas G., Jr., 30n4, 125, 218